FROM GATT TO THE WTO: THE MULTILATERAL TRADING SYSTEM IN THE NEW MILLENNIUM

From GATT to the WTO: The Multilateral Trading System in the New Millennium

The WTO Secretariat

KLUWER LAW INTERNATIONAL

THE HAGUE • LONDON • BOSTON

WORLD TRADE ORGANIZATION

Published by
Kluwer Law International
P.O. Box 85889, 2508 CN The Hague, The Netherlands.

Sold and distributed in the U.S.A. and Canada by
Kluwer Law International
675 Massachusetts Avenue, Cambridge, MA 02139, U.S.A.

In all other countries, sold and distributed by
Kluwer Law International
P.O. Box 322, 3300 AH Dordrecht, The Netherlands

Kluwer Law International incorporates the publishing programs of
Graham & Trotman Ltd, Kluwer Law and Taxation Publishers,
and Martinus Nijhoff Publishers.

British Library Cataloguing in Publication Data
A catalogue record for this book is available from the British Library

ISBN 90-411-1253-7 ✓
All Rights Reserved
© Kluwer Law International 2000
First published 2000

Typeset in 10/12pt Garamond by Midland Book Typesetting Company, Loughborough, Leics.
Printed and bound in Great Britain by Antony Rowe Ltd, Chippenham, Wiltshire.

Contents

CONTENTS

Preface

Introduction essay [handwritten annotation]

In 50 years the trading system has changed beyond recognition. Twenty-three countries signed the General Agreement on Tariffs and Trade (GATT) in 1947. GATT was intended as an interim arrangement, to be part of a much more comprehensive multilateral trade agreement. That comprehensive agreement was the International Trade Organization, which never came into existence. GATT, however, prospered. It focused in its early years on breaking down tariff and non-tariff barriers to trade, against the background of post-war reconstruction. Later, governments began to turn their attention to other aspects of international trade, responding to the growing complexity of trade relations and increasing interdependence among nations. But the world had to wait over four and a half decades for a more comprehensive multilateral trade agreement, which came into being with the birth of the World Trade Organization (WTO) in 1995. The WTO has more than 130 members and presides over a broad spectrum of rules on trade in goods, trade in services, and trade-related intellectual property rights. At the same time, like its predecessor, the WTO continues to promote trade liberalization through mutually advantageous negotiation and to offer a mechanism for countries to address trade disputes as they arise. The WTO faces many challenges arising from an ever-increasing level of interaction among its members, and from the emergence of new issues on the international economic agenda.

On the occasion of the 50th anniversary of the multilateral trading system, the WTO Secretariat and the Graduate Institute of International Studies jointly organized a symposium to examine issues facing the trading system, both past and present. Eleven scholars and trade policy practitioners, well known for their contributions over the years to the trade policy debate, were invited to participate in the symposium. They were each asked to write a paper for the symposium on any issue that they considered interesting in relation to GATT/WTO trading system, focusing both on lessons from the past and challenges in the present and future. These papers are reproduced in the present volume. Also included in the volume are the opening remarks made at the symposium by Mr Renato Ruggiero, Director General of the WTO, and Professor Alexander Swoboda, Director of the Graduate Institute of International Studies.

As might be expected from such an eclectic and talented group, the subjects chosen by the invited participants range across a wide spectrum, and each of the papers brings its own insights. The papers by Dr Sylvia Ostry, Professor Jagdish Bhagwati, Dr C. Fred Bergsten, Professor Robert E. Baldwin, Professor Horst Siebert and Professor Kym Anderson take a broad view of the trading system, past and present. Some of these papers focus more on understanding the past as a pointer to the future. Others examine particular themes more closely, and in particular the question of what should be on the WTO's negotiating agenda on the eve of a new century. Professor Augustine H.H. Tan examines problems of managing the trade relations against the background of the recent financial crisis. Professor John Jackson assesses the WTO dispute settlement system, tracing its evolution from the earlier GATT arrangements. Professor Ademola Oyejide analyzes the participation of developing countries in the multilateral trading system. Dr Jaime Serra Puche examines the evolution of regional trading arrangements and suggests how they should be viewed from a multilateral perspective. Finally, Professor Patrick Messerlin addresses the issue of public support for the objectives of a multilateral institution such as the WTO against the background of an increasingly integrated international economy.

List of Contributors

Kym Anderson

Kym Anderson is Professor at the School of Economics and Foundation Director of the Centre for International Economic Studies at the University of Adelaide in Australia, where he has been affiliated since 1984. He is a former Counsellor in the Research Division of GATT Secretariat and was a WTO Dispute Settlement Panellist on the most recent case involving the European Union's banana regime. He is a Research Fellow with the London-based Centre for Economic Policy Research and a Fellow of the Academy of Social Sciences in Australia.

Robert E. Baldwin

Robert E. Baldwin is Hilldale Professor of Economics, Emeritus, at the University of Wisconsin-Madison, where he previously served as Chairperson of both the Economics Department and of the Social Systems Research Institute. He taught at Harvard and the University of California at Los Angeles before moving to Wisconsin in 1964. Professor Baldwin is a Research Associate at the National Bureau of Economic Research and at the Centre for Economic Policy Research. He is a member of the Council on Foreign Relations and is on the Advisory Committee of the Institute for International Economics.

C. Fred Bergsten

C. Fred Bergsten has acted as Director of the Institute for International Economics since its creation in 1981. He is a graduate of the Fletcher School of Law and Diplomacy and the Central Methodist College in Missouri. He was Chairman of the Eminent Persons Group (EPG) of the Asia Pacific Economic Cooperation Forum throughout the EPG's existence from 1993 to 1995, and of the Competitive Policy Council created by the USA Congress throughout its existence from 1991 to 1997.

Jagdish Bhagwati

Jagdish Bhagwati is the Arthur Lehman Professor of Economics and Professor of Political Science at Columbia University, New York. He was Ford International Professor of Economics at MIT until 1980 as well as Economic Policy Adviser to the Director General of GATT. He is a Fellow of the American Academy of Arts and Sciences and the Econometric Society. Professor Bhagwati is also adviser to the Indian Finance Minister on India's economic reforms. His recent books include *Protectionism*, published in 1988 and *India in Transition*, published in 1993.

J. H. Jackson

Professor Jackson teaches international law and international economic law. From 1966 to 1998 he taught at the University of Michigan, and is currently University Professor of

Law at the Georgetown University Law Center in Washington, DC as well as Hessel E. Yntema Professor of Law Emeritus at the University of Michigan. In 1973 and 1974 he was General Counsel of the Office of the Trade Representative in the Office of the President, Washington, DC. In 1992, he received the Wolfgang Friedmann Memorial Award for life-long contribution to the field of international law, at Columbia University Law School.

Patrick A. Messerlin

Patrick A. Messerlin is a Professor of Economics, specializing in international trade and trade policy, at the Institut d'Etudes Politiques de Paris. He has taught as a visiting professor at the University of Houston and at Simon Fraser University. He holds a PhD in economics from the University of Paris. In 1996, he created the Groupe d'Economie Mondiale de Sciences Po, a research unit seeking to improve the performance of French and European public policies in a global world. From 1986 to 1990, he was a Senior Economist at the Research Department of the World Bank.

Sylvia Ostry

Dr Ostry is Distinguished Research Fellow at the Centre for International Studies at the University of Toronto. After teaching and researching at a number of Canadian universities and at the University of Oxford Institute of Statistics she joined the Canadian Federal Government in 1964, where she held a number of posts. She was also Chairman of the Centre for International Studies at the University of Toronto, Volvo Distinguished Visiting Fellow at the Council on Foreign Relations in New York, and Head of the Economics and Statistics Department of the OECD in Paris.

T. Ademola Oyejide

Professor Oyejide is Professor of Economics at the University of Ibadan, Nigeria. He is one of the leading trade specialists in Africa, and coordinated on behalf of the African Economic Research Consortium a recently completed major study related to regional integration and multilateral trade liberalization in sub-Saharan Africa. He is also Project Coordinator on a sequel study on 'Africa and the World Trading System', which aims to identify and examine issues related to Africa's trade links with the rest of the world, particularly in the context of the emerging global trading system.

Jaime Serra Puche

Dr Jaime Serra Puche was in 1996 the John Weinberg Visiting Professor at the Woodrow Wilson School, Princeton University, and a Distinguished Visiting Associate with the Carnegie Endowment for International Peace. He is now a senior partner at Serra & Associates International in Mexico City. Dr Serra Puche has served the Mexican Government as Secretary of Finance, Secretary of Trade and Industry, and Undersecretary of Finance. He has also taught at El Colegio de México, Universidad de Barcelona, and Stanford University. Dr Serra Puche is the recipient of numerous academic honours, including the Wilbur Lucius Cross Medal from Yale University, where he is now a trustee.

Horst Siebert
Professor Siebert is President of the Kiel Institute of World Economics, Germany, and Chair of Theoretical Economics at the University of Kiel. He is a member of the Council of Economic Advisers of Germany and an elected member of the Council of the European Economic Association. In addition, Professor Siebert is a member of the Scientific Council of the Ministry of Economics. He has overseen several research efforts including 'Allocation Policy in a Market Economy' at the University of Mannheim (1980–1984), and 'Economics of Natural Resources' of the German Research Association (1980–1991).

Augustine H.H. Tan
Augustine Tan is Associate Professor of Economics at the National University of Singapore, and the Coordinator of the Foundation Course Unit and of the Teaching, Learning and Resource Unit. He has served as a Member of Parliament, Chairman of the Parliamentary Committee on Finance, Trade and Industry and Chairman of the Estimates Committee in Parliament among various other positions. He has been a consultant with the Asian Development Bank, the International Labour Organization, the United Nations, the United Nations Conference on Trade and Development (UNCTAD), the United Nations Development Programme (UNDP), the Commonwealth Secretariat, Economic and Social Commission for Asia and Pacific (ESCAP), the East–West Centre, the World Bank and the Monetary Authority of Singapore.

List of Abbreviations

AD anti-dumping
AFTA ASEAN Free Trade Area
APEC Asia-Pacific Economic Cooperation Council
ASEAN Association of South-East Asian Nations
ASEM Asia Europe Meetings
CAP Common Agriculture Policy
CCII Cross-country Intra Industry
CETs common external tariffs
CFCs chlorofluorocarbons
CG18 Consultative Group of Eighteen
CPEs centrally planned economies
CU Customs Unions
DC-LDC developed country/least-developed country
DSB Dispute Settlement Body
DSU Dispute Settlement Understanding (Tokyo Round Understanding on Dispute Settlement)
ERM Exchange Rate Mechanism
EU European Union
FDI foreign direct investment
FOGS Functioning of the GATT System
FTA free trade agreements
FTAA Free Trade Agreement of the Americas
GATS General Agreement on Trade in Services
GSPs generalized system of preferences
ICT information and communication technology
ILO International Labour Organization
IMF International Monetary Fund
INGO International Non-Governmental Organizations
IPP intellectual property protection
ITA Information Technology Agreement
ITA II Information Technology Agreement (II)
ITO International Trade Organisation
LDCs least-developed countries
MAI Multilateral Agreement on Investment
MEA Multilateral Environmental Treaties
MERCOSUR Common Market of the Southern Cone
MFA Multi-fibre arrangement
MFN most-favoured-nation

MNE multinational enterprises
MRA mutual recognition agreements
MTN multilateral trade negotiations
NAFTA North American Free Trade Agreement
NGO Non-Governmental Organizations
OECD Organization for Economic Co-operation and Development
OEEC Organisation for European Economic Co-operation
OPEC Organisation of Petroleum Exporting Countries
OMA orderly marketing arrangements
PTA preferential trading agreements
RTAA Reciprocal Trade Agreements Act
S&D special and different, or special and differential
SPS sanitary and phytosanitary (measures and agreements)
SSA Sub-Saharan Africa
TPRM Trade Policy Review Mechanism
TRIMs trade related investment measures
TRIP Trade Related Intellectual Property
UNCTAD United Nations Conference on Trade and Development
USTR United States Trading Representative
VERs voluntary export restraints
WIPO World Intellectual Property Organization

Chapter 1

Opening Remarks at the 50th Anniversary Symposium

Renato Ruggiero,
Director General of the WTO

Next month we are celebrating the 50th anniversary of the multilateral trading system. This comes at a fascinating time. The end of the Cold War, the dramatic rise of many developing countries, and the massive increase in trade and investment flows around the globe have greatly expanded the frontiers of the trading system, and tested its ability to manage an economy of global dimensions. Trade, investment, technology and communications are linking a world of very different systems at very different levels of development into a single world market.

So, after 50 years, the multilateral trading system finds itself at a turning point. The new challenge is not just to advance free trade against the forces of protectionism. When we look to the trade agenda of the future, we are talking about much more than removing barriers to the flow of goods across borders – the traditional focus of GATT. We are talking about how investment and competition laws affect market access; whether differing labour or environmental standards confer a trade advantage and how best to take care of those issues; if taxation or innovation policies constitute a subsidy; or whether governments should be able to regulate content on the internet. These and many other issues are a world away from 'traditional' trade concerns such as tariffs or quotas; and yet all find themselves part, directly or indirectly, of the new trade agenda.

Why is this the case? The first point is that trade policy has always been about more than trade. By removing barriers to trade, we have also brought down barriers between nations and between people, which has in turn given the multilateral trading system a political and security role, as well as an economic role – as the post-war architects clearly envisaged.

A second point is that the historical success of the system in creating greater interdependence has also changed the international economy in important ways. Deeper integration means that trade and commercial exchanges do not take place in a vacuum. More than ever before, trade and the rules of the trading system intersect with a broad array of other policies and issues – from investment and competition policy, to environmental, development and health standards. We have to improve the relationship

© Kluwer Law International 2000. *From GATT to the WTO: The Mulilateral Trading System in the New Millennium.* The WTO Secretariat (ed.). Kluwer Law International, London, 2000; ISBN 90-411-1253-7.

between all these issues and the trade system so as to respond to the concern of a coherent and balanced consideration of different policies and objectives.

The third – and perhaps most important – point is that there is a human dimension of globalization. Television, telephones and fax machines are creating a global community as well as a global economy. And this global community – NGOs, civil society, the public at large – is demanding a much more integrated and interlinked approach in international relations. This trend will only increase as trade becomes more central to peoples' lives – to their hopes and fears about jobs, living standards, health and the environment. These issues are of course highly complex, perhaps too complex to be addressed adequately in the global media or internet chat groups, and yet at the same time too important to be left any longer to a few trade experts.

The financial crisis in south-east Asia has brought many of these challenges into immediate focus, and it has reinforced the fundamental point that in today's globalized world, domestic problems are shared problems and the responsibility for addressing them is a shared responsibility. If we seem to have weathered the worst of this storm, it is because, in this instance, we seem to have recognized this reality. We have collectively acknowledged the need to keep our markets open, to bite the reform bullet, and to ensure the responsiveness of the international financial system with the right kinds of policies.

Another challenge – as well as an opportunity – is the rapid expansion of regional arrangements. I have just been in Santiago for the Second Summit of the Americas. This initiative represents an important step towards freeing trade and investment in the hemisphere. But the challenge is deeper than moving things ahead on the regional level. When regionalism involves a growing number of countries and a growing share of world trade, there is now a challenge of ensuring the primacy of the multilateral system: the need to ensure coherence and complementarity, the need to keep moving on the multilateral front, to keep up with the regional initiatives, the need to ensure that the process remains one of dynamic interaction.

All this is occurring against the background of a rapidly changing world economy. One of the most interesting features of the post-Uruguay Round era is that multilateral trade liberalization has not slowed down: it has accelerated. Just in the last 18 months, we have negotiated agreements to free trade telecommunications, financial services and information technologies – with the possibility now of an ITA II. This is comparable to having achieved a new major round, the ninth one, the technological and financial round for the 21st century. Now ahead of us at the turn of the century, we have further important negotiations, with commitments already to negotiate agriculture, services and aspects of intellectual property. We have 31 accession negotiations underway, ranging from giants such as China and Russia, to small island states, and we are also working on bringing the least-developed countries into the system more meaningfully. Then there is the increasing momentum for work on electronic commerce, a medium which, more than any other form of trade, is pointing the way forward towards a world without barriers. The question of course is not whether technology and globalization should advance – that process is inevitable. The real question is whether we will help shape this new world, or have it forced upon us.

Heads of states and trade ministers will be gathering in Geneva in less than a month to celebrate the 50th anniversary, to assess the implementation process, taking into account particular problems of developing countries and to give a mandate to prepare the next negotiations at the end of this century. I urge them to give a very special attention to the integration problem of the least-developed countries. Furthermore, having committed ourselves to free trade across the Pacific, free trade in the western hemisphere, and free trade between Europe and the Mediterranean, it does not require a great leap of logic to envisage one global free trade area. What better moment than the 50th anniversary of the multilateral system to set our sights on the vision of worldwide free trade?

This is surely a large part of the answer to the broader political question of what kind of global system we want? What are our objectives for the 21st century? And how do we convince a wider public of the value of these goals? We are living through a major shift in the international landscape, a shift at least a significant as the post-war realignment. And we are witnessing a new polarity in the post-Cold War era – not between left and right, but between globalization and the forces lined up against it. In every country and every region, the same questions and anxieties are being expressed: People want the benefits of global trade and integration, but at the same time they fear the effects of globalization on the environment, wage levels, and cultural identities. They recognize the need for greater cooperation and coordination at the international level, but they instinctively resist interference in domestic affairs. They turn to global organizations to help manage our interdependence, but then begrudge these same organizations the resources and mandate they need to fulfil their roles.

Trade, investment, technology and communication will continue to move us towards a more integrated, even borderless, world economy. And the logic of global integration will continue to push us to find new means of cooperation and coordination at the international level. A particular effort needs to be made to improve the relationship between trade and the environment. But this will not happen automatically or inevitably, any more than the great success of the multilateral system over the last 50 years has been accidental. We need skill and a strong political commitment.

The multilateral trading system will be more important than ever to the international architecture of the new century, as an important element in bridging the gap between the national concerns of governments and the global issues they face. Our system must be dynamic. Our system must keep pace with technological and economic change. We must favour the creation of the resources needed to build a much more equitable world inside a strategy of sustainable development. We must respect cultural differences and values. We have to take the advantages of the equalizer potential of the new borderless technologies to permit least-developed countries to accelerate dramatically their human and economic development. We are not magicians and we cannot solve every problem that comes along – nor should we be expected to. But nor can we afford to ignore the political reality of the interdependent world we live in, or the widening circle of issues that must be addressed in a multilateral context. Trade agreements after all are not ends in themselves – they are a valuable means to important ends such as alleviating poverty and malnutrition, widening the circles of development, sharing technological progress, sustaining the health of our planet, and advancing the cause of peace. Over the next 50 years the multilateral trading system has an invaluable and indispensable contribution to make towards all of these goals – but only if we move forward with balance, coherence, and imagination.

Chapter 2

Opening Remarks at the 50th Anniversary Symposium

Alexander Swoboda,

Director of the Graduate Institute of International Studies

I am extremely pleased to be able to welcome you on behalf of the Graduate Institute of International Studies, also known to some of you as the Institut universitaire de hautes études internationales, to this symposium convened to celebrate the 50th anniversary of the birth of the multilateral trading system.

It is particularly appropriate that this celebration be sponsored both by the WTO and an academic institution devoted to the study of international relations, of international economic relations in particular. And I should like to thank the WTO and its Director General, Mr Renato Ruggiero, for taking this initiative.

It is particularly appropriate because there are few fields of economic and political life where policy, on the one hand, and academic thought and research, on the other, have been as closely intertwined – and economic analysis as influential – as in international trade and commercial policy. Concern with international trade issues has been a mainspring in the development of economic science. This is in a way not surprising. The question of why and what nations trade quite naturally motivates the theory of exchange, the theory of demand and supply, hence of production and of the gains from trade. The monetary theory of international adjustment takes its roots in Hume's attack on mercantilism. Adam Smith's enquiry into the sources of the wealth of nations, and of differences in that wealth across nations, is a cornerstone of both growth theory and the analysis of the division of labour, both within and across countries. Ricardo's analysis of comparative advantage yields the fundamental insight that countries trade because they are different and that they benefit from trade even though some are absolutely better at producing most goods (richer if you wish) than others. That trade, and trade liberalization, is of mutual benefit to all trading partners and is also the fundamental insight on which GATT, and now the WTO, are built.

That trade liberalization, though it benefits the nation as a whole, may hurt some groups within society; and that discriminatory liberalization may lead to trade diversion rather than trade creation are two reasons why the WTO is an indispensable organization to set the rules necessary for orderly trade liberalization and to translate the economists' insights and the potential benefits of freer trade into economic and political reality.

© Kluwer Law International 2000. *From GATT to the WTO: The Mulilateral Trading System in the New Millennium.* The WTO Secretariat (ed.). Kluwer Law International, London, 2000; ISBN 90-411-1253-7.

Reflections of academic economists on international trade, commercial policy and the trading system have not stopped with Ricardo. And we, at the Graduate Institute, are proud to have maintained a tradition of excellence in the study of that field. Great international economists from Ludwig von Mises and Wilhelm Röpke to Harry Johnson have held professorships at the Institute. Much of the work of the economics faculty has been and is dealing with trade theory, commercial policy and the international organization of trade relations, today with the likes of Professors Richard Baldwin, Slobodan Djajic or Henryk Kierzkowski.

GATT, first, the WTO now, have held special places at the Institute, as an object of research and teaching but also on a personal and collaborative basis. And after all we are neighbours in a lovely park. Several members of GATT and the WTO have or are serving as adjunct or visiting professors at the Institute, from former Director General Olivier Long to Richard Blackhurst and Hans-Ulrich Petersman. We have tried to help disentangle some of the thorny issues facing trade negotiators through a Ford Foundation-supported series of seminars that bring together negotiators with academics, first under the leadership of the late Professor Gerard Curzon – during the Tokyo Round – and at the onset of the Uruguay Round, now with the help of Richard Blackhurst.

I should also mention that the first major international conference on effective tariff protection was convened in December 1970 (and the proceedings published in 1971) under the joint sponsorship of the General Agreement on Tariffs and Trade and of the Graduate Institute. I am pleased to report that three participants in that conference are members of today's panel: Robert Baldwin, Jagdish Bhagwati and Augustine Tan.

If I may, I would like to express one wish at the outset of this symposium: that the interplay between ideas and policies that has characterized the evolution of the multilateral trading system, and the fruitful exchange between academics and policy-makers within the WTO, over the *past* 50 years continue over the *next* 50 years.

Speaking of the role of economic ideas, some of the most quoted sentences from John Maynard Keynes are those that appear in the concluding section of his General Theory:

> 'the ideas of economists and political philosophers, both when they are right and when they are wrong, are more powerful than is commonly understood. Indeed the world is ruled by little else. Practical men, who believe themselves to be quite exempt from any intellectual influences, are usually the slaves of some defunct economist.'

But it is one of the next sentences in Keynes' text that is most apposite here:

> 'I am sure that the power of vested interests is vastly exaggerated compared with the gradual encroachment of ideas.'

It is the WTO's accomplishment to have translated, and to keep translating, the powerful idea of the benefits of trade liberalization into reality in spite of the power of vested interests. For that we should all be grateful.

Chapter 3
The Future Agenda of the WTO

*Kym Anderson**

I. Summary

Despite the huge contribution the General Agreement on Tariffs and Trade (GATT) has made to the world economy since 1948, substantial scope remains for further contributions from and adaptations by its successor since 1995, the World Trade Organization (WTO). After first reviewing why the world needs the WTO, this paper examines the main challenges confronting the organization as we approach the new millennium, and assesses the WTO's potential to address each of these issues. They include completing the integration of agriculture and textiles and clothing into the mainstream of GATT, and coping with the WTO's much-expanded roles in monitoring compliance and settling disputes. The Uruguay Round certainly did not handle all the key issues confronting the international trading system, and new challenges have since arisen. Thus, as well as digesting the latest agreements, the WTO needs to address such issues as the calls to use the WTO and its dispute settlement procedures for issues only peripherally related to trade (environment, labour, human rights more generally), the continuing growth of regional trading arrangements, the rapidly expanding importance of foreign investment and competition policy, the surge in applications from (especially former socialist) countries wishing to join the WTO, the changing nature of services trade because of the information revolution, and the recent backlash against globalization. The paper suggests that most of these issues can best be addressed in the context of another comprehensive round of multilateral trade negotiations early next century, particularly given the built-in agenda for reviews of the agriculture, services and TRIPS agreements by 2000. In that case the non-trivial task of building a consensus among WTO members to launch that round needs to begin immediately. The paper concludes with a discussion of what it will take to build that needed consensus, and of the prospects for success.

In looking forward from this 50th year of the rules-based international trading system under GATT, it is important to realize that GATT's contributions to world

*   Without implicating them, thanks are due to the joint sponsors, the WTO Secretariat and the Graduate Institute for International Studies, for funding my participation. An earlier version of this paper appeared in Norwegian in V.D. Norman and A. Melchior (eds), *From GATT to WTO* (Norwegian Institute for International Affairs, Oslo, 1998).

economic growth, peace and prosperity were achieved despite what appeared at the time to be formidable obstacles. In the introductory chapter to her recently edited volume, Anne Krueger[1] described GATT's achievement as one of 'accidental success', for its history is full of ironies: plans were not achieved (eg, the failure to form the International Trade Organization (ITO) in 1947), and key tasks took a very long time to complete (eg, eight years negotiating the Uruguay Round agreements). Yet the ultimate outcomes far exceed anything that participants dared hope for at the outset.

Even though governments could not agree to form the ITO in 1947, they did sign up to GATT and subsequently to major multilateral trade liberalizations agreed to in ever-lengthier rounds of negotiations. It seems ironic that those liberalizations, together with reductions in international transport and communication costs (themselves partly induced by policy reforms), have been so successful in fostering interdependence among national economies that they have generated a new set of challenges for the trading system. But for the WTO (the GATT Secretariat's recent successor), there are also major opportunities to make the world a better place. It is the combination of those challenges and opportunities that are the subject of this paper.

To appreciate the WTO's potential, it is helpful to reflect first on why the world needs an organization to preside over international trade policy. Then the paper examines the systemic challenges that currently or soon may confront the WTO and its member states as we move into the next millennium. These include items of unfinished business already on the WTO's agenda as a result of the Uruguay Round, as well as new and prospective items. The paper concludes by assessing the opportunities available to the WTO to meet those challenges and in the process to strengthen both the organization and the trading system over which it presides.

II. Why the World Needs the WTO

II.1 Key objectives

The WTO has four key objectives: to set and enforce rules for international trade, to provide a forum to negotiate and monitor trade liberalization, to improve policy transparency, and to resolve trade disputes. The first two of these are discussed in this section; the other two in the next section. Apart from the transparency role, these were also the key objectives of its predecessor before the WTO came into being, but the WTO is much more comprehensive than GATT. For example, GATT's product coverage in practice was confined mainly to manufactures (effectively not including textiles and clothing), whereas the WTO encompasses all goods (including now the sensitive farm sector), services, capital to some extent, and ideas (intellectual property). As well,

---

[1]   A.O. Krueger (ed.), *The WTO as an International Organization* (University of Chicago Press, Chicago and London, 1998), p. 4.

following the conclusion of the Uruguay Round negotiations, the interim GATT Secretariat was converted to a permanent WTO Secretariat with greatly strengthened trade policy review and dispute settlement mechanisms. It also has a new role: cooperating with the International Monetary Fund (IMF) and World Bank with a view to achieving greater coherence in global economic policy making.

II.2   The purposes of WTO rules

GATT/WTO rules to govern international trade serve at least three purposes. First, they protect the welfare of small and weak nations against discriminatory trade policy actions of large and powerful nations. GATT Articles I (most-favoured-nation) and III (national treatment) promise that all WTO members will be given the same conditions of access to a particular country's market as the most favoured member, and all foreign suppliers will be treated the same as domestic suppliers. These fairness rules are fundamental to instilling confidence in the world trading system. In particular, they lower the risks that are associated with a nation's producers and consumers becoming more interdependent with foreigners – risks that otherwise could be used by a country as an excuse for not fully opening its borders.

Secondly, large economies have the potential to exploit their monopoly power by taxing their trade, but we know from trade theory that the rest of the world and the world as a whole are made worse off by such trade taxes. Thus while each large economy might be tempted to impose trade taxes, the effect of lots of them doing so simultaneously may well be to leave most if not all of them worse off – not to mention the welfare reductions that would result in many smaller countries. Hence the value of agreeing not to raise trade barriers and instead to 'bind' them in a tariff schedule at specified ceiling levels. This rule is embodied in GATT Article II, whereby WTO members are expected to limit trade only with tariffs and are obligated to continue to provide market access never less favourable than that agreed to in their tariff schedules. Again, the greater certainty which this tariff-binding rule brings to the international trading system adds to the preparedness of countries to become more interdependent.

And the third key reason as to why multilateral rules disciplining trade policy are beneficial is that they can help governments ward off domestic interest groups seeking special favours. This comes about partly via Article II, which outlaws the raising of bound tariffs, as well as via numerous other Articles aimed at ensuring that non-tariff measures are not used as substitutes for tariffs. This benefit of the system is sometimes referred to as the 'Ulysses effect': it helps prevent governments from being tempted, in this case to favour special interest groups at the expense of the rest of their economy.

While no one would argue that GATT rules have been applied without exception, the fact that they are there ensures the worst excesses are avoided. They therefore bring greater certainty and predictability to international markets, enhancing economic welfare in and reducing political tensions between nations. More than that, by promoting interdependence GATT/WTO indirectly has raised the price and hence reduced the likelihood of going to war.

II.3   Why countries need the WTO to negotiate freer trade

One of the clearest lessons from trade theory is that an economy unable to influence its international terms of trade cannot maximize its national income and economic growth without allowing free trade in all goods and services. Consumers lose directly from the higher domestic prices of importables, while exporters lose indirectly because import barriers cause the nation's currency to appreciate (there is less demand for foreign currency from importers) and raise the price of labour and other mobile resources.[2] More-open economies also grow faster. Why, then, do countries restrict their trade, and why do they need to get together to agree to liberalize those protectionist trade regimes multilaterally, when it is in their interests to do so unilaterally?

Numerous reasons have been suggested as to why a country imposes trade barriers in the first place, but almost all of them are found wanting.[3] The most compelling explanation is a political economy one. It has to do with the national income redistributive feature of trade policies: the gains are concentrated in the hands of a few who are prepared to support politicians who favour protection, while the losses are sufficiently small per consumer and export firm and are distributed sufficiently widely as to make it not worthwhile for those losers to get together to provide a counter-lobby, particularly given their greater free-rider problem in acting collectively.[4] Thus the observed pattern of protection in a country at a point in time may well be an equilibrium outcome in a national political market for policy intervention.

That political equilibrium in two or more countries might, however, be able to be altered for the better through an exchange of economic market access. If country A allows more imports it may well harm its import-competing producers if there are no compensation mechanisms; but if this liberalization is done in return for country A's trading partners lowering their barriers to A's exports, the producers of those exports will enjoy this additional benefit. The latter extra benefit may be sufficiently greater than the loss to A's import-competing producers that A's liberalizing politicians too become net gainers in terms of electoral support. Likewise, politicians in the countries trading with A may well be able to gain from this trade in market access, for equal and opposite reasons. That is, a new opportunity for trade negotiations can stimulate trade liberalization by

---

[2]   A. Lerner, 'The Symmetry Between Import and Export Taxes' (1936) 3 *Economica* 306–313.

[3]   W.M. Corden, *Trade Policy and Economic Welfare* (2nd edn, Clarendon Press, Oxford, 1997).

[4]   A.L. Hillman, *The Political Economy of Protection* (Harwood Academic, New York, 1989); G. Grossman and E. Helpman, 'Protection for Sale' (1994) 84 *American Economic Review* 833–850; and K. Anderson, 'Lobbying Incentives and the Pattern of Protection in Rich and Poor Countries' (1995) 43 *Economic Development and Cultural Change* 401–423.

altering the incentives to lobby politicians and thereby the political equilibrium in trading nations.[5]

Such gains from trade negotiations involving exchange of market access will tend to be greater nationally and globally, the larger the number of countries involved and the broader the product and issues coverage of the negotiations. Hence the wisdom in negotiating multilaterally with more than 100 countries over a wide range of sectors and issues, as in the Uruguay Round, despite the process being cumbersome. Now that there is so much more product coverage under the WTO than under GATT, and the number and extent of participation by member countries keeps growing, the scope for exchange of market access has increased dramatically. That is especially true for exchanges between more- and less-developed countries, now that agriculture and textiles and clothing are back in GATT mainstream and services and trade-related intellectual property have been added, making a wider range of intersectoral trade-offs possible.

III. Immediate Challenges with the Uruguay Round's Built-In Agenda

Implementation of Uruguay Round agreements that were concluded at the end of 1994 will continue for the rest of this decade (and beyond in the case of textiles and for some developing country commitments). As well, new commitments have been made in telecoms and financial services during 1997 by more than half the WTO member countries. These were unfinished parts of the negotiations leading to commitments under the General Agreement on Trade in Services (GATS). In aggregate, the Uruguay Round involves substantial promises to reduce import barriers and agricultural subsidies and to strengthen intellectual property rights, details of which need not be repeated since they are now widely available.[6]

---

[5]   Elaborations of this economists' perspective can be found in G. Grossman and E. Helpman, 'Trade Wars and Trade Talks' (1995) 103 *Journal of Political Economy* 675–708; A.L. Hillman and P. Moser, 'Trade Liberalization as Politically Optimal Exchange of Market Access' in M. Canzoneri et al. (eds), *The New Transatlantic Economy* (Cambridge University Press, Cambridge, 1995); B.M. Hoekman and M. Kostecki, *The Political Economy of the World Trading System: From GATT to WTO* (Oxford University Press, London and New York, 1995); A.V. Deardorff, 'An Economist's Overview of the World Trade Organization' (Discussion Paper No. 388, Research Seminar in International Economics, University of Michigan, Ann Arbor, MI, November 1996); and K. Anderson (ed.), *Strengthening the Global Trading System: From GATT to WTO* (Centre for International Economic Studies, Adelaide, 1996), chapter 1. Political scientists are beginning to take a similar view. See, for example, J. Goldstein, 'International Institutions and Domestic Politics: GATT, WTO, and the Liberalization of International Trade' in A.O. Krueger (ed.), *The WTO as an International Organization* (University of Chicago Press, Chicago and London, 1998), chapter 4.

[6]   See, for example, W. Martin and L.A. Winters (eds), *The Uruguay Round and the Developing Countries* (Cambridge University Press, Cambridge and New York, 1996).

Even if the WTO were to face no new challenges, simply digesting those Uruguay Round agreements and monitoring and adjudicating compliance constitute major increases in the workload for the WTO Secretariat, and for member states' delegates in Geneva and their support staff in national capitals. To illustrate, consider the contentious agriculture and textiles agreements, and then the WTO's expanded tasks of reviewing trade policy developments and settling disputes.

III.1   The agricultural and SPS agreements[7]

It is right to applaud the inclusion at last of agriculture in the rules-based trading system following the Uruguay Round. Agricultural policies more than most sectoral policies need to be disciplined under GATT/WTO. This is because, without such discipline, the empirical evidence across countries and over time strongly suggests domestic political pressures are such that many countries would eventually adopt policies that increasingly assist and insulate their farmers from foreign competition.[8] Such policies in a subset of countries lower the mean and increase the variance of international food prices, thereby encouraging additional countries to adopt similar policies. Their perpetuation, though wasteful, is affordable in advanced economies because of the sector's small and declining shares of GDP and employment.

While farm policies had proved to be too politically contentious to be included in previous GATT rounds, their inclusion in the Uruguay Round was considered unavoidable because the farm policies of OECD countries had become extremely distortionary by the 1980s, both absolutely and relative to non-farm trade policies. Since there was every indication that agricultural protection growth would continue to spread, cancer-like, unless explicitly checked, the Cairns Group of agricultural-exporting countries formed and took it upon themselves to ensure the Round was not concluded until an agricultural agreement was in place.

In the light of the long history of agricultural protection growth in industrial countries, even achieving a standstill in agricultural protection via the Uruguay Round would have to be described as progress. It would be an advance over what otherwise might have been the case in part because it would reduce the risk of newly industrializing countries following the more advanced ones down the agricultural protection growth path.

As it turned out, only a little more than a standstill was agreed to in the three key areas of farm export subsidies, import market access, and domestic producer subsidies. The fact that farm export subsidies are still to be tolerated continues to distinguish agricultural from industrial goods in GATT, a distinction that stems from the 1950s when the USA insisted on a waiver for agriculture of the prohibition of export subsidies.

---

[7]   This subsection draws on K. Anderson, 'Agriculture and the WTO into the 21st Century' (paper presented at the Farm Leaders' Trade Strategy Seminar at the Cairns Group Ministerial Meeting, Sydney, 2–3 April 1998). See also T. Josling, *Agricultural Trade Policy: Completing the Reform* (Institute for International Economics, Washington, DC, 1998).

[8]   See K. Anderson, 'Lobbying Incentives and the Pattern of Protection in Rich and Poor Countries' (1995) 43 *Economic Development and Cultural Change* 401–423 and the references therein.

Moreover, even by the turn of the century farm export subsidies may be only about one-fifth lower than they were in the late 1980s to comply with the agreement.

A second distinguishing feature of the agricultural agreement is that it requires all non-tariff import barriers to be converted to tariffs. Those tariffs are then to be reduced and bound. However, the extent of tariff reduction by the end of the century is even more modest than for export subsidies. Indeed, the claimed tariff equivalents for the base period 1986–1988, and hence the initial tariff bindings, are in many cases far higher than the actual tariff equivalents of the time. This 'dirty' tariffication, shown in column 4 of Table 1, has two consequences. One is that actual tariffs may provide no less protection by the turn of the century than did the non-tariff import barriers of the early 1990s. The other consequence is that countries can set the actual tariff below their bound rate but vary it so as to stabilize the domestic market in much the same way as the EU has done in the past with its system of variable import levies and export subsidies. This means there will be much less than the hoped-for reduction in fluctuations in international food markets that tariffication was expected to deliver.[9]

It is true that some countries have agreed also to provide a minimum market access opportunity. But that access in some cases is subject to special safeguard provisions, where it only offers potential rather than actual access (another form of contingent protection). As well, there is scope to minimize the impact of those imports on the domestic market: Japan's required rice imports could be of low feed quality and/or could be re-exported as food aid, for example. Furthermore, market access rules formally introduce scope for discriminating in the allocation between countries of these tariff quotas. And perhaps even more importantly, the administration of such quotas tends to legitimize a role for state trading agencies. When such agencies have selling rights on the domestic market in addition to a monopoly on imports and exports of farm products, they can choose to charge 'mark-ups' and thereby distort domestic prices easily and relatively covertly. There are thus elements of quantitative management of both export and import trade in farm products now under the WTO, including scope for discriminatory limitations on trade volumes, rather than just limitations on price distortions.

The third main component of the agriculture agreement is that the aggregate level of domestic support for farmers is to be reduced to four-fifths of its 1986–1988 level by the turn of the century. That too will require only modest reform in most industrial countries because much of the decline in that measure of support had already occurred by the time the Uruguay Round was completed.

---

[9]   Dirty tariffication is not confined to industrial countries. On the contrary, developing countries are even more involved in the practice. This is possible because they were allowed to convert unbound tariffs into 'ceiling bindings' unrelated to previous actual rates of protection. Many developing countries have chosen to bind their tariffs on agricultural imports at more than 50 per cent and some as high as 150 per cent – far above the tariff equivalents of their restrictions actually in place in the 1980s and early 1990s (K. Anderson, 'On the Complexities of China's WTO Accession' (1997) 20 *World Economy* 749–772).

Table 1 – Uruguay Round tariff bindings and actual tariff equivalents of agricultural protection, European Union and United States, 1986–2000

	Actual tariff equivalent (%) 1989–1993	Tariff binding		Dirty tariffication[a] 1986–1988	Binding 2000/ actual tariff equivalent 1989–1993
		Final period 2000 (%)	Proportional reduction by 2000 (%)		
European Union					
Wheat	68	109	36	1.60	1.60
Coarse grains	89	121	36	1.42	1.36
Rice	103	231	36	2.36	2.24
Beef and veal	97	87	10	1.00	0.90
Other meat	27	34	36	1.32	1.26
Dairy products	147	205	29	1.63	1.39
Sugar	144	279	6	1.27	1.94
All agricultural unweighted average	45	73		1.61	1.63
Standard deviation	57	96		1.58	1.68
United States					
Wheat	20	4	36	0.30	0.20
Coarse grains	2	2	74	2.00	1.00
Rice	2	3	36	5.00	1.50
Beef and veal	2	26	15	10.33	13.00
Other meat	1	3	36	0.67	3.00
Dairy products	46	93	15	1.09	2.02
Sugar	67	91	15	1.50	1.36
All agricultural unweighted average	13	23		1.44	1.77
Standard deviation	22	35		1.20	1.59

Note: [a] Announced base tariff rate as a ratio of actual tariff equivalent in the base period.

Source: M. Ingco, 'Agricultural Trade Liberalization in the Uruguay Round: One Step Forward, One Step Back?' (supplementary paper prepared for a World Bank Conference on the Uruguay Round and the Developing Countries, Washington, DC, 26–27 January 1995)

Because of a concern among agricultural exporters that the hard-won benefits to them from the agriculture agreement would be reduced by current farm protectionist measures being replaced by alternative measures such as quarantine restrictions, an agreement on sanitary (human and animal health) and phytosanitary (plant health) measures (SPS agreement) was also negotiated. The SPS agreement seeks to ensure that any such SPS import restrictions are imposed only to the extent necessary to ensure food safety and animal and plant health on the basis of scientific information, and are the least trade-restrictive measures available to achieve the risk reduction desired. Although there is sufficient vagueness in the wording to ensure that the protectionist abuse of SPS measures is still possible, the dispute settlement evidence to date shows that exporting countries can succeed in getting WTO panels to rule against the most excessive cases.

In short, implementing the agricultural reforms agreed to in the Uruguay Round will involve only very modest liberalization over the next six years in industrial countries and even less in developing countries, with plenty of room for disputes over compliance during the implementation period and for further reductions in the new millennium (see column 2 of Table 1). But at least agriculture is now in the mainstream of the WTO (which allowed the other agreements in the Uruguay Round to be concluded), and it has been agreed to reopen agricultural negotiations in 1999 to continue the process of farm reform. Moreover, the important need to tariffy non-tariff import barriers and to include domestic producer subsidies and a quantified Aggregate Measure of Support in the reform package has been recognized. The new rules and obligations eventually will further constrain farm protection growth in both advanced and newly industrialized countries, thereby promising greater certainty and stability to international food markets next century.

III.2 The agreement on textiles and clothing

Another major achievement of the Uruguay Round was to bring textiles and clothing back into the mainstream of GATT/WTO activities. Since the early 1960s these industries had been treated differently from other manufacturing. Specifically, their protection in advanced economies from import competition from newly industrializing countries had grown enormously, contrary to the policy trend for most other manufacturing industries. That had been most unfortunate for developing countries seeking to export their way out of poverty, and it meant they had much less reason to become active participants in previous GATT negotiations in which policies affecting textiles were not seriously under challenge.

Like agriculture, the textiles and clothing sector of economies above middle-income status tends to be in relative decline as a share of GDP or exports, and in absolute decline in terms of employment. Also like agriculture, textile and clothing producers in many instances have been successful in securing rising levels of protection from import competition. Having reached the point of extraordinarily high rates of protection in high-income countries and a very considerable degree of managed trade by the mid-1980s when the Uruguay Round was due to be launched, developing country members of GATT made it clear they would not participate actively in the Round unless textiles and clothing trade policies were high on the agenda for liberalization. That was a credible threat in this case, unlike in previous rounds, because of the inclusion on the Uruguay Round agenda of new sectors and issues: advanced economies were keen to improve their access to services and capital markets, and the protection of their intellectual property, in developing countries.

What was achieved in terms of commitments under the Uruguay Round to dismantle textile and clothing protection? As with agriculture, not a lot was achieved in absolute terms but a great deal was achieved relative to the past and relative to what might otherwise have been the case. That is, import protection in high-wage countries will continue to be higher for this sector than any other manufacturing sector for the foreseeable future, but there may have been at least a standstill – and possibly some reversal – in protection growth.

It is a remarkable agreement not least because it adopts the goal of tariff-only restraints on trade. Again as with agriculture, however, the devil is in the details. In this case, the tariffs are unlikely to be the key constraint on trade for a long time. True, quotas on trade are to grow faster, but nowhere near fast enough to become redundant by the end of the transition decade. According to Hertel et al.,[10] by 2005 the quotas will have increased by only about half the amount necessary for them to become redundant, in which case full tariffication would require the other half of the increase to occur at the end of the ten-year transition period. This seems an unlikely event, and raises questions about the political likelihood of commitments being less than fully implemented.

Another challenge that lies ahead for this group of products has to do with the uncertainties associated with China, Taiwan, Vietnam and other possible new WTO members. While they remain outside the WTO, they are likely to enjoy little if any extra growth in their access to EU and USA textile and clothing markets as those liberalizing countries are pressured to honour commitments to developing countries that *are* WTO members. Countries such as China may even suffer reductions to growth in their access to advanced-country markets. On the other hand, what might happen should such countries be admitted to the WTO before the Multi-Fibre Arrangement (MFA) phase-out is completed in 2005? Certainly China is expecting greater access once it joins the WTO. In so far as that is provided, these countries' accession would add to structural adjustment pressures for the declining industries of advanced economies, and reduce the quota rents to other developing country suppliers. The least competitive firms and workers in both sets of countries are unhappy about that prospect, and may use China's accession as an excuse for not completing the phase-out of the MFA by 2005. Should that happen, Anderson et al.[11] have shown empirically that a great deal of the potential

---

[10]   T.W. Hertel, W. Martin, K. Yanagishima and B. Dimaranan, 'Liberalizing Manufactures Trade in a Changing World Economy' in W. Martin and L.A. Winters (eds), *The Uruguay Round and the Developing Countries* (Cambridge University Press, Cambridge and New York, 1996), chapter 7.

[11]   K. Anderson, B. Dimaranan, T. Hertel and W. Martin, 'Asia–Pacific Food Markets and Trade in 2005: A Global, Economy-Wide Perspective' (1997) 41 *Australian Journal of Agricultural and Resource Economics* 19–44.

national and global economic benefits from both the Uruguay Round and China's WTO accession would be foregone.

In short, the implementation of this agreement is one which developing countries will have to monitor carefully, in the hope both of minimizing any slippage (particularly if/when China joins the WTO) and of making sure further progress is made in the next round of multilateral trade negotiations as it affects this still highly protected group of products.

III.3 The WTO's role in monitoring trade policies and providing information

One of the reasons protectionist trade policies persist is that the losers from those policies (suppliers of imports from abroad as well as domestic consumers and domestic producers of exportables) are poorly informed about the nature and extent of their loss. In so far as they underestimate the loss, so they under-invest in lobbying against such distortionary policies. In these circumstances there is an economic return to society from supplying more information on the effects of interventionist policies. Yet many governments choose to under-supply such information, presumably at the request of those interest groups gaining from incomplete transparency.[12]

The shortfall in national transparency agencies can be offset somewhat at least by the WTO Secretariat providing that service. It now does so, in the form both of annual notification requirements and of the Trade Policy Review Mechanism (TPRM). Notices of all changes in trade and trade-related policies must be published and made accessible to a country's trading partners, which means that that information is also more accessible to groups within the protective country. For countries acceding to the WTO, particularly developing and former centrally planned economies, this requirement of WTO membership is a major step towards more transparent governance.

Begun on a trial basis during the Uruguay Round, the WTO reviews each country's policies on a regular basis: once every two years in the case of the EU, the USA, Japan and Canada; every four years in the case of the next 16 biggest traders; and every six years in the case of others except for the smallest and poorest developing countries where the interval may be longer. After extensive consultations in the national capital, the WTO Secretariat publishes its TPRM review together with a companion review by the government concerned. The process thus monitors the extent to which members are meeting their commitments and obligations, as well as providing information on newly opened trading and investment opportunities. These activities are not costless, however. On the contrary, they put a considerable strain not only on WTO Secretariat resources but also on delegates in Geneva and on staff in national capitals – especially in smaller and poorer economies. Unless sufficient funds are budgeted for the provision of these public goods, the quantity and especially quality of their provision will suffer to the detriment of both global and national economies.

---

[12] G.A. Rattingan and W.B. Carmichael, *Trade Liberalization: A Domestic Challenge for Industrial Nations* (National Centre for Development Studies, Australian National University, Canberra, 1996).

III.4 The WTO's expanded role in dispute resolution

In the absence of a global government, another key contribution of GATT has been to provide an avenue for resolving trade disputes. That role has been strengthened very substantially under the WTO, whereby members are committed not to take unilateral action against a trading partner but rather to seek recourse through the WTO's Dispute Settlement Body (DSB) and to abide by its rules and findings. The process and timetable for dispute resolution has been tightened up, made much more automatic, and otherwise greatly streamlined relative to what operated under GATT before 1995.[13]

The experience over the first two years of this new system has been highly successful.[14] During that time developed countries have brought around 50 matters to the DSB; developing countries have brought more than 20 cases; and a further four have been brought by both developed and developing country members. About two-thirds of these have been against developed countries, the other one-third against developing countries. This total of more than 70 in the first two years compares with a mere 300 cases in the total 48-year history of GATT. Moreover, the DSB's panel reports are causing countries to implement significant policy changes, unlike many GATT dispute reports. One prominent international trade law commentator believes that the establishment of the DSB in the WTO 'is likely to be seen in the future as one of the most important, and perhaps even watershed, developments of international economic relations in the twentieth century'.[15]

Again, though, this public good is not costless. The huge growth in the number and complexity of new panel cases has been such that the legal resources of the WTO Secretariat are continually stretched to their limit despite their expansion. It also means national governments need to mount more sophisticated legal teams than previously, which raises equity questions since smaller and poorer members are less able to fund such activities. Finding ways to ensure that this new dispute settlement system is reasonably equally accessible to all members will be important, otherwise some developing country members may feel they are marginalized within the institution.

IV. New and Prospective Challenges for the WTO

The above are but a sample of the challenges facing the WTO as a direct result of the Uruguay Round. Yet the Round certainly did not address all the key issues confronting the international trading system during the past decade. Moreover, new challenges have since arisen and others are on the horizon. These need to be addressed at the same time as digesting the latest agreements.

---

[13] R.E. Hudec, 'Strengthening of Procedures for Settling Disputes' in H. Corbet (ed.), *Remaking the World Trading System* (University of Michigan Press, Ann Arbor, MI, 1995).

[14] J. Cameron and K. Campbell (eds), *Dispute Resolution in the World Trade Organization* (Cameron May, London, 1997).

[15] J.H. Jackson, *The World Trading System: Law and Policy of International Economic Relations* (2nd edn, MIT Press, Cambridge, MA, 1997), p.176.

Specifically, WTO member governments and the WTO Secretariat need to address such issues as the calls to use the WTO and its dispute settlement procedures for issues only peripherally related to trade (environment, labour, human rights and political matters such as the Helms–Burton Act regarding Cuba), the continuing growth of regional trading arrangements, the surge in applications from (especially former socialist) countries wishing to join the WTO, the rapidly expanding importance of foreign investment and competition policy, the changing nature of services trade particularly with the growth of electronic commerce, and the recent backlash against globalization. Each of these issues is considered in turn below.

It is worth noting at the outset that to some extent these new issues are all due to the very success of GATT/WTO in reducing traditional barriers to trade that hamper economic growth. The lowering of those barriers, together with falling costs of transport and communication between countries (themselves partly induced by policy reforms), has raised the relative importance of domestic economic and social policies in determining the international competitiveness of different industries. For that reason, and because the outlawing of traditional trade policies has encouraged groups to seek government assistance by means of other (typically domestic) policy measures, attention needs to focus increasingly on the more trade-related of those domestic policy measures. One was formally recognized at the signing of the Uruguay Round agreements in 1994, to the extent that it was decided to establish a WTO Committee on Trade and Environment. Subsequently, the growing importance of the linkages between trade and investment policies, and trade and competition policies, was acknowledged at the WTO's first ministerial meeting in late 1996, where it was agreed to establish working groups to study these two issues as part of the WTO's work programme. On both occasions, pressure from some members to have the WTO address also the issue of trade and labour standards was not taken up, but the pressure remains. Meanwhile, countries have sought and will continue to seek faster progress on these issues through existing or new groupings of subsets of WTO members, most notably through regional integration agreements such as the EU, the North American Free Trade Agreement (NAFTA), the ASEAN Free Trade Area (AFTA) and the Asia–Pacific Economic Cooperation Council (APEC).

IV.1 Issues peripherally related to trade: environmental and labour standards[16]

The perceived need for international rules and institutions to address environmental and labour concerns arises in part from the long-standing concern in high-standard countries that some of their firms suffer a competitive disadvantage because of lower environmental

---

[16] Section IV.1 draws on K. Anderson, 'Environmental Standards and International Trade' in M. Bruno and B. Pleskovic (eds), *Annual World Bank Conference on Development Economics 1996* (World Bank, Washington, DC, 1997), pp. 317–338; K. Anderson, 'Environmental and Labour Standards: What Role for the WTO?' in A.O. Krueger (ed.), *The WTO as an International Organization* (University of Chicago Press, Chicago and London, 1998), chapter 8; and K. Anderson and R. Blackhurst (eds), *The Greening of World Trade Issues* (University of Michigan Press, Ann Arbor, MI, and Harvester Wheatsheaf, London, 1992).

and labour standards abroad. Even though differences in standards across countries are a natural consequence of differences in national incomes, tastes and preferences, they none the less give rise to claims of 'unfair' trade, which can undermine support for a GATT/ WTO rules-based trading system. Such differences become ever more important as traditional barriers to trade and investment between countries fall.[17] On the one hand, they lead to claims in developed countries of eco- or social-dumping, and fears of a 'race to the bottom' as governments compete to attract and keep investments in their territory by lowering standards. In poor countries, on the other hand, people fear being forced to raise standards at an earlier stage of development than they would otherwise choose, thereby reducing their comparative advantage in products whose production is intensive in the use of natural resources or unskilled labour.

The issues are made more complicated by the fact that they also involve some externalities that spill over national boundaries. The most obvious examples are physical spillovers associated with global environmental problems. Since greenhouse gases contribute to climate change and CFCs deplete the ozone layer regardless of which country they are emitted from, there is a concern that, if one set of countries seeks to tax or otherwise induce less of these emissions by firms located in their region, the environmental benefits from those measures will be offset in so far as the activities responsible relocate to countries with lower standards. The freer international trade and investment flows are, the less effective subglobal regulation will be and hence the greater the need for international cooperation or coercion.

To what extent is there a parallel claim with respect to labour standards? Many economists would say there is none, because they perceive no physical labour spillovers of the global-warming or ozone-depleting kind. In addition to physical spillovers, though, people can be affected emotionally by and have humanitarian concerns for activities abroad. An example is that people in one country may grieve if another country's activities threaten a particular animal or plant species,[18] or involve abuse of worker rights or poor working conditions in that other country. Or they may grieve if they believe that the desires of another country's citizens for higher environmental or labour standards in their country are not being recognized sufficiently by their national government (a political market failure). Whether this type of spillover is worthy of any international action, however, is even more contentious than the case of physical spillovers.

---

[17]   J.N. Bhagwati, 'The Demand to Reduce Domestic Diversity among Trading Nations' in J.N. Bhagwati and R.E. Hudec (eds), *Fair Trade and Harmonization: Prerequisites for Free Trade?* (MIT Press, Cambridge, MA, 1996), vol. I, chapter 1.

[18]   The latest case to come before the WTO Dispute Settlement Body, by India, Malaysia, Pakistan and Thailand against the USA, involves the catching of turtles in shrimp trawling nets. Like the previous tuna–dolphin case, by Mexico against the USA, the issue is made more complex by the fact that the production process is not physically detectable in the final product that is traded (shrimp or tuna). Labelling is a much more efficient way of dealing with this issue than simply banning imports of the final product. (See United States – Restrictions on imports of tuna, DS21 and United States – Import prohibition of certain shrimp and shrimp products, WT/0558.)

What role is there for the WTO in any of these situations? The demands for greater harmonization across countries of domestic policies, for competitiveness reasons, coupled with the greening of world politics and the growing interest in worker rights and conditions beyond national borders, are likely to put the WTO and trade policy under pressure to perform tasks for which they were not designed and are not well suited – and at a time when the WTO needs first to consolidate its role in the world and ensure the completion of unfinished business from and implementation of the Uruguay Round. Supporters of the WTO therefore are tempted to say the institution should resist all attempts to become involved in these issues. That strategy is risky, however. While many developing countries might support it, we might see more aggressive unilateral use of trade measures by advanced economies against countries with lower social standards and/ or less willingness in advanced economies to maintain liberal trade policies and to participate in future multilateral trade negotiations. Hence some engagement in the debate by the WTO may be wise. At the very least, that could involve reminding the world of some of the non-trade measures and actions available to address these problems. It could also involve participating in studies aimed at showing whether and to what extent trade and investment liberalizations are accompanied or followed by a reduction in these problems directly or through a rise in social standards – to see if trade reform might be part of the *solution* to the problem.

IV.2   Embracing socialist and least-developed economies in the WTO

With more than 130 members, the WTO is approaching the status of a truly global trade organization except for under-representation by two groups: the former centrally planned economies (CPEs) seeking to transform from plan to market orientations, and some of the smallest and poorest economies. Most of the CPEs not already members are seeking WTO accession, the most notable being China (whose accession would allow Taiwan to join) and Russia. Their accession negotiations are not moving rapidly, however. The problem is partly that members want more access to those countries' markets than their governments have been willing to give. This is especially so with respect to bound tariffs, signing the WTO's plurilateral government procurement agreement, and assurances over intellectual property rights. Additional problems include their lack of policy transparency and their high degree of state trading (the WTO rules for which are still not well developed), not to mention the need to overcome political opposition (for human rights reasons) in the USA Congress and elsewhere to their joining. In China's case the 'concessions' available to developing country WTO members are also being sought. The USA and others are very reluctant to allow China those 'concessions', however, because that could effectively make meaningless the negotiated access to Chinese markets.[19]

The other group feeling marginalized is the world's least-developed countries (LDCs), particularly those that are not yet WTO members. For them the cost of the

---

[19]   K. Anderson, 'On the Complexities of China's WTO Accession' (1997) 20 *World Economy* 749–772.

accession process, and subsequently of maintaining a mission in Geneva that is large enough to cover the expanding number of items of key concern to them, is prohibitive without some financial and technical aid. A programme of multilateral assistance does exist, and was expanded following a high-level meeting between LDCs and the WTO and five other international agencies in October 1997. Many bilateral assistance programmes also exist.[20] But with so many new countries seeking membership and so many more issues to get on top of following the Uruguay Round, the budgets for those programmes may need to expand further, especially if a new round is launched soon.

In addition to the 30 or more countries in the queue for membership currently, perhaps another 20 will apply soon. It takes up to six years to accede on average, so within another decade the WTO will have much the same membership number and composition as the United Nations. The WTO began as a club of industrial countries, but their share had fallen to one-quarter by the start of the Uruguay Round – and could be as small as one-sixth by the start of the next round.

To understand how well the WTO club is managing its own globalization, consider the following four questions: to what extent are less-advanced economies (a) opening up to trade, (b) able to get their exports into markets of more-advanced economies, (c) engaged in WTO activities such as improving the rules, and (d) able to accede expeditiously?

On the first question, to what extent are less-advanced economies opening up to trade, the answer is generally that they are opening up. During the past decade or so an ever-larger number of developing countries – including in Africa – have embraced trade liberalization. Some of those reform programmes have been adopted with reluctance as conditions for receiving IMF or World Bank loans, while others have been unconditional unilateral decisions. Until they are bound under the WTO, though, there is a risk of back-sliding in the future. Furthermore, tariffs need to be bound at levels close to applied rates to be taken seriously, unlike during the Uruguay Round when many developing countries just committed to ceiling bindings at several times the level of applied rates.

On the second question, to what extent are less-advanced economies able to get their exports into markets of more-advanced economies, the answer is clearly that they are not able to do this. The two sectors of most interest to less-advanced economies are agriculture and textiles/clothing, and protection levels in more-advanced economies for those items are more than ten times the average on other merchandise. And even though commitments have been made in the Uruguay Round to lower those barriers, only modest reductions will have resulted by the turn of the century.

On the third question, to what extent are less-advanced economies engaged in WTO activities such as improving the rules, the answer is that, while there are ample opportunities for less-advanced economies to become engaged in WTO activities such as chairing committees, they are taken up infrequently. Michalopoulos[21] suggests that

[20]   OECD, *Survey of DAC Members' Co-operation for Capacity Development in Trade* (DCD/DAC(97)24/REV1, OECD, Paris, 1997).

[21]   C. Michalopoulos, 'The Participation of Developing Countries in the WTO' (Policy Research Working Paper 1906, Washington, DC, World Bank, 1998).

this is because poor and especially small countries have few if any delegates in Geneva, and those that are there are relatively poorly serviced by their national capitals and so are always over-stretched. The pooling of efforts by members forming a group has been one way of coping. Perhaps further aid funding is warranted for the smaller and least-developed countries to raise the quality and quantity of representation by them.

As to the final question concerning the pace of accession of new members, the answer is unclear. Certainly an average time of six years to accede sounds long, and certainly politics may have contributed, as with China. But much of the delay appears to be on the part of the acceding country. Sometimes this is because of a lack of internal political support to push ahead with reform commitments. More often it is because of insufficient bureaucratic horsepower to get on top of the issues and to move the necessary papers forward any faster.[22] The obvious solution is to raise the quantity and quality of staffing in national capitals, and in particular to boost training. Further education is needed not only about the WTO institution but also in analytical capability. The domestic political commitment to do that may not be in place, however, in which case the question again arises as to whether more development assistance funds need to be directed to that cause.

IV.3   Ensuring regional trade agreements are not seen as a WTO substitute

For much of the post-war period regional integration agreements have complemented and supplemented the multilateral trading system rather than marginalized or undermined it.[23] But that may have been more due to good luck or special circumstances than to GATT/WTO rules and procedures governing such preferential arrangements (which continue to be weak). Hence there is no room for complacency on this issue, particularly given the recent rise in the number of regional integration agreements.[24] The proliferation recently of 'hub and spoke' agreements involving the USA and EU is especially worrying, not just because of the trade and investment diversion they cause but also because they divert trade diplomats' attention away from the multilateral trading system. The more successful the WTO is in meeting its other challenges, however, the less likely it is that

---

[22]   C. Michalopoulos, 'WTO Membership for Countries in Transition' (Policy Research Working Paper, Washington, DC, World Bank, 1998).

[23]   K. Anderson and R. Blackhurst (eds), *Regional Integration and the Global Trading System* (Harvester Wheatsheaf, London, and St Martin's Press, New York, 1993); and WTO, *Regionalism and the World Trading System* (World Trade Organization, Geneva, 1995).

[24]   See J.A. Frankel, *Regional Trading Blocs in the World Economic System* (Institute for International Economics, Washington, DC, 1997); L.A. Winters, 'Regionalism versus Multilateralism' in R. Baldwin, D. Cole, A. Sapir and A. Venables (eds), *Regional Integration* (Cambridge University Press, Cambridge and New York, 1998); and L.A. Winters, 'Regionalism and the Next Round of Multilateral Trade Negotiations' (paper presented at a conference on the World Trading System at Fifty: Global Challenges and USA Interests, Institute for International Economics, Washington, DC, 15 April 1998). There are now at least 90 regional integration agreements, three-quarters of which were formed in the past four years.

regionalism will present a systemic threat. In particular, reducing scope for member countries to use anti-dumping duties as a form of contingent protection could greatly reduce the incentive for small 'spoke' countries to sign on to an economic integration agreement with a major 'hub'.

IV.4   Integrating foreign investment and competition policies into the WTO

The Uruguay Round agreement on trade-related investment measures barely began to address the issue of distortions caused by foreign investment policies and procedures. Given the massive growth in foreign investment flows in the past decade or so, the OECD's initiative in this area, the current Asian financial crisis, and the WTO Secretariat's own assessment arguing for the need to bring national foreign direct investment (FDI) policies under WTO discipline,[25] it is not surprising that the WTO ministerial meeting in late 1996 in Singapore decided to establish a working group to examine the full range of issues surrounding the relationship between international trade and investment.

That 1996 ministerial meeting also decided to examine the interaction between international trade and competition policy. Initial studies of this issue suggest there is already plenty of scope for GATT rules to be used to discipline the contestability of domestic markets,[26] and that any move towards harmonization or simply mutual recognition of national competition policies, even if desirable, would be long in getting started and difficult to negotiate.[27] Part of the difficulty with bringing this issue into the WTO is that many anti-competitive practices are the actions of private producers rather than of governments.[28]

The Singapore Ministerial Declaration stated:

'It is clearly understood that future negotiations, if any, regarding multilateral disciplines in these areas, will take place only after an explicit consensus decision is taken among WTO members regarding such negotiations.'[29]

In the case of investment at least, that is likely to come sooner rather than later, because the OECD has already drafted a Multilateral Agreement on Investment and United Nations Conference on Trade and Development (UNCTAD) too has a substantial role in setting standards and monitoring developments in the area. Since the EU is very keen

---

[25]   WTO, *Annual Report 1996* (World Trade Organization, Geneva, 1996), vol. I.

[26]   E.g., B.M. Hoekman and P. Mavroidis, 'Competition, Competition Policy, and GATT' (CEPR Discussion Paper No. 876, Centre for Economic Policy, London, January 1994).

[27]   P.J. Lloyd and G. Sampson, 'International Competition Policy after the Uruguay Round' (1995) 18 *World Economy* 681–705.

[28]   For an extensive coverage of this issue, see E.M. Graham and J.D. Richardson (eds), *Global Competition Policy* (Institute for International Economics, Washington, DC, 1997).

[29]   WT/MIN(96)/DEC, World Trade Organization, 1996.

to see a broader multilateral investment agreement embedded in the WTO, this is bound to be something developing countries will use to bargain for better deals on agriculture and textiles early next century.

An important aspect of the growth of foreign investment is associated with the globalization of production. With the decline in trade barriers (governmental as well as transport and communication costs) has come greater scope for firms to break up the production process into subprocesses located in different countries.[30] The resulting FDI and intra-firm trade in components/intermediate inputs has contributed to the trebling of trade as a share of global output since 1950 (from 7 per cent to 22 per cent), with intra-firm trade of multinational corporations now accounting for two-thirds of world trade, according to WTO Director General Ruggiero.[31]

One of the implications of this phenomenon for the WTO has to do with dispute settlement. Since member governments are the complainants or respondents in WTO panel cases, the question arises as to which member government should look after the interests of a particular multinational firm. In the WTO's latest dispute settlement case against the EU's banana regime, for example, the USA (which grows almost no bananas) was a complainant ostensibly because of its interest in services associated with EU banana imports from Latin America, but presumably also because a major producer of bananas in Latin America is a USA multinational firm. The dispute settlement system is not well designed for this reality of multinationals having much of their production in other than their host country. Nor is it designed to cope with the inevitable conflicts that will arise between host governments and multinational firms,[32] including those involving bribery and corruption.[33]

Another area where deregulation and rapid technological change are combining to create newly tradable products has to do with the supply of electricity. The reform of policies that held energy (especially coal) prices low in developing countries and high in some high-income countries, the privatization and/or de-monopolization of utilities supplying electricity, and the advent of small-scale, natural-gas-fired generators along with advances in information technologies have combined to make electricity a much more tradable product in recent years.[34] Likewise, privatization of water, sewerage, health and education services all open up new areas of international trade and/or investment where WTO disciplines and market access negotiations are relevant. As with government procurement (for which so far only a plurilateral agreement has been secured among a subset of WTO members) and telecoms, both

---

[30]   J.R. Markusen, 'Trade versus Investment Liberalization' (NBER Working Paper No. 6231, Cambridge, MA, 1997).

[31]   R. Ruggiero, 'Charting the Trade Routes of the Future: Towards a Borderless Economy' (paper presented to the International Industrial Conference, San Francisco, 29 September 1997).

[32]   E.M. Graham, *Global Corporations and National Governments* (Institute for International Economics, Washington, DC, 1996).

[33]   K.A. Elliot (ed.), *Corruption and the Global Economy* (Institute for International Economics, Washington, DC, 1997).

[34]   *Economist*, 28 March 1998, pp. 65–67.

nationalist and protectionist forces will resist efforts to bring these big-ticket items under the WTO.

IV.5   The changing nature of services trade

The above-mentioned recognition of the need to address investment and competition policy issues in the WTO coincides with a new appreciation of a difficulty with the General Agreement on Trade in Services (GATS). Snape[35] argues that the GATS is probably too general in its attempt to cover all modes of service delivery and all forms of barriers to access, but not general enough in terms of obligations on countries making liberalization commitments. On the former, he believes that, since the parts of the GATS dealing with investment, competition policy and movement of people also could apply to goods trade, they should be taken out of GATS and renegotiated as more general agreements covering both goods and services. He expects that would allow faster progress on services negotiations, since they could then focus just on cross-border trade and measures discriminating between domestic and foreign suppliers, as with goods trade negotiations. In terms of obligations, Snape argues for the GATS to embrace most-favoured nation (MFN) and national treatment principles, again as with goods trade under GATT, in place of the current arrangement whereby countries can take MFN and national treatment exceptions.

More fundamentally, the impact of the information revolution in lowering communication and computing costs is adding a whole new dimension to global economic integration.[36] Just as the globalization of goods trade and investment changed the face of manufacturing in the 1980s, so this digital revolution (again helped by deregulation and the transferring of many services from the public to the private sector) is transforming services and ideas-based industries. It is making many previously non-traded services now highly tradable internationally to the point where for some products national borders are becoming irrelevant. It is also making information one of the key factors of production and, unlike land, labour and physical capital, that factor is highly mobile internationally. With financial capital also increasingly having that property of great international mobility (witness the speed of contagion in East Asia's financial crisis during 1997–1998), economies are going to be rewarded more than ever for having sound policies in place – and penalized more than ever for having restrictive policies. That is, we may see liberal economies leapfrogging poorer performing ones even more in the future than in the past 30 years or so. Income gaps within and between countries will depend much more on differences in access to information relative to differences in endowments of traditional factors of production.

This phenomenon underscores the significance of the telecom services, financial services and information technology agreements signed by WTO members in the past year and the TRIPS agreement of the Uruguay Round. They represent the beginning of

---

[35]   R.H. Snape, 'Reaching Effective Agreements Covering Services' in A.O. Krueger (ed.), *The WTO as an International Organization* (University of Chicago Press, Chicago and London, 1998), chapter 10.

[36]   R. Ruggiero, 'Charting the Trade Routes of the Future: Towards a Borderless Economy' (paper presented to the International Industrial Conference, San Francisco, 29 September 1997).

systematic reform of those very sectors that are crucial for making the most of the information revolution. But this phenomenon also calls into question the adequacy of the GATS and the TRIPS agreement in the light of the recent and forthcoming explosion in electronic commerce,[37] something that may have to be addressed when GATS and TRIPS are reviewed at the end of this decade.

IV.6   Dealing with the recent backlash against globalization

Not surprisingly, the accelerated pace of globalization in the past 15 or so years, to which both new information technologies and policy reforms have contributed, has generated resentment by some groups in numerous countries. In the richer economies the greater flow of imports from and FDI to newly industrializing countries are alleged to be causing job losses and/or lower relative wages for less-skilled workers in those rich countries (when really the main cause is probably the new information technologies). And most recently the openness to trade and FDI flows in East Asian economies is said to have left them vulnerable to the whim of international financial markets and now to IMF conditionality as they accept loans contingent on strict policy reforms being adopted and kept in place. Whatever is behind each of these developments, proponents of globalization ignore them at their peril.[38] Appropriate reactions might include the following, according to Blackhurst:[39]

(i)   governments need to make it more widely understood that while policy reforms are good for the overall economy, there will always be some groups who benefit less than others and some of those may even be made worse off if not compensated;

(ii)   it also needs to be better understood that, while globalization can bestow huge benefits on participants, it also raises the cost of bad policies (as some East Asian countries have learnt, the hard way, during recent months); and yet

(iii) increased protectionism and resistance to further policy reform will make matters *worse*, particularly if it slows the extent to which a country can take advantage of the information revolution.

V.   Opportunities to Further Strengthen the Multilateral Trading System

The completion of the Uruguay Round negotiations, the subsequent agreements on telecoms, financial services and information technology, and the on-going

---

[37]   WTO, *Electronic Commerce and the Role of the WTO* (World Trade Organization, Geneva, 1998).

[38]   D. Rodrik, *Has Globalization Gone Too Far?* (Institute for International Economics, Washington, DC, 1997).

[39]   R. Blackhurst, 'The WTO and the Global Economy' (1997) 20 *World Economy* 527–544.

implementation of the commitments made in those various agreements all indicate that the rules-based multilateral trading system is very much alive and well in its 50th year. The strong desire expressed at the political level of the WTO ministerial meeting in Singapore in December 1996, to continue to strengthen the system, also is reassuring for the institution's future. Yet as the previous two sections indicate, a huge built-in work programme and many new challenges confront the WTO collective: delegates in Geneva, their support staff and masters in national capitals, and Secretariat staff.

Moreover, even after the Uruguay Round agreements are implemented, by which time tariffs will be down to very low levels for imports of most manufactured goods by developed countries, there will still be considerable scope for further gains from traditional multilateral trade reform. This has been demonstrated empirically by Francois and McDonald[40] with recent global modelling results. In particular, they make clear that:

(i)   some manufactures will still have high tariffs (offering even higher effective rates of protection), including for processed primary products exported by developing countries;

(ii)   even though non-tariff barriers on imports of agricultural products have been tariffied, because of 'dirty tariffication' those tariffs will still remain high at the end of the implementation period (2000 for developed countries, 2004 for developing countries) and farm producer and export subsidies will be tolerated rather than outlawed and will only be reduced by about one-fifth or less;

(iii) non-tariff barriers remain on numerous manufactures and the threat of contingent protection in the form of anti-dumping duties remains considerable in some markets, most notably textiles and clothing where reneging on Uruguay Round commitments is a real possibility especially if China and Vietnam join the WTO and India continues to open up;

(iv)   services trade barrier reduction commitments remain very limited and those agreed to will have barely begun to open the service sector to trade by the turn of the century;

(v)   the government procurement agreement is only plurilateral rather than multilateral and so is only a beginning to freeing up to international competition that very considerable portion of each nation's economy; and

(vi)   great scope still remains for trade facilitation measures, especially in developing countries where customs procedures and the like continue to make trading difficult.

Given the plethora of issues needing to be addressed by the WTO, and the built-in agenda for reviews of the agriculture, SPS, technical barriers, services and TRIPS agreements by 2000 anyway, the case for launching a comprehensive round of multilateral trade negotiations early next century is compelling.

For that to occur, the non-trivial task of building a consensus among WTO members to launch that round needs to begin immediately. Sir Leon Brittan, the EU Commission

---

[40]   J.F. Francois and B. McDonald, 'The Multilateral Trade Agenda: Uruguay Round Implementation and Beyond' (CIES Seminar Paper 96-16, University of Adelaide, November 1996).

Vice-President responsible for relations between the EU and the WTO, has already lent his support from the EU, and smaller advanced economies including Australia and New Zealand are strongly supportive. Many developing countries also would be willing participants, at least under certain conditions.[41] One of those conditions is that issues on which they would be asked to liberalize more than some of them might like (services, TRIPS, investment) be counter-balanced with issues of direct interest to their exporters (particularly agriculture and textiles). Another condition is that more aid funds be made available to the smaller and poorer developing country members (and aspirants) so they can mount an adequate presence in Geneva and fund sufficient preparatory work in their national capitals.

A key component of the latter requires building a stronger domestic constituency for national policy reform. That could be helped considerably by more analytical work (including using national and global economy-wide models) which clearly demonstrate the indirect benefits from trade liberalization. The capacity of the economics profession to do that well was made clear in the recent ex post evaluations of the Uruguay Round.[42] Now is the time for similar but ex ante analytical evaluations for a millennium round, with follow-up dissemination and training seminars to spread the findings widely.

However, a new round of multilateral trade negotiations is not going to happen without the USA Government behind the idea. Unfortunately, trade policy is not currently high on the present USA Administration's agenda.[43] It is to be hoped that the various 50th birthday celebrations for GATT during 1998 will, among other things, at least bring the issue to the attention of the USA (and any other member that has yet to see the need to consolidate the WTO's very considerable achievements in its first two plus years). Having the next WTO ministerial meeting in the USA in the autumn of 1999 should help. Would dubbing it the Clinton Round raise USA interest enough for the current administration to commit to launching a new comprehensive round before the next presidential election in 2000?

VI. Bibliography

Anderson, K., 'Lobbying Incentives and the Pattern of Protection in Rich and Poor Countries' (1995) 43 *Economic Development and Cultural Change* 401–423

---

[41]   Those developing countries that are Cairns Group members are especially anxious that the agricultural negotiations scheduled to restart next year be part of a more comprehensive round so that intersectoral and cross-issue trade-offs are possible.

[42]   See, for example, the project that culminated in the Martin and Winters World Bank conference volume, W. Martin and L.A. Winters (eds), *The Uruguay Round and the Developing Countries* (Cambridge University Press, Cambridge and New York, 1996).

[43]   J.J. Schott (ed.), *Restarting Fast Track* (Institute for International Economics, Washington, DC, 1998).

—— (ed.), *Strengthening the Global Trading System: From GATT to WTO* (Centre for International Economic Studies, Adelaide, 1996)

—— 'Agricultural Policy Reform under the Uruguay Round: Impact on Asian-Pacific Developing Countries' (1997) 2 *Journal of the Asia Pacific Economy* 303–331

—— 'Environmental Standards and International Trade' in M. Bruno and B. Pleskovic (eds), *Annual World Bank Conference on Development Economics 1996* (World Bank, Washington, DC, 1997), pp. 317–338

—— 'On the Complexities of China's WTO Accession' (1997) 20 *World Economy* 749–772

—— 'Agriculture and the WTO into the 21st Century' (paper presented at the Farm Leaders' Trade Strategy Seminar at the Cairns Group Ministerial Meeting, Sydney, 2–3 April, 1998)

—— 'Environmental and Labour Standards: What Role for the WTO?' in A.O. Krueger (ed.), *The WTO as an International Organization* (University of Chicago Press, Chicago and London, 1998), chapter 8

Anderson, K. and R. Blackhurst (eds), *The Greening of World Trade Issues* (University of Michigan Press, Ann Arbor, MI, and Harvester Wheatsheaf, London, 1992)

—— *Regional Integration and the Global Trading System* (Harvester Wheatsheaf, London, and St Martin's Press, New York, 1993)

Anderson, K., B. Dimaranan, T. Hertel and W. Martin, 'Asia–Pacific Food Markets and Trade in 2005: A Global, Economy-Wide Perspective' (1997) 41 *Australian Journal of Agricultural and Resource Economics* 19–44

—— 'Economic Growth and Policy Reforms in the APEC Region: Trade and Welfare Implications by 2005' (1997) 3 *Asia–Pacific Economic Review* 1–18

Anderson, K. and Y. Hayami, *The Political Economy of Agricultural Protection* (Allen and Unwin, London and Sydney, 1986)

Anderson, K. and H. Norheim, 'From Imperial to Regional Trade Preferences: Its Effect on Europe's Intra- and Extra-Regional Trade' (1993) 129 *Weltwirtschaftliches Archiv* 78–102

Bhagwati, J.N., 'The Demand to Reduce Domestic Diversity among Trading Nations' in J.N. Bhagwati and R.E. Hudec (eds), *Fair Trade and Harmonization: Prerequisites for Free Trade?* (MIT Press, Cambridge, MA, 1996), vol. I, chapter 1

Blackhurst, R., 'The WTO and the Global Economy' (1997) 20 *World Economy* 527–544

Cameron, J. and K. Campbell (eds), *Dispute Resolution in the World Trade Organization* (Cameron May, London, 1997)

Charnovitz, S., 'Exploring the Environmental Exceptions in GATT Article XX' (1991) 25 *Journal of World Trade*, issue 5

Corden, W.M., *Trade Policy and Economic Welfare* (2nd edn, Clarendon Press, Oxford, 1997)

Deardorff, A.V., 'An Economist's Overview of the World Trade Organization' (Discussion Paper No. 388, Research Seminar in International Economics, University of Michigan, Ann Arbor, MI, November 1996)

Elliot, K.A. (ed.), *Corruption and the Global Economy* (Institute for International Economics, Washington, DC, 1997)

Esty, D.C., *Greening GATT: Trade, Environment, and the Future* (Institute for International Economics, Washington, DC, 1994)

Francois, J.F. and B. McDonald, 'The Multilateral Trade Agenda: Uruguay Round Implementation and Beyond' (CIES Seminar Paper 96-16, University of Adelaide, November 1996)

Francois, J.F., B. McDonald and H. Nordstrom, 'Assessing the Uruguay Round' in W. Martin and L.A. Winters (eds), *The Uruguay Round and the Developing Countries* (Cambridge University Press, Cambridge and New York, 1996)

Frankel, J.A., *Regional Trading Blocs in the World Economic System* (Institute for International Economics, Washington, DC, 1997)

GATT, *The Results of the Uruguay Round of Multilateral Trade Negotiations: The Legal Texts* (GATT Secretariat, Geneva, 1994)

Goldstein, J., 'International Institutions and Domestic Politics: GATT, WTO, and the Liberalization of International Trade' in A.O. Krueger (ed.), *The WTO as an International Organization* (University of Chicago Press, Chicago and London, 1998), chapter 4

Graham, E.M., *Global Corporations and National Governments* (Institute for International Economics, Washington, DC, 1996)

Graham, E.M. and J.D. Richardson (eds), *Global Competition Policy* (Institute for International Economics, Washington, DC, 1997)

Grossman, G.M. and E. Helpman, *Innovation and Growth in the Global Economy* (MIT Press, Cambridge, MA, 1991)

—— 'Protection for Sale' (1994) 84 *American Economic Review* 833–850

—— 'Trade Wars and Trade Talks' (1995) 103 *Journal of Political Economy* 675–708

Hertel, T.W., W. Martin, K. Yanagishima and B. Dimaranan, 'Liberalizing Manufactures Trade in a Changing World Economy' in W. Martin and L.A. Winters (eds), *The Uruguay Round and the Developing Countries* (Cambridge University Press, Cambridge and New York, 1996), chapter 7

Hillman, A.L., *The Political Economy of Protection* (Harwood Academic, New York, 1989)

Hillman, A.L. and P. Moser, 'Trade Liberalization as Politically Optimal Exchange of Market Access' in M. Canzoneri et al. (eds), *The New Transatlantic Economy* (Cambridge University Press, Cambridge, 1995)

Hoekman, B., 'Trade Laws and Institutions: Good Practices and the World Trade Organization' (Supplementary Paper for the World Bank Conference on the Uruguay Round and the Developing Countries, Washington, DC, 26–27 January 1995)

Hoekman, B.M. and M. Kostecki, *The Political Economy of the World Trading System: From GATT to WTO* (Oxford University Press, London and New York, 1995)

Hoekman, B.M. and P. Mavroidis, 'Competition, Competition Policy, and GATT' (CEPR Discussion Paper No. 876, Centre for Economic Policy, London, January 1994)

Hudec, R.E., 'Strengthening of Procedures for Settling Disputes' in H. Corbet (ed.), *Remaking the World Trading System* (University of Michigan Press, Ann Arbor, MI, 1995)

Ingco, M., 'Agricultural Trade Liberalization in the Uruguay Round: One Step Forward, One Step Back?' (supplementary paper prepared for a World Bank Conference on the Uruguay Round and the Developing Countries, Washington, DC, 26–27 January 1995)

Jackson, J.H., *The World Trading System: Law and Policy of International Economic Relations* (2nd edn, MIT Press, Cambridge, MA, 1997)

Johnson, D.G., *World Agriculture in Disarray* (2nd edn, St Martin's Press, New York, 1991)

Josling, T., *Agricultural Trade Policy: Completing the Reform* (Institute for International Economics, Washington, DC, 1998)

Kindleberger, 'The Rise of Free Trade in Western Europe, 1820–1875' (1975) 35 *Journal of Economic History* 20–55

Krueger, A.O. (ed.), *The WTO as an International Organization* (University of Chicago Press, Chicago and London, 1998)

Lerner, A., 'The Symmetry Between Import and Export Taxes' (1936) 3 *Economica* 306–313

Lloyd, P.J. and G. Sampson, 'International Competition Policy after the Uruguay Round' (1995) 18 *World Economy* 681–705

Markusen, J.R., 'Trade versus Investment Liberalization' (NBER Working Paper No. 6231, Cambridge, MA, 1997)

Martin, W. and L.A. Winters (eds), *The Uruguay Round and the Developing Countries* (Cambridge University Press, Cambridge and New York, 1996)

Michalopoulos, C., 'The Participation of Developing Countries in the WTO' (Policy Research Working Paper 1906, Washington, DC, World Bank, 1998)

—— 'WTO Membership for Countries in Transition' (Policy Research Working Paper, Washington, DC, World Bank, 1998)

OECD, *Survey of DAC Members' Co-operation for Capacity Development in Trade* (DCD/DAC(97)24/REV1, OECD, Paris, 1998)

Rattingan, G.A. and W.B. Carmichael, *Trade Liberalization: A Domestic Challenge for Industrial Nations* (National Centre for Development Studies, Australian National University, Canberra, 1996)

Rodrik, D., *Has Globalization Gone Too Far?* (Institute for International Economics, Washington, DC, 1997)

Ruggiero, R., 'Charting the Trade Routes of the Future: Towards a Borderless Economy' (paper presented to the International Industrial Conference, San Francisco, 29 September 1997)

Schott, J.J. (ed.), *Restarting Fast Track* (Institute for International Economics, Washington, DC, 1998)

Snape, R.H., 'Reaching Effective Agreements Covering Services' in A.O. Krueger (ed.), *The WTO as an International Organization* (University of Chicago Press, Chicago and London, 1998), chapter 10

Srinivasan, T.N., 'International Trade and Labour Standards from an Economic Perspective' in P. van Dijck and G. Faber (eds), *Challenges to the New World Trade Organization* (Kluwer Law International, Dordrecht, 1996), chapter 11

Tangermann, S., 'An Assessment of the Uruguay Round Agreement on Agriculture' (paper prepared for the OECD's Agriculture Directorate, Paris, 1994)

Winters, L.A., 'Regionalism and the Next Round of Multilateral Trade Negotiations' (paper presented at a conference on the World Trading System at Fifty: Global Challenges and USA Interests, Institute for International Economics, Washington, DC, 15 April 1998)

—— 'Regionalism versus Multilateralism' in R. Baldwin, D. Cole, A. Sapir and A. Venables (eds), *Regional Integration* (Cambridge University Press, Cambridge and New York, 1998)

WTO, *Regionalism and the World Trading System* (World Trade Organization, Geneva, 1995)

—— *Annual Report 1996* (World Trade Organization, Geneva, 1996), vol. I

—— *Electronic Commerce and the Role of the WTO* (World Trade Organization, Geneva, 1998)

Chapter 4

Pragmatism Versus Principle in GATT Decision-Making: A Brief Historical Perspective

Robert E. Baldwin

I. Introduction

When I first came to Geneva in the early 1960s as part of the USA delegation to the Kennedy Round negotiations, GATT was dominated by so-called old GATT hands – delegates and trade officials in the respective capitals who had participated in most of the previous five rounds of trade negotiations. While economists played a major role in drafting GATT (eg, James Meade of the United Kingdom and Clair Wilcox of the USA), diplomats and individuals trained in public administration had been given primary responsibility for directing the operations of the organization. They were rightly very proud of the accomplishments of GATT since 1948 and did not hesitate to lecture newcomers like myself on why the organization had been so successful. In doing so, they stressed the fragility of GATT and the danger of it becoming ineffective or even breaking up should new hands like me insist on the application of GATT's underlying general economic principles without sufficient regard for the special economic and political circumstance of particular members.

The attitude of this group towards the tariff disparity issue that arose in the Kennedy Round, namely, the existence of many more high-duty and low-duty items in the USA tariff schedule than in the schedule of the European Community, illustrates their negotiating perspective. Although the overall average duty levels were comparable in the USA and the Community, EC negotiators argued that tariffs on products with especially high duties should be reduced by a greater percentage than tariffs on low duty items. Specifically, they initially proposed cutting duties on manufactures by 50 per cent of the *difference* between their existing level and 10 per cent, whereas the USA proposed an across-the-board cut in tariffs of 50 per cent. As the staff person in the US Trade Representative primarily responsible for following this issue, I argued, along with others in the USA delegation, that the economic reasoning put forth by the Community in support of their proposal had little merit and, therefore, that the USA should strongly oppose the proposal, especially since it would significantly reduce the overall average

© Kluwer Law International 2000. *From GATT to the WTO: The Multilateral Trading System in the New Millennium*, The WTO Secretariat (ed.), Kluwer Law International, London, 2000; ISBN 90–411–1253–7

depth of the tariff cuts.[1] The USA did, in fact, adopt this negotiating position and, despite various compromising efforts by both the EC and the USA, no duty-cutting rule to deal with the tariff disparities issue was ever agreed on. The issue was eventually shelved for the rest of the Kennedy Round negotiations.[2]

Many of the old GATT hands were quite critical of the USA position. They were concerned that USA negotiators were endangering the success of the Round over an issue they did not regard to be of major significance. In their view, even if the EC argument did not have economic merit (and they were not too sure about this), the fact that EC negotiators strongly believed in their position was in itself sufficient to require that a compromise be reached. They believed that progress towards trade liberalization within a framework of respect for the strongly held views of any important member should take precedence over economic logic.

The outcome of the so-called 'chicken war' in 1962–1963 further illustrates the view that 'keeping peace in the family' is more important than closely following the economic and organizational principles on which GATT is based. This dispute between the USA and EC arose because the introduction of the variable levy agricultural system by the EC in 1962 sharply increased the EC import duty on exports of broiler chickens from the USA. Consequently, the USA invoked its GATT right either to receive compensation in the form of tariff cuts on other products or to retaliate by raising duties against an equivalent amount of EC exports to the USA. The USA claimed that the EC actions had resulted in a loss of US$46 million of USA exports of chickens to the EC, whereas the Community argued that the loss was only US$19 million. After consultations between the two trading powers failed to resolve the issue and the USA announced its intention to raise duties on US$46 million of EC trade, a GATT panel was appointed to judge the merits of the USA case. The panel's decision that a reasonable figure for the amount of trade affected was US$26 million struck me at the time as based on little more than the old GATT hands' policy of trying not to upset either party in a dispute too much.[3] In my view, an objective economic assessment of the value of USA trade adversely affected or, to use the language of Article XXVIII of GATT, 'the substantially equivalent concessions initially negotiated with the applicant contracting party' had to be much closer to the USA figure.

The tariff disparities issue and the chicken war are two, comparatively minor negotiating matters illustrating the pragmatic decision-making approach of the old GATT hands – an approach still favoured by many trade officials. However, it has been

---

[1]   See Robert E. Baldwin, 'Tariff-Cutting Techniques in the Kennedy Round' in Richard Caves, Harry Johnson and Peter Kenen (eds), *Trade, Growth, and Balance of Payments: Essays in Honor of Gottfried Haberler* (Rand McNally and Co., Chicago, 1965) for a detailed discussion of the disparities issue.

[2]   The tariff-cutting rule adopted in the Tokyo Round did reduce tariffs on high-duty products by a greater percentage than tariffs on low-duty products.

[3]   See Ernest H. Preeg, *Traders and Diplomats: An Analysis of the Kennedy Round of Negotiations under the General Agreement of Tariffs and Trade* (Brookings Institution, Washington, DC, 1970) for a more complete discussion of this incident.

applied in dealing with many more important issues over the years. Moreover, the approach has involved much more than just ignoring assessments based on standard economic reasoning, as in the disparities and chicken-war incidents. It has also involved a willingness to introduce new forms of discrimination between countries and to utilize quantitative and other non-price means to limit imports on the grounds that these derogations were needed to maintain harmony among members and continue the general liberalization process.

This paper appraises some of the important GATT decisions over the last 50 years in which the pragmatic approach was followed in terms of whether the decisions made actually contributed to long-run trade liberalization or perhaps held it back in certain sectors and countries. Most economists believe that adhering to GATT principles of most-favoured-nation treatment, national treatment on internal taxation and regulation, and the general elimination of quantitative restrictions is the best decision-making strategy not only for maximizing collective economic benefits but for achieving long-run economic harmony among nations. Thus, from a 50-year perspective, one might conclude that backing away from these principles under the short-run negotiating pressures of maintaining harmony has turned out not to have been the best negotiating approach. In contrast, one may conclude that 'practicality over principle' has prevented a fragile international organization from disintegrating or becoming ineffective, thereby enabling the international community to enjoy the enormous benefits of the trade liberalization of the last 50 years.

In observing decision-making in GATT and WTO over the last 35 years, I have come to hold mixed views on the merits of the pragmatic approach of the old GATT hands. The main theme I would like to develop is that this approach has been successful from a long-run viewpoint when applied to negotiating initiatives that mainly involved increasing market access for some or all countries. However, when basic GATT principles have been bent or circumvented by waivers or new rules to accommodate pressures to reduce market access, this approach has, in my view, brought about less long-run liberalization and growth than would have occurred by utilizing the basic price-oriented policies of GATT.

II. Market-Opening Trade Initiatives

An example where a pragmatic approach not closely tied to basic GATT principles proved to be successful in contributing to long-run trade liberalization is the acceptance by GATT of the General System of Preferences (GSP) for developing countries. This scheme emerged as a serious proposal in the first United Nations Conference on Trade and Development (UNCTAD) in 1963 as part of the efforts at that time to narrow the then widening income gap between developing and developed countries. The proposal called for developed countries to set import duties at lower rates on manufactured goods if they were produced in developing countries in contrast to developed nations. A number of developed countries promptly agreed to introduce the scheme for a selected number of products. However, they needed a GATT waiver to implement the arrangement, since it was inconsistent with the non-discrimination principle embodied in Article I of GATT. Not only were these waivers granted but also a general waiver was extended for GSP schemes in 1971.

At the time, most American trade economists thought that GSP was a bad idea. We strongly favoured effects to help the developed countries to grow more rapidly but believed this was best accomplished by MFN tariff cuts by the developed countries on labour-intensive products such as apparel and footwear coupled with the abandonment by the developing countries of their import-substitution policies. However, many trade negotiators thought that neither of these actions was politically realistic. The GSP scheme was, consequently, put forth as a practical alternative means of providing greater trade benefit to the developing countries. Among the objections by economists to the scheme was that it would lead to the establishment of industries in the developing countries that would not prove to be viable in the long run as tariffs came down generally through periodic rounds of GATT multilateral negotiations or as the developed countries withdrew the preferences because of domestic political pressures. Either of these actions would then cause considerable hardship in the countries that the scheme was aimed at benefiting. It could also lead to increased resistance on their part to further GATT rounds of MFN tariff cuts, thus slowing down general trade liberalization.

It turned out that those of us who opposed GSP were overly concerned about the unfavourable consequences of the scheme. Eliminating duties on exports of selected manufactured goods from developing countries served as an important catalyst in these countries for moving away from the import-substitution development route in favour of a more export-oriented approach. Furthermore, the economic benefits resulting from being able to take advantage of economies of scale, from the knowledge spillovers associated with increased trade between developed and least-developed countries, and from the unleashing of the latent entrepreneurial and labour talents in the poorer countries have enabled most GSP beneficiaries to adjust comparatively easily to new competition as general duty levels have declined, new countries have been made eligible for the preferences and some preferences have been withdrawn.

A good case can thus be made, I think, that the opening up of the developing countries to market-oriented policies was promoted to an important extent by the granting of tariff preferences. Moreover, as these countries discovered the significant growth benefits from outward-looking policies, they became much more willing to open their own markets to the products of the developed nations. It might well have taken longer to reach the existing degree of liberalization in most developing countries had we not been willing to permit this violation of the most-favoured-nation principle.

A current market-opening issue of considerable concern that involves the abrogation of most-favoured-nation treatment is the proliferation of regional trading agreements. Article XXIV, which permits such agreements, was included in GATT as part of a compromise to achieve harmony, and the lax enforcement over the years of the requirement that each agreement be appraised for compatibility with the general provisions of this article attests to the willingness of members to continue to indulge the special interests of particular members. It is still too early to reach a firm view on whether the recent increase in the number and importance of free trade agreements is serving to stimulate the long-run liberalization of international and domestic resource-distorting policies or to retard such liberalization. Particularly troubling with respect to free trade agreements is the exploitation by protectionist groups of the need for rules of origin to introduce non-transparent trade restrictions that they would not be able to obtain in multilateral trade-liberalizing negotiations. Thus, even if such agreements stimulate liberalization in many areas, they could end up creating more hard-core protectionism than the liberalization benefits are worth.

The failure of the efforts by President Clinton to extend fast-track authority so that presidents can present trade agreements to Congress on an up or down basis without amendments has revealed another danger from free trade agreements to the goal of greater multilateral liberalization. With most new free trade proposals involving trade between developed and developing countries rather than either between developed countries or between developing countries, many equity-minded legislators in the developed countries are becoming increasingly concerned that their less skilled, less educated constituents will be adversely affected by further trade liberalization. This view is evident from an examination of the actual votes of members of the USA House of Representatives on the North American Free Trade Agreement (NAFTA) and the agreements concluded under the Uruguay Round trade negotiations (GATT) as well as from their planned Fast-Track votes. There was a tendency in both the NAFTA and Fast-Track votes (especially strong in the Fast-Track case) for legislators to vote against these measures the higher the proportion of workers in their districts who did not have a high school education and the higher the proportion of workers in industries with a net import surplus. In GATT vote neither of these factors was statistically significant for explaining the pattern of voting. As legislators' statements explaining their votes indicate, the trade liberalization associated with the Uruguay Round agreements was viewed as providing a more equitable distribution of the benefits and costs from trade liberalization than NAFTA or Fast-Track. The voting implications of these different perceptions were that GATT passed the USA House of Representatives by a margin of 142 votes, whereas NAFTA passed by only 34 votes and Fast-Track was expected to fail (and thus was withdrawn from consideration) by a margin of between five and 20 votes.

It appears, therefore, that the emphasis of recent USA administrations on negotiating free trade agreements with the developing countries in South America and the Pacific Rim may have produced a backlash against further trade liberalization. It may be that the failure of WTO/GATT members to require a greater degree of compliance with the provisions of Article XXIV and thereby perhaps to slow down the proliferation of free trade agreements is partly responsible for this result.

III.   Import-Restricting Policies

When bending or abandoning basic GATT principles has involved restricting market access, the old GATT hands' negotiating approach has proved, in my view, to have retarded long-run trade liberalization. The main GATT decisions resulting in this outcome have been the exclusion of textile and clothing products and agricultural products from normal GATT discipline from the 1950s until the textile-apparel and agricultural agreements of the Uruguay Round.

The introduction of discriminatory quantitative restrictions to regulate international trade in textiles and clothing is closely related to the fear by many GATT members in the 1950s of a flood of market-disrupting imports from Japan.[4] Japan had quickly emerged at the end of World War II as a fairly high-tech but low-wage country capable of becoming a major competitor in international markets, especially in labour-intensive products. Prior to Japan becoming a GATT member, countries concerned about this problem were able to use quantitative restrictions against Japanese imports without being in violation of GATT. Furthermore, when Japan did join GATT in 1955, a number of countries invoked Article XXXV, the non-application of the agreement between particular contracting parties, in order to be able to continue their discriminatory practices. These countries gradually disinvoked this Article but, in agreeing to do so, they pressured Japan into signing various bilateral agreements outside of GATT in which Japan voluntarily agreed to limit its exports of various products, especially textiles and apparel. Even countries that had not invoked Article XXXV, such as the USA, entered into such arrangements with Japan.

The initiative to exclude textiles and apparel formally from the normal discipline of GATT, not just with respect to Japanese exports but market-disrupting exports from other countries as well, was led by the USA. A short-term (one year) agreement permitting discriminatory restrictions against cotton textile imports was negotiated within GATT in 1961 and quickly followed a few months later by the negotiation of the Long-Term Arrangement Regarding International Trade in Cotton Textiles. As stated in the preamble, the goal of the agreement was 'to promote on a sound basis the development of production and expansion of trade in textile products and progressively to achieve the reduction of trade barriers and the liberalization of world trade in these products'.[5]

Unfortunately, world trade in textile and apparel products did not proceed in the manner described in the preamble. Instead, the Long Term Arrangement on Cotton Textiles began a process of increasing protection in these product sectors. The 1961 agreement was extended twice through to 1973, and then replaced in 1974 by the Multi-Fibre Arrangement (MFA). This agreement extended the right to impose discriminatory quantitative restrictions to imports of textile and apparel products made of wool and man-made fibres as well as cotton. In the four renewals of the MFA prior to the Uruguay Round agreement on textiles, such restrictions were applied to an increasing number of countries (eg, the USA had bilateral quota agreements with 41 countries by 1993) and an increasing number of man-made and natural products (eg, ramie). However, in a truly remarkable shift in trade policy, GATT members decided in the Uruguay Round to phase

---

[4]   See Patterson *Discrimination in International Trade: the Policy Issues, 1955–1965* (Princeton University Press, NJ, 1966) for an excellent discussion of the circumstances leading to the exclusion of the textile and apparel sectors from normal GATT discipline.

[5]   GATT, *Arrangement Regarding International Trade in Textiles* (GATT Secretariat, Geneva, 1974).

out the MFA gradually over a ten-year period. By 2005 textile and apparel products can only be protected by tariffs, thus bringing these sectors back within the normal discipline of the WTO/GATT.

The MFA forcefully demonstrates the unfortunate outcome of following a decision-making strategy that, in my view, has too readily granted exceptions to basic GATT principles in order to ease the adjustment problems of certain nations. For over one-third of a century economic resources have been tied up in the textile-apparel sectors that could be used more productively in other activities. The cost to American consumers of these import controls was estimated to be US$24 billion in 1990,[6] which meant that the average family paid about US$350 more annually for textile and apparel products than if the controls had not existed. Of course, GATT members were under strong domestic and international political pressure in the 1950s and early 1960s to do something about market-disrupting imports from Japan and developing countries. They could have insisted that the non-discriminatory procedures of Article XIX be followed, even though this would have forced resource adjustments in those exporting countries that were losing competitive position relative to Japan and the developing countries. A gradual phase out of the discriminatory quantitative restrictions, such as is taking place as a result of the Uruguay Round agreement, could also have been implemented.

Agricultural trade has also long been characterized by policies inconsistent with basic GATT principles. Granting of a waiver to the USA in 1955 in order to implement domestic legislation raising domestic prices for various agricultural products above international prices provided the basis for a general disregard of GATT discipline in this sector. Especially disturbing to countries who are efficient exporters of agricultural products has been the use of export subsidies by other countries in order to dispose of domestic surpluses stimulated by artificially high domestic prices. Such policies have led to massive misallocations of world economic resources and distortions of world trade in agricultural products. Fortunately, as in the case of textiles and apparel, the Uruguay Round negotiations produced an agreement that begins the process of bringing agriculture within the normal discipline of GATT. Non-tariff import barriers are being replaced by tariffs, which will then be gradually reduced, and members are required to implement progressively larger minimum access commitments. In addition, progress has been made in reducing export subsidies. Eventually, income support subsidies are likely to become the only means by which countries' inefficient agricultural sectors can be supported.

IV. Fair Trade Policies

There has also been a tendency for members to tolerate the misuse of GATT's 'fair trade' rules, especially its anti-dumping provisions, to accommodate the protectionist goals of certain members. Since advanced industrial trading powers such as the USA and the EC

---

[6]   Clyde G. Hufbauer and Kimberly Ann Elliott, *Measuring the Costs of Protection in the United States* (Institute for International Economics, Washington, DC, 1994).

began to face increasing competition from developing nations in the early 1970s, they have relied to an increasing extent on the anti-dumping provisions of GATT, which permit the imposition of discriminatory tariffs, to limit imports. In the USA, for example, the number of anti-dumping cases reaching the International Trade Commission (ITC) for a material injury determination was less than five per year in the 1960s, 20 per year in the 1970s, and more than 40 per year from 1980 to 1994.[7] The non-discriminatory safeguard provisions of Article XIX are now seldom used in the USA to gain temporary import relief. This increase in anti-dumping actions has been facilitated both by the introduction of new provisions in USA anti-dumping law making it easier for petitioners to gain a favourable decision and by a more protectionist administration of existing provisions. The result has been that the anti-dumping law is now the preferred means by which some industries gain relief from increased import competition. Furthermore, there is empirical evidence that the anti-dumping law is now actually being used to promote collusive practices among international competitors.[8]

Unfortunately, negotiators in the Uruguay Round did not choose to restrain this misuse of the anti-dumping provisions of the WTO/GATT for protective and collusive purposes. Indeed, some provisions of the new anti-dumping agreement in the WTO seem to make it easier to misuse the anti-dumping laws for these purposes. It is hoped that the WTO review of this agreement that is due within the next few years will focus closely on this problem. The safeguard provisions of the WTO should become the standard route for seeking import protections. Furthermore, if rules covering competition policy are introduced into the WTO, it may be best to deal with international dumping under these rules.

Introducing labour standard provisions into the WTO is another fair trade issue that has been the subject of considerable recent discussion, particularly in the USA. As with the recent increases in anti-dumping actions, the motivations behind these pressures are, to a considerable extent, protectionist in nature, in my view. Labour unions in the advanced industrial countries rather than worldwide human rights groups are the main force exerting political pressure to permit countries with high labour standards to be able to introduce discriminatory trade restrictions against those with lower standards.

In my view, the negotiating experiences of the last 50 years suggest that the WTO should be very cautious about providing an exception to the non-discrimination rule at this time for labour-standard reasons. Unlike the provision in Article XX permitting discrimination against products produced by prison labour, there is a wide divergence of views among WTO members concerning the desirability of permitting discriminatory import restrictions against countries who, for example, allow the employment of children in certain sectors. Most developing-country members of the WTO maintain that, while they are as concerned about the welfare of workers as any developed country, permitting

---

[7]   Robert E. Baldwin, 'Imposing Multilateral Discipline on Administered Protection' in Anne O. Krueger (ed.), *The WTO as an International Organization* (University of Chicago Press, Chicago, 1998).

[8]   Ibid.

discriminatory import restrictions on these grounds would have disastrous domestic economic consequences because of their relatively low levels of development and would lead to trade frictions much more serious than those arising from anti-dumping actions. They point out that stricter labour standards will be introduced voluntarily as their per capita incomes rise, as has occurred in the more developed countries.[9] In the meantime, international bodies such as the International Labour Organization rather than the WTO should be utilized for the purposes of monitoring international labour conditions and coordinating efforts to improve these conditions on a voluntary basis.

V. Some Conclusions

There can be no doubt but that GATT's record over the last 50 years of liberalizing trade and of maintaining reasonably harmonious trade relations among an increasing number of members makes it one of the most successful international organizations of the twentieth century. It is useful, nevertheless, to ask if there were policies that could have been followed to produce even greater economic growth and political harmony. The conclusion of this paper is that there are such policies and that they would have involved closer adherence to basic GATT principles such as most-favoured-nation treatment and the use of tariffs rather than quantitative restrictions to control imports. There was, in my view, an excessive willingness for many years to bend or seek exceptions from these principles to accommodate the special concerns of particular members. This pragmatic approach was justified on the grounds that to do otherwise would jeopardize the effectiveness of the organization in liberalizing trade and maintaining harmonious relations among trading nations.

When exceptions to basic GATT principles were made in market-opening initiatives, such as the approval of GSP, the pragmatic approach to trade policy does not seem to have produced significant worldwide efficiency and growth losses and, indeed, may have actually promoted general economic growth in the GSP case. However, it is still too early to determine if the recent proliferation of market-opening but discriminatory free trade agreements have increased or decreased overall trade liberalization and raised or lowered long-run economic growth compared with what would have been achieved by following the traditional multilateral trade-liberalizing techniques of GATT.

In contrast, the discriminatory quantitative restrictions permitted by GATT in the textile and apparel sectors and in agriculture for market-protecting purposes have, in my view, brought about resource misallocations that have appreciably reduced worldwide economic welfare and growth. In addition, discriminatory measures permitted to achieve 'fair trade' have sometimes, as in anti-dumping actions, been utilized for narrow protectionist purposes and consequently reduced the gains from trade-liberalizing multilateral negotiations. I also conclude that members should be cautious at this time

---

[9]   See Alan B. Krueger, 'International Labor Standards and Trade', in *Annual World Bank Conference on Development Economics 1996* (World Bank, Washington, DC, 1996).

about introducing into the WTO the new rules on labour standards that some countries have recently called for on grounds of fairness.

Rather remarkably, negotiators in the Uruguay Round turned away from the 'go along–get along' negotiating approach to a surprising extent. They approved agreements bringing the textiles and apparel sectors and agriculture back under normal GATT discipline and eliminating such discriminatory measures as voluntary export restraints and performance requirements for foreign direct investors. In addition, they insisted that all members gradually stage-in the rules covering such new GATT issues as trade in services and the protection of intellectual property rights rather than granting indefinite exemptions from these rules for some members. Most members seem to appreciate to a greater extent than in earlier years that following the basic principles underlying the WTO/GATT best promotes both harmonious long-run economic relations between trading nations and world economic growth. If negotiators continue to behave in a manner consistent with this view, we can look forward to even greater benefits from the WTO/GATT in the next century than were achieved in the current one.

Chapter 5

Fifty Years Of the GATT/WTO: Lessons from the Past for Strategies for the Future

C. Fred Bergsten[*]
Director, Institute for International Economics

I.   Summary and Conclusions

Five major lessons for successful global trade management emerge from the first fifty years of the GATT/WTO system. They need to be applied to the present situation to set the stage for another half century of successful multilateral trade cooperation. I will summarize the key headings at the outset and then elaborate each, concluding with proposals for the upcoming Fiftieth Anniversary Ministerial and the WTO agenda for the early part of the twenty-first century.

(i)   *The Bicycle Must Keep Moving.* Forward momentum is essential to avoid backsliding into protectionism and mercantilism. A major new initiative is sorely needed at the present time to restart the bicycle.

(ii)   *Big is Beautiful.* Large-scale initiatives work better than small ones in keeping the bicycle moving. The time has come to launch the largest liberalization effort in the history of the global system, an effort to achieve global free trade by a date certain (probably 2010 or 2020) via a new Millennium Round and perhaps one or two successors.

(iii) *Building Blocks, Not Stumbling Blocks.* Regional trade arrangements have been a major source of liberalization momentum throughout the postwar period, especially over the past decade, but also pose potential risks to the global system. Hence, they provide both the foundation for the next big multilateral initiative and another motivation to launch it.

(iv) *Money is Central.* The international monetary and macroeconomic environment has been a critical determinant of the launch of all three major postwar trade rounds. Prospective monetary developments, particularly the onset of record trade deficits in the United States, suggest a similar imperative over the next year or two.

*   The author expresses deep appreciation for very helpful comments on an initial draft from Isaiah Frank, Joseph Greenwald, Julius Katz, Ernest Preeg and Alan Winters.

(v) *Leadership is Essential.* The United States has galvanized each of the previous rounds but the European Union has been an essential partner in de facto 'G-2' management of the system. With the creation of the euro, G-2 management will extend into the monetary arena and become more apparent – including for the next major WTO negotiation.

II. The Bicycle

Momentum has been a decisive factor in the direction of trade policy throughout the postwar period, both internationally and within the major countries. The political economy is straightforward: new liberalization initiatives force protectionist forces onto the defensive, while the absence thereof creates a vacuum that protectionists fill quite successfully.

The history of the GATT itself reveals an ebb and flow reflecting this principle. When the institution became largely comatose for several years after the completion of the Kennedy and Tokyo Rounds, major new protectionist efforts were undertaken and succeeded for at least a while: most notably the installation of the MFA and the US import surcharge in the early 1970s, and the panoply of new VERs (autos, steel, machine tools, expanded in textiles/apparel) in the early 1980s. By contrast, the ongoing agenda of sector negotiations after the completion of the bulk of the Uruguay Round in 1994 has precluded significant backsliding.

The periodic absence of international momentum has had a particularly profound effect on the trade policy of the United States, the largest and most influential member of the system. *Its* protectionists took advantage of the post-Kennedy Round malaise to ram the 'Mills bill' through the House, with its textile and shoe quotas and other far-reaching protectionist provisions; threaten the even broader Burke-Hartke legislation to control all imports and outward direct investment; and prompt the Nixon Administration to negotiate the MFA and apply an import surcharge. *Its* protectionists successfully achieved the series of new VERs listed above, forced a wholesale reversal of the Reagan Administration's trade policy in September 1985, and enacted the 'Super 301' provision even after the Administration had successfully preempted more negative legislation. And the current antiglobalization forces in the United States have taken advantage of the present lack of forward momentum, short-lived and modest though it is, to win a stunning victory in late 1997 with their defeat of new fast track negotiating authority for the President.

As will be noted below, these temporary (but extremely costly) periods of major American protectionism were driven initially by (largely self-inflicted) imbalances in US monetary and macroeconomic policy. However, the absence of any major GATT initiatives at the time left the door open for such relapses. This explains why American trade negotiators are always anxious to begin a new initiative as soon as the prior one ends, or even sooner, and why the rest of the world errs to demur in the name of 'trade fatigue' or some other excuse that ignores the fundamental interplay between external and internal politics in American trade policy.

The lesson for 1998 and beyond is clear: launch a new liberalizing initiative in the WTO to restart the bicycle as soon as possible. As noted, the sectoral follow-ups to the Uruguay Round – in telecommunications services, financial services and information technology products – maintained a degree of momentum after its conclusion. The APEC summit initiative of November 1997, committing its members (who make up half of the world economy) to new liberalization in 9–15 additional sectors, is a promising start in the needed direction if it can be multilateralized (as will be elaborated below). And the Uruguay Round wrap-up was extremely wise to incorporate a 'built-in agenda' for the future, including such major topics as agriculture and overall services.

Hence the WTO system is teed up to launch the needed new initiative. Sir Leon Brittan, and now the EU more officially, has proposed a Millennium Round for that purpose. But no significant liberalizing progress is underway at present. The United States, the developing countries and the rest of the WTO membership hence need to embrace the EU initiative promptly to restart the bicycle and regain the momentum for liberalization. It is urgent for them to do so in light of the evident strength of the backlash against globalization, as indicated in the continuing rejection of fast track in the United States and the growing Asian calls to reduce their vulnerabilities to future crises by partial separation from the global system rather than the full-scale outward orientation of the past.

III. Big is Beautiful

The history of the GATT/WTO, and especially trade policy in the United States, clearly reveals that large-scale initiatives fare better than modest ones. The political economy is again straightforward: big-picture proposals capture the imagination of top political leaders and thus induce them to provide the leadership needed to win domestic support, provide a foreign policy/national security rationale to amplify the purely economic case for proceeding, and generate such huge stakes that no political leader is willing to accept blame for failure of the enterprise once it has been launched. 'Big is beautiful,' therefore, at both the start-up and completion of the process.

The key example of the United States is again instructive. Extension of NAFTA to tiny Chile would have been so small that it failed to command any Presidential leadership and business support. The defeat of fast track was due importantly to the Administration's failure to indicate how it would use the authority and thus the absence of any apparent stakes worth fighting for.

Each succeeding GATT round has had the important advantage of being more ambitious than its predecessors. The Kennedy Round sharply increased the amount of multilateral cuts in tariffs, which remained an important impediment to trade at that time. The Tokyo Round began the process of extending the GATT system to nontariff measures. The Uruguay Round brought agriculture and textiles into the system, seriously addressed services and intellectual property rights, and dramatically improved the dispute settlement mechanism. 'Bigger was better' in attracting sufficient political support to bring each succeeding negotiation to a successful conclusion, despite the bigger battles that had to be taken on to do so.

There is a natural extension, to the next phase of multilateral liberalization and rulemaking, from this past progression of escalating increasing negotiating goals: setting a goal of global free trade by a date certain, perhaps 2010 or 2020.[1] Over 60 per cent of world trade is already free, or en route to being free (see Table 1), as a result of the initiatives already completed or undertaken by the several large regional arrangements (EU, NAFTA, Mercosur, AFTA, Australia-New Zealand, FTAA and APEC). It is thus a relatively short step to global free trade, and rolling the regionals into such a multilateral context is in any event the only way to assure the avoidance of conflict among them. Hence a global free trade goal appears feasible, as well as being a highly desirable big-picture proposal to capture political imagination and support around the world.

Table 1 – Regional Tree Trade Arrangements Share of World Trade, 1998

EU	22.8
Euromed	2.3
Nafta	7.9
Mercosur	0.3
FTAA	2.6*
AFTA	1.3
Australia-New Zealand	0.1
APEC	23.7*
Total	61.0

*   Excluding Subregionals

The route to that goal will clearly encompass one or two major 'rounds' of WTO negotiation. A corollary of 'big is beautiful' is that multi-issue rounds have been crucial to the outcome of the successive GATT negotiations. Trade-offs across issue-areas are required to meet the needs of the ever-growing number of country participants, and to induce a critical mass to sign on. The three recent sectoral agreements have probably completed the roster of potential stand-alone deals, and their negotiation may have even jeopardized later agreements on agriculture and other difficult topics by 'using up' some of the trade-offs that could otherwise have been employed for that purpose. It must also be remembered that several sectoral efforts, including maritime services in the WTO and a Multilateral Agreement on Investment in the OECD, have failed largely because of the absence of potential trade-offs with other issue-areas.

The current APEC sector initiatives, which represent the major liberalization effort now underway and may provide one of the foundations for the Millennium Round, are

---

[1]   As originally proposed in C. Fred Bergsten, 'Globalizing Free Trade', *Foreign Affairs*, May/June 1996.

instructive in this regard. After their success in galvanizing global agreement on the Information Technology Agreement (ITA) in late 1996, the APEC leaders decided to try to replicate that event in additional sectors in 1997. They originally envisaged agreeing on two or three sectors, at their Vancouver summit in late 1997, but found that 'balance among the parties' required a much larger number – so they decided to proceed on 15, including nine in 1998. APEC of course hopes to multilateralize these negotiations, as it did with the ITA, and the EU (and presumably others) have already indicated that they will propose additional sectors. This broad group of sectors will then undoubtedly be meshed with the built-in agenda already endorsed by the WTO, setting the stage for the Millennium Round (with or without the 'global free trade by 2010/2020' goal recommended here).

The basic lesson of GATT/WTO history, as well as of trade policy in the United States, is that larger initiatives fare better than small ones. Application of that lesson to the period ahead is of crucial importance because of the severe threat to the open trading system from opponents of globalization in the United States, Europe and some key developing countries. The complaint that rounds take too long to complete is actually a virtue because, as long as their eventual success remains a realistic prospect, it is the very existence of the negotiations that propels the bicycle forward and provides a bulwark against backsliding. If one worries about excessive duration, however, the answer is to divide the total negotiations into a series of self-balancing, but smaller, 'roundups' every two or three years to assure the credibility of the process.[2] The prescribed course of action is, in any event, the earliest possible launch of a Millennium Round within the context of setting a policy objective of achieving global free trade by 2010 or 2020.

IV. Building Blocks, Not Stumbling Blocs

Debate continues to rage in some quarters over the compatibility of regional trade agreements with the multilateral system. Some observers fear that regional participants, once having liberalized regionally, will not want to give up their preferential arrangements and/or will have 'used up' their liberalization potential and/or trade attention. There are, indeed, a few disquieting signs. NAFTA employs rules of origin in the textile/apparel sector that discriminate sharply against non-members. Mercosur raised its common external tariff in late 1997 and sometimes expresses doubts about extending its liberalization to broader groupings. History also suggests the real possibility of clashes among regional blocs if their relationships are not managed in the context of a successful global system.

Fortunately, however, the postwar record is an unbroken chain of positive interaction between the global system and its main regional subsystems. There are clear

---

[2] As advocated by Jeffrey J. Schott, *WTO 2000: Setting the Course for the World Trading System* (Policy Analyses 45. Washington: Institute for International Economics, 1996).

theoretical grounds for this outcome: modest liberalization begets broader liberalization by demonstrating its payoff and familiarizing domestic politics with the issue, regional deals can provide useful models for broader global agreements, and the adverse impact of new preferential arrangements on outsiders induces the latter to seek new multilateral compacts.

The regionals have in fact kept the bicycle moving forward both through their own liberalization and through the impetus they have provided to the successive multilateral initiatives. They have indeed been a major driving force behind each of the rounds that have been the primary channels for global progress. Hence the regionals have been key elements in the successful evolution of the two principles already enumerated, the forward momentum of the bicycle and 'big is beautiful'.

The key regional arrangement is by far the European Union, and its evolution has been central to the entire postwar history of the multilateral trading system. The initial creation of the Common Market, in the late 1950s, was the most important driver of the American initiative to launch the Kennedy Round in the early 1960s – both for defensive reasons, to start reducing the newly created discrimination against American exports, and to build the 'new Atlantic partnership' enunciated by President Kennedy. The expansion of the European Community to include the United Kingdom and others, with the extension of its discrimination to important new markets, was an important factor in the American decision to insist on the Tokyo Round in the 1970s. The EU decision to launch the 'single market' strategy in 1985, with the implied broadening of discrimination to many new functional areas, likewise added to the US determination to begin the Uruguay Round a year later. To its great credit, the EU has agreed to reduce its barriers on a multilateral basis in each of these rounds – though with great reluctance in agriculture – and thus to sustain the bicycle of global liberalization.

The positive thrust of regionalism for global liberalization has broadened considerably over the last decade or so. When the EU and others refused to proceed with the new round that the United States was seeking in the early 1980s, the United States reversed its traditional policy of sole reliance on multilateral liberalization and agreed to negotiate bilateral free trade agreements with Israel and then Canada; the EU and others took notice and subsequently agreed to restart the multilateral bicycle. When the Uruguay Round faltered in the late 1980s, Mexico successfully sought US and Canadian agreement to negotiate NAFTA and several Asian countries (notably Japan and Australia) took the lead in creating APEC; the EU and others took notice and the Round regained momentum. When the Round faltered once more in the early 1990s, APEC's decision to hold annual summits and create 'a community of Asian Pacific economies' oriented toward 'free and open trade and investment in the region by 2010/2020', as formally agreed a year later, quickly persuaded the Europeans to overcome their problems and participate in a successful wrap-up.

For their part, all of the new regionals have so far emulated the willingness of the EU to multilateralize at least part of their liberalization (on a fully reciprocal basis). APEC, potentially the second most important regional grouping because its external trade level closely approximates that of the EU, has to date remained wholly faithful to its precept of 'open regionalism'[3] and has in fact played a key role in galvanizing the conclusion of both the Uruguay Round and the ITA.

It will of course be essential for the major countries, who are at the same time central to both the global system and the main regionals, to manage the interaction between them in a manner that will continue to be mutually supportive – as the United States did while simultaneously negotiating NAFTA and the Uruguay Round. Assuming that the United States (with NAFTA, APEC and the FTAA) and the European Union (with its expanding network, including Euromed and perhaps EU-Mercosur), do so, the lesson for 1998 and beyond is clear: implement the liberalization commitments of the regional arrangements as rapidly and successfully as possible, and roll them into global agreements especially via the Millennium Round as promptly as possible.

For example, APEC should proceed speedily with its new sectoral approach but offer to include other countries and indeed the entire WTO, as it did with the ITA, as part of the new Round. APEC should indeed go even further and challenge the rest of the world to pursue the proposed multilateral agreement to emulate, on the world level, APEC's own commitment to achieve 'free and open trade and investment' by 2010 (for the industrial countries that account for 90 per cent of its trade) and 2020 (for the rest). For their part, even short of such a new global compact, the other regional arrangements should publicly indicate their willingness, à la APEC, to globalize their regional liberalization (on a reciprocal basis).

V. Money Is Central

International monetary conditions and the related macroeconomic environment, though outside the purview of the GATT/WTO itself, have been central factors in the postwar evolution of the multilateral trading system. They have been particularly critical to the launch of the successive major negotiations, and to the determination of the United States to push for such agreements.

This was particularly true for the Tokyo and Uruguay Rounds. The Tokyo Round was in fact launched as part of the agreement, insisted upon by the United States, to restore fixed exchange rates among the major countries and terminate the import surcharge that it had instituted in August 1971 – the most frontal assault on the principles of the GATT in the history of that institution. The American strategy was twofold: to accomplish a substantial devaluation of the dollar, to restore American competitiveness and reverse the sharp deterioration (for those days) of its trade balance, and to launch a new international trade negotiation to help resist the intense protectionist pressure which had developed by 1971 as described above. (Dollar devaluation was also essential to enable the Administration to win Congressional support for the new trade round, which it did in 1974.)

---

[3]   As described by C. Fred Bergsten in 'Open Regionalism', *Global Trade Policy 1997*, edited by Sven Arndt and Chris Milner (London: Blackwell Publishers, 1998 and in Working Paper 97-3, Washington: Institute for International Economics, 1997).

The launch of the Uruguay Round was similarly linked to a monetary crisis. The huge dollar overvaluation of the early 1980s, stemming from the massive budget deficits and benign neglect of the first Reagan Administration, generated a huge current account deficit and converted the United States from the world's largest creditor country to the world's largest debtor. As a result, protectionist pressure escalated rapidly and Reagan himself, despite his devotion to open markets in general and free trade in particular, 'granted more import relief to US industry than any of his predecessors in more than half a century'.[4] In addition, leading Congressmen commented that 'the Smoot Hawley tariff itself would have passed had it come to the House floor in the fall of 1985'. The Administration therefore adopted a two-part strategy similar to 1971: depreciate the dollar sharply, primarily through the Plaza Agreement of 1985, and launch a new multilateral negotiation to counter the protectionist pressure. Dollar devaluation was again essential to achieving the stronger trade position that would garner Congressional approval for the new trade talks, as ultimately achieved in 1988.

The Kennedy Round also originated partially in a monetary crisis. The first run on gold in the postwar period occurred during the Presidential campaign in 1960, and President Kennedy reportedly viewed the balance-of-payments problem along with the risk of nuclear war as his top policy priorities. The Administration's strategy for correcting the deficit (as defined at the time), as developed during its first year in office, included a major effort to open foreign markets to American exports. This in turn led to the proposal to launch the Kennedy Round.

Today's circumstances replicate these previous episodes to an important extent. The US merchandise trade deficit has already reached an annual rate of $225 billion and, with the adverse affect of the Asian crisis, will probably rise to $250–300 billion later this year and into 1999. The IMF has predicted that our current account deficit will reach $230 billion this year, almost 3 per cent of GDP, and the actual outcome could be even higher. The imbalance is of course primarily a macroeconomic phenomenon, as in the past, and will require substantial correction in the exchange rate of the dollar – which is currently overvalued by 15–20 per cent in trade terms.[5]

Meanwhile, however, substantial protectionist pressures will undoubtedly arise once the US economy slows and unemployment begins to increase – and be blamed on the record trade deficit. As noted above, the opponents of globalization have successfully resisted new Presidential negotiating authority even while the economy has been proceeding successfully. The monetary imbalance will thus again require the United States to press for a new multilateral negotiation, to restart the bicycle and help resist the backlash against liberalization.

In this particular circumstance, monetary and macroeconomic events elsewhere reinforce the need for an early start on a new Millennium Round. The new euro will start at a level that is undervalued, in trade terms, by 15–20 per cent – the natural mirror image

---

[4]   Remarks by Treasury Secretary James A. Baker III before a conference sponsored by the Institute for International Economics, 14 September 1987.

[5]   Simon Wren-Lewis and Rebecca Driver, *Real Exchange Rates for the Year 2000* (Washington: Institute for International Economics, May 1998).

of the dollar's overvaluation.[6] Once the new European Central Bank establishes the credibility of the new currency, it is likely to start assuming an important role in world finance and a major portfolio diversification from dollars into euro will ensue.[7] This will produce an appreciation of the euro and a sharp fall in Europe's trade balance, in the face of unemployment levels already running above 10 per cent in all the major countries, and trigger protectionist pressures there. It will be extremely prudent to launch a new WTO negotiation in time to generate forward momentum with which to resist these tendencies as well.

The Asian macro situation adds to these requirements. As the real effects of the region's crisis unfold over the next year or two, with millions of unemployed and thousands of bankruptcies, calls for withdrawal from the liberalization pattern of the past are bound to increase. Here too it will be highly desirable to commit governments to renewed progress, as APEC has already done to an important extent, before the pressures in the opposite direction become too great.

There is thus an intimate relationship between the global trading system and monetary/macroeconomic imbalances. The latter trigger changes in trade balances that generate protectionist processes. The imbalances cannot be corrected by changes in trade policy but rather must be resolved by changes in macroeconomic and currency policies. These changes take time (usually two to three years) to play through, however, and the trade policy pressures must meanwhile be countered by restarting the bicycle of liberalization. This pattern has played a significant role in the launch of all three major GATT negotiations and is likely to do so again for the first major WTO effort.

VI. Leadership

The final key variable in the successful management of the GATT regime was leadership, usually exercised most visibly by the United States. As noted throughout this essay, American events and initiatives played a central role in the launch of all three GATT rounds (and most of the smaller negotiations as well, including the recent sectoral talks).

It must be remembered, however, that the European Union has been an essential partner in each of these ventures. The reason is simple: the EU, since it expanded beyond the original six members in the early 1970s, has had an economy as large as that of the United States, has been an even larger trading entity, and has spoken with a single voice on most trade policy issues. Hence Europe has been a fully equal partner to the United States on trade issues, has been able to veto any global trade accord, and hence has been a necessary co-leader of all multilateral enterprises.

---

[6]   Wren-Lewis, cited. The recent 'convergence report' of the Commission of the European Community notes 'the unusual European trade surplus of 1–1.5 per cent of its GDP for the first time since 1986,' when the European currencies were clearly undervalued and subsequently rose sharply as counterpart to the huge dollar depreciation.

[7]   C. Fred Bergsten, 'The Dollar and the Euro', *Foreign Affairs*, July/August 1997.

With the creation of the euro, the EU will shortly achieve a similar degree of equality on monetary and macroeconomic issues. Particularly in light of the critical importance for trade policy of prospective monetary developments, in both the United States and the European Union, it is thus even more important than before for this de facto G-2 to provide leadership for the WTO system.

In recent years, the United States has sought to magnify its leadership by mobilizing Asian cooperation through APEC. As noted above, APEC has already played a crucial leadership role in the global system on at least two occasions – the conclusion of the Uruguay Round and the negotiation of the ITA. The United States generally takes the lead on trade issues within APEC but the group as a whole must now be viewed as an important player in the global trading system. But the new bipolar power structure will still require joint US-EU leadership to launch the Millennium Round and all other global trade initiatives for the foreseeable future.

VII.   Conclusion

My assessment of the last 50 years thus identifies five key principles as explaining the essential success of the global trade regime. The five have generally worked together in mutually reinforcing ways:

(i)   Monetary and macroeconomic imbalances trigger a need for new global negotiations, to contain the protectionist impulses generated by large trade deficits.

(ii) New regional arrangements, which create new trade discrimination and thus motivate outsiders to negotiate globally in response, also trigger such a need.

(iii) New multilateral rounds are then undertaken to restart the bicycle of liberalization, in order to counter the risks of backsliding and even reversal of previous openings.

(iv) Large initiatives, especially comprehensive rounds, are utilized in implementing the strategy to appeal to the widest possible group of participating countries and thus to propel the bicycle most effectively.

(v)   Leadership is provided by the largest trading entities, heretofore the United States and the European Union, as the natural de facto stewards of the system.

This five-part pattern largely explains the inauguration, course and completion of the three large rounds which have represented the dominant developments of the postwar trading system. The pattern is re-emerging today and is likely to do so clearly over the next year or so. I hope that the system will respond with the Millennium Round on this occasion as it did with the Kennedy, Tokyo, and Uruguay Rounds in the past.

It must be recognized, however, that today's circumstances differ in important ways from those of the past. For example, the threat to the open trading system – at least so far – is not the crude protectionism of the past that, in the case of the United States, produced a 'Mills bill' and import surcharges in the early 1970s and a series of VERs in the middle 1980s. The ostensible threat is a more nuanced reaction to globalization, accepting the inevitability of that phenomenon but seeking to manage it in potentially destructive ways.

One set of these efforts focuses on neomercantilistic devices, like the 'super 301' provision of 1988 US trade legislation. Another promotes linkages between trade policy and non trade objectives, notably regarding international labour standards and environmental issues. Most important is the explicit effort to stop the bicycle by calling a 'strategic pause' in further liberalization,[8] perhaps as a prelude to reintroducing traditional protectionist efforts if the system's forward momentum can be decisively broken. The advocates of that strategy in the United States can claim at least two recent successes with their defeat of fast track negotiating authority and the MAI.[9]

This 'new face of protectionism' offers both opportunities and risks. It poses opportunities to address a series of real problems which its advocates identify, including barriers to trade not yet covered by the WTO (eg, centred on competition policy in Japan) and interrelationships between trade, on the one hand, and labour and environmental issues, on the other. The risk is of course the derailing of the bicycle of liberalization and thus a potential reversal of the progress of the past 50 years.

It is also important, at this point in time, to note the backlash against globalization in other parts of the world. There is a minority, but nevertheless strong and perhaps growing, sentiment of this type in Europe – with the creation of the euro as something of a symbolic equivalent to NAFTA in the United States. The Asian crisis, as its real economic costs unfold over the next year or two, will undoubtedly trigger a similar backlash in Asia (though one that may focus more on separation from the international capital markets than from trade). The issue for the global trading system is thus far more than 'simply' countering the risk of backsliding in the United States, important as that consideration alone continues to be.

The monetary impetus for a new trade initiative also now takes on a broader geographical dimension. As noted above, the prospect of record trade deficits in the United States – largely as a result of renewed dollar overvaluation – is again the chief consideration. But the prospective sharp decline in high-unemployment Europe's trade balance, as the creation of the euro and the inevitable depreciation of the dollar lead to a sharp fall in the region's competitive position, adds substantially to the case. So does Asia's need for continued access to the American and European markets to enable it to recover from its current financial crisis.

The third key reason to launch a new negotiation, the need to channel the regional arrangements in a cohesive global direction, is also more extensive than in the past. This dimension of the prior rounds aimed primarily to reduce the discriminatory impact of the

---

[8]   Jeffrey Faux, 'Fast Track's Problem – Not the Marketing, the Product' in *Future Visions for U.S. Trade Policy, Four Contrasting Views* (Washington, Council on Foreign Relations, March 1998).

[9]   The difficulties experienced by the pending IMF legislation in the Congress are often cited as a third case in point, and there is some overlap between the opponents of trade liberalization and the IMF. However, many of the strongest opponents of the IMF (on moral hazard grounds) are conservatives who strongly support free trade, and the chief opponents of globalization (eg, the AFL-CIO and Minority Leader Gephardt) have either supported the IMF or adopted a neutral stance on it. Hence it would be a mistake to lump these developments together in any facile manner.

European Union. Now, however, it is also important to generate a similar opening by NAFTA, Mercosur, and several other regional groupings that have become economically significant in the 1990s. The need for a new global trade negotiation, again, has varied geographical as well as substantive dimensions.

In pursuing that negotiation, I have argued for the most far-reaching application in GATT/WTO history of the principle that 'big is beautiful.' All of the past rounds were quite ambitious, by contemporary standards, but they sought merely to *reduce* barriers (and write new rules) in the search for *freer* trade. Now that so many regional arrangements have already blazed the trail to *free* trade, I believe the time has come for the global system to adopt a goal of *eliminating* all barriers by a date certain (perhaps 2010 and 2020, à la APEC and Euromed). In addition to all its substantive benefits, this would keep the bicycle of liberalization moving forward – in the Millennium Round and perhaps even a successor – for at least the next decade or two.

When our successors meet in 2048 or so, I hope they will be able to look back and see that we, at the turn of the century, met the challenges of the global trading system as successfully as did our forebears in creating the GATT system a half century ago. We can only do so if we learn the lessons of this enormously fruitful period of global cooperation, draw the appropriate lessons for the future, and proceed courageously to implement those conclusions. I hope this paper will contribute to that purpose.

Chapter 6
Fifty Years: Looking Back, Looking Forward

Jagdish Bhagwati

The 50 years of the multilateral trading system, as spanned by the birth of the General Agreement on Tariffs and Trade (GATT) at the beginning and the blossoming of the World Trade Organization (WTO) at the end, merit unrestrained applause. Dividing the normal centennial celebratory period by half is truly appropriate: while much has been accomplished in the past 50 years, much remains to be done in the next 50 as well. There is little that I can add, however, to the experience and insights that my many friends at this symposium will provide on this occasion.

But perhaps I can provide a unique perspective since I happen to combine contrasting personas. I was born in a developing country (India) but now am a citizen of a developed one (the USA). I am a scholar of trade theory but I also write on trade policy (unlike many who are not handicapped by scientific pursuits and know-how). I am an academic (and the epithet 'professor' is occasionally thrown at me in debate as if it was an affliction) but have also been 'on the inside' (since Arthur Dunkel made me Economic Policy Adviser to the Director General of GATT during 1991–1993).[1]

I. Looking Back

The achievements of GATT in liberalizing trade through *reduced border trade barriers* are too well known to need recounting. Successive rounds of multilateral trade negotiations (MTNs), culminating in the successful Uruguay Round, have brought down trade tariffs to dramatically low levels around the world. True, there are still developing countries such as India whose tariffs call for significant reductions. But it is a mistake to believe, as Mr

---

[1]   I should not overdo this as I have limitations as well, which I was made aware of during the ill-fated negotiations for fast-track authority for President Clinton recently. I am informed that, on being faced by the USA Ways and Means Committee with my *Wall Street Journal* (10 September 1997) article arguing against linking fast-track to environmental and labour requirements, Ambassador Charlene Barshefsky is alleged to have remarked: 'Bhagwati does not understand trade: he has never been in a trade negotiation.' Since a good lawyer friend of mine teaches mock trade negotiations at my university, I hope to sit in on one of them in the near future and rid myself of this crippling limitation.

©   Kluwer Law International 2000. *From GATT to the WTO: The Multilateral Trading System in the New Millennium*, The WTO Secretariat (ed.), Kluwer Law International, London, 2000; ISBN 90–411–1253–7

Bergsten has argued recently in *Foreign Affairs*, that the future task for the WTO will be to exchange 'fair trade' disciplines offered by the developed countries for lower trade tariffs and restrictions by the developing countries. In agriculture alone, the tariffication brought about by the Uruguay Round has now led to sufficiently high tariffs in the developed countries that they cry out to be reduced in future MTN rounds.

In the same vein, a steadily wider range of sectors with trade barriers has been brought under GATT's axe. Take just two major examples: agriculture, having escaped GATT owing to the 1955 waiver, is now back in the picture, with definite steps taken towards freeing of trade therein with the Uruguay Round; and we now have also made progress on services in GATT under the umbrella of the General Agreement on Trade in Services (GATS).

Equally, the list of GATT's achievements must include the establishment of some, though woefully inadequate, discipline on 'fair trade' rules. Economists understand only too well the misuse that has occurred of rules such as on anti-dumping measures, with continued capture of these ironically for 'unfair' trade protectionism. It is an open secret that anti-dumping actions have in reality nothing to do with predation, and that GATT has been unable to impose the necessary discipline in this area. On the other hand, it is not hard to imagine what chaos could have reigned in the absence of GATT.

The Uruguay Round must also be credited with having brought about a single Undertaking, with common rules and obligations for all members, with exceptions largely reduced to transitional periods for developing countries. Thus we finally have a WTO which aims to have a single set of rules to govern world trade. This is a considerable achievement as few of us believe now, as many of us did in the 1950s through to the 1970s, that there should be 'special and differential' (S&D) treatment for the developing countries. The earlier view was based on the belief that there were different economics governing developing countries, requiring a different policy framework and special exemptions permitting readier resort to trade barriers for balance-of-payments reasons and on infant industry protection grounds, thus effectively exempting them also from the expected reciprocity in reductions of trade barriers in MTNs. Now, we believe that letting developing countries hold on to their trade restrictions is to let them shoot themselves in the foot, that the same economics apply to them as to others. Their growing importance in world trade also makes it politically impossible to maintain huge asymmetries of market access. The imposition of the same rules on both sets of nations has therefore become the norm, implying a Single Undertaking.[2]

Next, the WTO now has a more effective dispute settlement mechanism. We have moved away from an ineffective system where a defendant could veto the adoption by GATT Council of an adverse finding. This has removed the incentive to exercise 'aggressive unilateralism' of the section 301 variety (US Trade Act of 1979) in cases where the defendant did act this way, as in the soyabean case (EEC – Measures on Animal Feed Proteins, L/4599) where the EU had blocked two successive adverse findings at GATT

---

[2]   In this context, the notion that the 'least developed countries' should still be accorded S&D status is to ignore these fundamental lessons.

and then the USA had resorted unilaterally to retaliatory tariffs.[3] The strengthened dispute settlement mechanism has also led to increased resort to its impartial procedures to cool bilateral disputes which, as in the USA–Japan automobile case,[4] were marked by acrimonious friction inherent in bilateral confrontations. The WTO resolution of the Eastman Kodak–Fuji dispute[5] has also served to underline the fact that unilateral determination of 'unfair trade' by national bodies such as the US Trade Representative (USTR), on the basis of complaints by interested national parties, and threats based thereon are simply an unacceptable way of proceeding in such disputes: the total defeat of Eastman Kodak shows how baseless the USA complaints against Japan are likely to have been, exactly as argued by some of us over the years in the teeth of assertions backed by few or no arguments. All this is to the good.

You will note that I do not list the inclusion of TRIPS in the Uruguay Round agreement as an 'achievement'. It is better regarded as an *unprincipled compromise* that had to be made, in order to reach agreement on the entire negotiation, at the insistence of corporate groups and their allies in national governments in influential developed countries. It has led to problems down the line.

At the level of theoretical principle, intellectual property protection (IPP) is precisely 'protection' and would normally be considered incompatible with the notion of 'free' as indeed many have argued historically and as many nations (now arguing otherwise) have also practised. But it is justified on grounds of world efficiency on the argument that, while it has an adverse effect on the use of technology and hence its benefits, it also creates a necessary incentive to create the technology. But it cannot be shown that increasing it to levels as high as 20-year patent protection is desirable even though most of us will agree that the optimal level of IPP will lie between zero and 20 years, and nearly all scholars will agree that 20 years is certain to be undesirable and hence too high.

Besides, it cannot be argued that IPP, even when formulated at the level conducive to world efficiency, will lead to mutual gain for all, and the presumption is that the producer nations will benefit whereas user nations could be losers. On the other hand, free trade will generally benefit all. Hence, it can be properly contended that, at the intellectual level, IPP does not belong to the WTO at all. Nonetheless, it was included because, speaking plainly, it was a way of legitimating trade sanctions in order to enforce IPP: the unilateral use of Special 301 actions to force other nations into compliance with USA demands was obviously less legitimate in the public eye.

---

[3]   Section 301 actions where the USA is seeking to impose new obligations on others, not covered by earlier treaty commitments, are still a problem, however, for the USA administration if it wishes to abide by the spirit of multilateralism in the teeth of repeated attempts by USA lobbying groups, and Congress, to impose their demands on foreign nations. The distinction between these two types of 301 actions was noted and explored in contributions by me and by Professor Robert Hudec in Jagdish Bhagwati and Hugh Patrick (eds), *Aggressive Unilateralism* (University of Michigan Press, 1991).

[4]   United States – Imposition of import duties on automobiles from Japan under sections 301 and 304 of the Trade Act of 1974, WT/D56.

[5]   Japan – Measures affecting consumer photographic film and paper, WT/D5GG.

That lesson has not been lost on the labour and environmental groups who now see the inclusion of the essentially extraneous issue of IPP in the WTO as providing them with a precedent for the inclusion of their own extraneous demands for such inclusion as well. Thus, when I get into public debates on the question of linkage between trade treaties and institutions, on the one hand, and labour and environmental standards demands, on the other hand, this precedent is invariably cited: 'If you did it for capital, why not for labour, why not for nature?' In fact, this mindset has been reinforced also by efforts to include the multilateral agreement on investment (MAI) in the future WTO agenda.

II.   Looking Ahead

This brings me immediately to the question: where should the WTO head? It can be answered in two ways: by looking at the unfinished agenda before the WTO, and by defining the vision we should have today of the world trading system for the next half-century.

The two issues are obviously not unrelated. They unite, in particular, on the issue of whether there should be another round at the end of this century, as I and many others have long pleaded for and as Sir Leon Brittan, the EU Commission Vice-President responsible for relations between the EU and the WTO, has dramatized by asking for and christening it as the Millennium Round, prompting the witticisms that MTNs always prompt: that it will take a millennium to start it, and that it will take a millennium to end it! Evidently, both the unfinished agenda of the Uruguay Round, with the ongoing negotiations in services and agriculture for instance which are built into it, and also the further agenda defined by our long-term vision and mainly untouched by that round, define the agenda of the step (in the shape of the Millennium Round) that we need to take towards that vision.

Let me concentrate on what that long-term vision should be, since the unfinished agenda of the Uruguay Round is a well-worn issue where the contours of what we aim for are well known and the matter is largely one of successful negotiations. I would like to address all too briefly five key issues: (1) regionalism or rather preferential trade agreements (PTAs) versus multilateralism; (2) the question of labour standards; (3) the environmental problem; (4) multilateral agreement on investment; and (5) competition policy.

II.1   PTAs or regionalism: Article XXIV

I believe that the huge enthusiasm for PTAs in the 1980s, and economists' complacency towards them, has eroded. I will take a full measure of credit for having persistently raised the issues raised by them when the tide was fully in favour of these discriminatory arrangements and multilateralism was considered an 'extended four-letter word'. In fact, in a recent article I edited where the author was defending multilateralism, the printer had mistakenly converted the word in the title into the more favoured 'multiculturalism'!

We today have a real problem with the proliferation of these PTAs, all sanctioned by Article XXIV of GATT, or with lesser preferential trade agreements under waivers or the

Enabling Clause. Increasing numbers of studies have underlined that trade diversion does occur under these PTAs, exactly as theory would predict. Besides, they create a 'systemic' problem of criss-crossing preferences that lead to non-uniformity of trade barriers depending on where a product is supposed to originate from: leading to what I have called a 'spaghetti bowl' phenomenon. It is simply wrong therefore to think that these PTAs are the same as free trade, as many politicians, bureaucrats and journalists believe.

A justification produced for these PTAs today is that they help propel the multilateral trade negotiations forward. I believe that this was true in 1982 when the USA turned to Article XXIV because the MTN route was not functioning. This is no longer true.

Thus, on grounds of efficiency, PTAs should be anathema to the architects of the world trading system. On grounds of necessity, as leading us to worldwide free trade, the case is also moot. None of this is to say that, if a set of nations wants to go for deep political and economic integration, using the core EU model, then that makes it a different animal, turning the PTA in question into a pet from a wild beast. My objections are to agreements such as free trade agreements and CUs which are essentially centred on trade preferences for members.[6]

I find it good to see that the regionalism issue, as the PTA problem is misleadingly called, is on the WTO agenda. But there does not seem to be the political will to see the solution that is necessary and which can be defined as follows:

(i)   rewrite Article XXIV to permit non-MFN discrimination only when deep integration of the EU-core variety is formally the objective, outlawing all new FTAs and CUs otherwise;

(ii)   build into Article XXIV a 'sunset clause' on all existing PTAs so as to bring their external tariffs, whether unified or not, in line on schedule with the internal tariffs on PTA members;

(iii) pursue regionalism, for all sorts of objectives (such as human rights, security, launching multilateral trade initiatives etc) without sacrificing MFN, pursuing trade liberalization through unilateral as well as reciprocity-based MFN liberalization.

It is up to us supporters of the multilateral principles of free trade to support these objectives and one can only appeal to the WTO leadership to take the lead in pushing for these alternatives instead of seeking only palliatives.

II.2   Labour standards etc

It is plain that the WTO is now faced with considerable political demands from NGOs and unions to incorporate labour standards etc as exceptions to market access rights at the

---

[6]   Many of these arguments have been developed by me, Arvind Panagariya and T.N. Srinivasan in recent writings, singly or jointly. Others who have made compelling objections of one kind or another to regionalism are Phil Levy, Pravin Krishna, Anne Krueger and Alan Winters. The recent Carnegie Commission report, chaired by Jaime Serra Puche, also contains a fine analysis of the problems raised by PTAs and makes a number of very useful, if less radical, proposals to limit the damage from PTAs and enlarge the benefits from them.

WTO, almost always on the basis that this is within the sovereign right of the groups and nations to demand without any intervening procedure or restrictions on automaticity defined by existing WTO procedures.

Thus, where the WTO would subject such exercise of unilateral suspension of market access to the dispute settlement mechanism, and require 'compensation' in the absence of compliance if the ruling is adverse, these groups want to have blanket exemptions such as the enshrining of 'core' labour standards, seen essentially as 'rights' of universal value, in a Social Clause or, worse still, simply through automatic exemptions from WTO scrutiny altogether.[7]

The problem is that, viewed as 'labour rights', the labour standards become indistinguishable from general human rights. We then must ask: why should one set of rights be subject to WTO sanctions and not others? Thus, if exploitative child labour is to be proscribed at the WTO, why not use WTO sanctions to protect children from capital punishment as well; after all, this is proscribed by the International Covenant on Civil and Political Rights that embodies the human rights 'law' today. Then, we would have legitimated the use of sanctions against USA trade because several states now have legislation under which children of the age below the limit defined in human rights law can be treated as adults, and adults in turn are subject to capital punishment, and so children can be executed. In short, the WTO turns then into an instrument for use of sanctions against selective human rights violations rather than against a much wider set.

So, the question arises: why? Here, the protectionist intent of the selected set becomes manifest and worries the developing countries. Issues such as child labour have been singled out, not just because they appeal to one's conscience – as many have pointed out, these very groups frequently do nothing to open up immigration to workers from

---

[7]   Thus, Dani Rodrik has proposed that a domestic procedure such as International Trade Commission scrutiny of anti-dumping petitions be established to ensure that there is a legitimate, nationally shared ethical preference being exercised, and then to permit automatic exemption by the WTO of suspension of market access that follows thereafter. This is a plainly absurd idea, of course, and it is plain that Rodrik, whose economic analysis can be acute, has not given serious thought to, or read the intricate philosophical, economic and legal analyses of this matter which has agitated many distinguished analysts and policy-makers for several years now (see, for example, the two huge volumes on questions such as these, produced and edited by me and Professor Robert Hudec in 1996, *Fair Trade and Harmonization: Prerequisites for Free Trade?* (MIT Press, 1996)). For one thing, it makes no sense to deny that the democratic passage of ethics-related legislation is already a valid expression of a national preference. To suggest that this be double-guessed by a national administrative process that might overturn the legislated preference (as in the US Marine Mammal Protection Act or s609 of US Public Law 101–62) surely removes the proposal from any serious discussion. Then again, the problem arises, not because anyone denies that such preferences exist within nations and must be accommodated: the issue rather is that if you permit automatic exemptions, based exclusively on national preferences, then there is no constraint on what can be asserted – morality is not subject to a 'scientific test', for instance – and hence the trade experts feel that this could lead to chaos and hence some constraint needs be put on such automaticity. I can only refer the reader to the two Bhagwati–Hudec volumes for a serious discussion of the resulting issues; they also contain references to the entire literature.

abroad to ensure their rights by having them work in countries with better standards; nor do the Congressmen who are active in supporting the imposition of such demands on other nations have any track record on trying to remedy similar human rights conditions in their own backyards – but because of the fear of competition.

Here, I feel that the widespread fear that trade with poor countries has hurt the poor in the rich countries needs to be addressed much more forcefully than the WTO has done. I believe, on the basis of my research, that the effect of trade with poor countries on real wages in the rich countries is likely to have been even favourable, moderating the fall coming from unskilled-labour-saving technical change.[8] If I am right, then one should be able to tell the unions that, and to argue that the pursuit of labour rights must become part of the general strategy of pursuing human rights of all kinds, with instrumentalities that might include trade sanctions for which we have a number of instruments and agencies, other than the WTO. And where we have problems for specific sanctions with the WTO rules, we also have the possibility of waivers where we have persuaded several others of our convictions, and where we want to go alone, we can always do so but by providing for 'compensation' under existing rules.

In short, I believe that we need to keep the Social Clause out of the WTO, turning the labour standards issues (now narrowed down to human rights issues) over to the ILO and to instrumentalities that address human rights issues, and to get the WTO generally out of this issue. It is simply not the appropriate agency for the problem; and whatever rules we agree on how to deal with human rights violations, including procedures to suspend nations' trade rights at the WTO and at the UN for embargo procedures, they must be applied to human rights generally.[9]

II.3   Environmental problems

The environmental interface with WTO rules is also a matter of considerable controversy and I believe that the time has come to take a concerted look at the problems that have emerged.

First, the basic idea that purely domestic, as against global, environmental pollution should be dealt with by harmonization or upward movement of lower tax burdens abroad, has an intuitive appeal. But, as I and Professor Srinivasan have argued,[10] there is a perfectly legitimate case for diversity in pollution tax rates for identical pollution across countries in the same industries (what we call CCII tax burden differences). Besides, the fears of a race to the bottom, which is theoretically possible, are unjustified by the empirical findings that corporations seem to use the more environmentally friendly

---

[8]   Cf. 'Play It Again Sam: A New Look at Trade and Wages' (mimeo, Columbia University, 1997).

[9]   I have dealt with the issue of human rights and trade sanctions and trade rules in my contribution to the festschrift for Arthur Dunkel, *Uruguay Round and Beyond*, edited by me and Mathias Hirsch, published by Springer Verlag and by Michigan University Press in May 1998.

[10]   In Bhagwati and Hudec, *Fair Trade and Harmonization: Prerequisites for Free Trade?* (MIT Press, 1996), chapter 4.

technologies even where the requirements are more lax. So, the argument that free trade requires fair trade in the sense of harmonization or upgrading of foreign tax burdens with one's own is ill-taken. Thus, most of the arguments advanced against free trade on this account, and the demands that the WTO should have 'social dumping' clauses to permit countervailing duties when the foreign pollution tax burden is lower, are simply mistaken.

Next, this still leaves open questions of the type raised by the shrimp–turtle and the dolphin–tuna decisions.[11] In all these cases, GATT and WTO judgments are quite sound, in my view. Speaking very broadly, it makes little sense to legitimate unilateral assertion of environmental and social preferences and thereby suspend other WTO members' access to one's markets. It is surely more desirable to reach agreement on these matters through negotiations and, failing that, to suspend such trade while paying, if challenged at the WTO, suitable compensation for such unilateral suspension. If we do not do that, the road will open to everyone to make such unilateral assertions and disrupt trade in consequence. The issue requires accommodation of the kind embodied in the entire set of WTO procedures and ideas on how to handle such conflicts. The more militant environmentalists and NGOs such as The Public Citizen portray the WTO in demonized and distorted form on this question when, in fact, their own views are unbending, unaccommodating and destructive.

Finally, I believe that, on the global environmental issues, we badly need to grandfather in the trade sanctions against free riders in the existing multilateral environmental agreements, taking them (quickly) one by one to ensure that these potentially targeted 'free-riding' nations have no justifiable case against such a procedure (for instance, a pacifist in a war is a 'conscientious objector', not a 'free rider'). My own impression is that the multilateral environmental agreements have taken good care to carry most nations on board through suitable accommodations of the objections raised by hesitant countries.

II.4 Multilateral agreement on investment

It is probably a heresy to say that the multilateral agreement on investment (MAI), as presently drafted, and at the present time, is not a good idea and that it should be shelved temporarily. But the adverse reception accorded to the unveiling of the OECD-produced draft and the temporary withdrawal of it from any agenda indicate that there are basic problems with MAI. True, with trade and investment closely tied together today, an agreement on investment at the WTO seems a good idea.

But such an agreement must be balanced in at least two ways: first, it should not be just about removing obstacles to investment but should also address subventions and subsidies to it; and, secondly, it must be formulated with the active participation of both developing and developed countries. Neither has been done.

Besides, tricky questions such as the use of state power against specific foreign firms with a view to extracting concessions from their governments have not been addressed.

---

[11]   United States – Import prohibition of certain shrimp and shrimp products WT/D58; United States – Restriction on imports of tuna DS21.

Thus, during the USA–Japan auto dispute,[12] it was remarkable that the USA was threatening to zero in on Japanese auto firms' luxury model exports to the USA with punitive tariffs of 100 per cent simply to impose import targets, component-purchase targets etc. All this, while asserting in other contexts the need to leave multinationals free from political interference in matters of production and trade! Again, the USA was jawboning Japanese transplants into buying more USA components, virtually intimidating these firms into a 'local purchase' policy, while pushing for the adoption of trade-related investment measures (TRIMs) outlawing the use of 'local content' clauses by host countries for multinationals. MAI does not adequately come to grips with such transgressions by the powerful countries, while seeking to impose constraints on the weaker countries. But it should if it is to be credible.

In addition, I feel that the timing of the MAI is precipitous and bad. Developing countries are pushing their direct foreign investment (DFI) doors open quite dramatically on their own. If obstacles are created for DFI, you lose out in the race for more DFI that almost every country is engaged in. Why then get into devising MAI and selling it at the WTO when market forces are already leading countries to several pro-DFI practices? By formalizing all this into an explicit MAI, we make this into a political issue, and invite the anti-DFI lobbies, the anti-WTO lobbies and all the wackos in every country onto centre stage. The WTO is in enough trouble from such lobbies, which played *some* role in President Clinton's defeat on fast-track renewal; it seems a foolish idea to add to these troubles gratuitously. In fact, as every informed scholar of the politics of international economic policy knows, the level of political difficulty escalates as you go from free trade in goods to free trade in services, to freedom of DFI, to freedom of all capital flows, to freedom of labour flows. We seem to have forgotten all this in the flush of the victory (still incomplete) of free trade forces at Geneva; but we do so at our peril.

II.5 Competition policy

Finally, I believe that we have to get what Sylvia Ostry has called 'system friction' under some form of managed control at the WTO. This involves getting into what is best called 'competition policy'. Two sets of problems in particular are important to distinguish.

First, problems of market access in our exports, and predation by foreign companies continue to create trade conflicts and we need to come to agreed parameters on what is acceptable practice and what is not.

Secondly, while we trade economists correctly view trade as the best antidote to domestic monopoly, it is also true that international cartelization can kill that therapeutic effect. Clearly, some form of agreed anti-trust policy, which is not just 'anti-big' on a knee-jerk basis, has to be evolved. That is an important, unfinished task.

---

[12] United States – Imposition of import duties on automobiles from Japan under sections 301 and 309 of the Trade Act of 1979, WT/DS6.

Chapter 7
Dispute Settlement and the WTO: Emerging Problems

*John H. Jackson**

On 1 January 1995, a new international economic organization, the World Trade Organization (WTO), came into being, resulting from the lengthy, extensive and complex Uruguay Round trade negotiation in the context of General Agreement on Tariffs and Trade (GATT). The Uruguay Round Agreement of GATT/WTO has been described as 'the most important event in recent economic history'. In addition the WTO has been described as the 'central international economic institution',[1] and nations are more and more engaged with the detailed processes of the WTO, especially its dispute settlement procedure. But the WTO Agreement, including all of its elaborate annexes, is probably fully understood by no nation which has accepted it, including some of the richest and most powerful trading nations that are members.

We now have more than three years' experience under the new organization and its 'constitution'. At this point in time, appraisals of the launch and early experience of the WTO are almost uniformly optimistic and approving.

The purpose of this paper is to put forward some generalizations or tentative hypotheses about the meaning and potential of these early years of experience. It will do this in four parts. First, it will give a brief overview of the history, background and 'landscape' of the new organization, illustrating not only the continuity from its predecessor, GATT, but also some of the major problems of GATT and how the Uruguay Round negotiators approached those problems in developing the new organization and the extraordinarily extensive treaty text of the Uruguay Round.

Secondly, this paper will examine the jurisprudence of the new organization during the early years up to the present.[2] A brief overview of the dispute settlement cases will be

---

    *   All rights reserved. Portions of this manuscript are partly drawn from several other recent works of this author, which may be of interest to the readers. See J.H. Jackson, 'The Great 1994 Sovereignty Debate: United States Acceptance and Implementation of the Uruguay Round Results' (1997) 36 *Columbia Journal of Transnational Law* 157–188; and J.H. Jackson, *The World Trade Organization: Constitution and Jurisprudence* (Chatham House Papers, RIIA/Pinter, 1998). See also J.H. Jackson, 'Global Economics and International Economic Law' (1998) 1 *Journal of International Economics Law* 1.

    [1]   Leonard Bierman et al., 'The General Agreement on Tariffs and Trade from a Market Perspective' (1996) 17 *University of Pennsylvania Journal of International Economic Law* 821 at 845.

    [2]   May 1998.

    ©   John H. Jackson 2000. *From GATT to the WTO: The Multilateral Trading System in the New Millennium*, The WTO Secretariat (ed.), Kluwer Law International, London, 2000; ISBN 90–411–1253–7.

presented, along with some indications of the potential meaning of those cases and some hypotheses about the directions of the new Appellate Body.

Thirdly, this paper will discuss some of the emerging constitutional problems, particularly questions about allocation of power within the WTO, and between the WTO and the member states. Particular attention will be given to the potential ability or inability of the WTO to cope with some of the many problems of 'globalization' which are emerging.

Finally, this paper will, in section IV, suggest some possible solutions or partial solutions to some problems, and draw some conclusions and prognoses.

I.   Overview of GATT History and the WTO

Looking back over the 1946–1994 history of GATT allows one to reflect on how surprising it was that this relatively feeble institution with many 'birth defects' managed to play such a significant role for almost five decades. It certainly was far more successful than could have been fairly predicted in the late 1940s.

World economic developments pushed GATT to a central role during the past few decades.

The growing economic interdependence of the world has been increasingly commented upon. Events that occur halfway around the world have a powerful influence on the other side of the globe. Armed conflict and social unrest in the Middle East affect the farmers in Iowa and France and the auto workers in Michigan and Germany. Interest rate decisions in Washington have a profound influence on the external debt of many countries of the world which, in turn, affects their ability to purchase goods made in industrial countries and their ability to provide economic advancement to their citizenry. Environmental problems have obvious cross-border effects. More and more frequently, government leaders find their freedom of action circumscribed because of the impact of external economic factors on their national economies.

One of the interesting and certainly more controversial aspects of GATT as an institution was its dispute settlement mechanism. It is probably fair to say that this mechanism was unique. It was also flawed, due in part to the troubled beginnings of GATT. Yet these procedures worked better than might have been expected, and some could argue that in fact they worked better than those of the World Court and many other international dispute procedures. A number of interesting policy questions are raised by the experience of the procedure, not the least of which is the question of what should be the fundamental objective of the system – to solve the instant dispute (by conciliation, obfuscation, power threats, or otherwise), or to promote certain longer-term systemic goals such as predictability and stability of interpretations of the treaty text.

Even though some argued that GATT dispute settlement was merely a facilitation of negotiations designed to reach a settlement, the original intention was for GATT to be placed in the institutional setting of the ITO, and the draft International Trade Organization (ITO) Charter called for a rigorous dispute settlement procedure which contemplated effective use of arbitration (not always mandatory, however), and even

al to the World Court in some circumstances.[3] Clair Wilcox, Vice-Chairman of the
Delegation to the Havana Conference, notes that the possibility of suspending trade
essions under this procedure was:

regarded as a method of restoring a balance of benefits and obligations that, for
ny reason, may have been disturbed. It is nowhere described as a penalty to be
mposed on members who may violate their obligations or as a sanction to insure
1at these obligations will be observed. But even though it is not so regarded, it
ill operate in fact as a sanction and a penalty.'

rther noted that the procedure for obtaining a World Court opinion on the law
ived in a dispute, and says: 'A basis is thus provided for the development of a body of
international law to govern trade relationships.'

When one reflects on the almost 50 years of pre-WTO history of the GATT dispute
settlement process, some generalizations seem both apparent and quite remarkable. With
very meagre treaty language as a start, plus divergent alternative views about the policy
goals of the system, GATT, like so many human institutions, took on a life of its own.
Both as to the dispute procedures (a shift from 'working parties' to 'panels'), and as to the
substantive focus of the system (a shift from general ambiguous ideas about 'nullification
or impairment', to more analytical or 'legalistic' approaches to interpreting rules of treaty
obligation), the GATT panel procedure evolved towards more rule orientation.

GATT dispute settlement process became admired enough that various trade policy
interests sought to bring their subjects under it. This was one of the motivations which
led both the intellectual property interests and the services trade interests to urge those
subjects to be included in the Uruguay Round. The Uruguay Round results, of course,
apply the new Dispute Settlement Understanding (DSU) procedures to those subjects.

II. The Early Years of WTO Jurisprudence

II.1 The first years of the new WTO dispute settlement procedures

The WTO Secretariat listings of 5 June 1998 show that 135 cases[4] have been brought
under the new procedures. This is a remarkable increase, about fourfold, over the rate of
cases under GATT. Various conclusions can be made. Perhaps the numbers represent a
great deal of confidence by the nation-state members of the WTO in the new procedure.
Or perhaps they are testing it, trying it out by bringing cases. Or perhaps the new texts of
the Uruguay Round Agreements have sufficient ambiguity (fairly typical at the beginning
of practice under a treaty text) that they engender more cases. Finally, most likely it is a
combination of all these factors.

---

[3] Havana Charter for an International Trade Organization, Articles 92–97 in UN
Conference on Trade and Employment – Final Act and Related Documents, UN Doc. E/Conf. 2/
78 (1948). See also C. Wilcox, *A Charter For World Trade* (1949), p. 159 and pp. 305–308.

[4] See <www.wto.org/wto/dispute/bulletin.htm>.

One of the more optimistic indicia of the figures is the relatively large number of settlements that are apparently occurring. This could be an indication that the procedures are enhancing and inducing settlements, and that these settlements are consistent with the 'rule orientation' principles of the procedures. Governments start a procedure, and then as the procedure advances more becomes known about the case. At some point, the jurisprudence will suggest to the participants the likely outcome of the case and this will induce settlement, consistent with the rules as interpreted in prior cases. Thus the jurisprudence contributes to predictability which assists the governments in coming to agreement about their case, consistent with the rules themselves.

Another optimistic indication is the general spirit of compliance with the result of the dispute settlement procedures. Even the major powers have indicated that they will comply with the mandates of the dispute settlement reports when they are finalized and formally adopted (which is virtually automatic). Of course there are grumblings and complaints, particularly by special interests within societies, about the rulings of the panels and the Appellate Body. Nevertheless, this observer has attended meetings where officials from the major participating members in the WTO have all indicated that their governments intend to comply with the results of holdings against their governments.[5] So far, there seems to be no exception to this spirit of compliance, although the question of what is appropriate 'compliance' is controverted from time to time.[6]

There is also some controversy about whether a WTO member who is subject to a dispute panel report directing action to become consistent with WTO treaty rules is obligated as a matter of international law to comply (as this author has opined), or has the option merely to 'compensate' by other trade measures.[7]

Another interesting facet of the cases brought so far is the much greater participation by developing countries. Developing countries have brought a number of the cases themselves, even against some of the big industrial countries (with rather satisfying wins).

---

[5]   Conference on WTO dispute settlement organized by the American Bar Association at Georgetown University Law Center, 20 February 1998.

[6]   For several cases the new procedural rules (DSU) calling for an arbitrator to resolve a controversy over the reasonable time allowed to conform to a panel report were invoked. See 'US Asks for Arbitrator in Fight with EU over WTO Banana Ruling', *Inside US Trade*, 5 December 1997; 'US Requests Arbitration over Japan's Implementation of Liquor Panel', *Inside US Trade*, 10 January 1998; and 'EU Asks for WTO Arbitration on Implementation of Hormone Panel', *Inside US Trade*, 10 April 1998. See also Japan – Taxes on Alcoholic Beverages: Arbitration under Article 21(3)(c) of the Understanding on Rules and Procedures Governing the Settlement of Disputes, WT/DS8/15, WT/DS/10/15 and WT/DS11/13, 14 February 1997; and European Communities – Measures Affecting Livestock and Meat (Hormones), WT/DS26 and 48/AB/R, 16 January 1998.

[7]   See John H. Jackson, 'The WTO Dispute Settlement Understanding: Misunderstandings on the Nature of Legal Obligation' (1997) 91 *American Journal of International Law* 60 (editorial comment); cf. Judith Hippler Bello, 'The WTO Dispute Settlement Understanding: Less is More' (1996) 90 *American Journal of International Law* 416 (editorial comment).

In addition, for virtually the first time in GATT/WTO history, developing countries have brought cases against other developing countries.

II.2 Some tentative generalizations about the developing jurisprudence

The addition of the right to appeal to an Appellate Body made up of a permanent cadre (a roster of seven, sitting in divisions of three), in conjunction with the automaticity of approval of panel reports, has already had a very profound impact on the world trading system as embodied in GATT and WTO (GATT continues as a treaty, although the WTO has taken over all of the organizational functions of what used to be GATT).

Some of these impacts will be discussed in section II.3 below, but several aspects of the nine or ten reports that we now have from the Appellate Body divisions indicate characteristics and general approaches that are of considerable interest.

II.2.a Relevance of general international law principles

First, the Appellate Body has made it reasonably clear that general international law is relevant and applies in the case of the WTO and its treaty annexes, including GATT. In the past there has been some question about this, with certain parties arguing that GATT was a 'separate regime', in some way insulated from the general body of international law. The Appellate Body has made it quite clear that this is not the case and has made reference to general international law principles, particularly as embodied in the Vienna Convention on the Law of Treaties, which the Appellate Body calls upon for principles of treaty interpretation.

II.2.b Formal juridical approach

The Appellate Body also has produced reports which, while arguably not entirely free of possible error, have been very carefully crafted, and give the strong impression of opinions that judicial institutions in many legal systems follow. The Appellate Body reasoning has been quite thorough, and generally careful (especially considering the very short time limits within which they have to operate). The Appellate Body has also been quite independent and impartial. I think it is fair to say that one cannot detect nationality influence on the Appellate Body. There is no indication of particular authorship of any part of an Appellate Body report and no provision for dissenting opinions. Thus an Appellate Body report is only attributed generally to the three members of the roster which sat in the division. One can also say that the Appellate Body work has been more 'juridical', or some might say 'legalistic', in tenor than before in GATT, and indeed more so than in many if not most international tribunals.

II.2.c Deference to national decisions

Another characteristic that seems to be emerging from the jurisprudence with the Appellate Body is a more deferential attitude by the Appellate Body towards national government decisions (or in other words more deference to national 'sovereignty') than sometimes has been the case for the first-level panels or the panels under GATT.[8] In some sense, therefore, the Appellate Body has been exercising more 'judicial restraint' and has been more hesitant to develop new ideas of interpreting the treaty language than sometimes has been the case in the first-level panels themselves. It is not clear why this is so, but one can note that the Appellate Body roster contains relatively few GATT specialists; rather the Appellate Body, which generally is considered to have outstanding members, has members that are more 'generalists' than one would typically find on the first-level panels or in GATT panels in previous years. This could be a very good omen, because the care and appropriate deference to national decisions may be a significant factor in the long-run general acceptance of the work of the WTO Dispute Settlement Body among a great variety and large number of nations of the world.

II.3   Role of the WTO dispute settlement system in the new world trading framework

It has already been mentioned that under the new procedures the dispute settlement system is having a profound impact on the world trade system. In particular, diplomats find themselves in new territory. Rather than operating in what is thoroughly a 'negotiating atmosphere', diplomats find themselves acting as lawyers, or relying on lawyers, much more heavily than before, and much more heavily than some of them would like. The dispute settlement procedure itself becomes part of the negotiating tactics for various dispute settlement attempts. One hears or sees in the media reference to 'nation A' arguing against 'nation B's' measures, and 'threatening to bring a case in the WTO' if it does not get the matter resolved.[9] The negotiations concerning potential and threatened USA action against Japanese automobile imports is a case in point, where the

---

[8]   Examples of some attitudinal statements of this type (not necessarily supported by the 'holding' of the case) include: United States – Standards for Reformulated and Conventional Gasoline, WT/DS2/AB/R, 29 April 1996, p. 30 ('WTO Members have a large measure of autonomy to determine their own policies on the environment (including its relationship with trade), their environmental objectives and the environmental legislation they enact and implement'); Japan – Taxes on Alcoholic Beverages, WT/DS8, 10, and 11/AB/R, 4 October 1996, p. 22 ('WTO rules are not so rigid or so inflexible as not to leave room for reasoned judgments in confronting the endless and ever-changing ebb and flow of real facts in real cases in the real world'); and European Communities – Measures Affecting Livestock and Meat (Hormones), WT/DS26 and 48/AB/R, 16 January 1998, see especially para. 165 and the language ('We cannot lightly assume that sovereign states intended to impose upon themselves the more onerous, rather than the less burdensome obligation by mandating conformity or compliance with such standards, guidelines and recommendations. To sustain such an assumption and to warrant such a far-reaching interpretation, treaty language far more specific and compelling than that found in Article 3 of the SPS Agreement would be necessary.').

[9]   See, eg, 'US Threatens Canada with WTO Case, Hints at Mexico Challenge', *Inside US Trade*, 3 April 1998; John Zarocostas, 'US to Request a WTO Panel on Duty Hikes', *Journal of Commerce*, 20 February 1997, p. 2A; John Zarocostas, 'EU May Go to WTO over US Textiles Rules', *Journal of Commerce*, 10 March 1997, p. 3A; 'US Considering WTO Talks on Japanese Barriers to Apples', *Inside US Trade*, 29 November 1996.

option to bring the case in the WTO apparently worked in a way that was deemed by the Japanese appropriately favourable to their negotiating position.[10] In another case, Costa Rica, small as it is, brought a case against the giant of the north – the USA – concerning import quotas in the USA against the importation of cotton underwear and some other textile products. Costa Rica won the case, both at the first level and on appeal, and to some this is quite an eye-opener.[11]

One interesting set of developments that has been evolving, first of all under GATT and now under the WTO, is the participation of private attorneys who are retained by governments involved in the WTO dispute settlement process. Small governments in particular often do not have in-house expertise that is adequate to handle some of the complex cases (or even some of the simple cases) which are finding their way into the WTO dispute settlement arena. Such states are put at a substantial disadvantage against large entities like the USA or the European Community which have such in-house expertise. These smaller states consequently have in some circumstances been eager to retain the services of private attorneys, usually Europeans or Americans. But there has been some objection made, most often by the USA, to the practice. During the course of the last year, developments seem to have moved very substantially in the direction of permitting this practice of governments retaining private attorneys, with certain limitations. In their 1997 Bananas Case report,[12] the Appellate Body division indicated that there were few valid grounds for refusing the participation of government-retained private counsel at the appellate proceeding, and this reasoning could very well apply to first-level panel proceedings. Subsequently there have been indications that some first-level panels have accepted the practice. I believe this is a welcome move, but it will necessitate a certain amount of careful thinking about the role and relationship of the private attorneys vis-à-vis their government clients, and vis-à-vis the WTO system. It will be wise for the DSB or other appropriate bodies to develop certain standards and ethical rules, perhaps including conflict-of-interest rules as well as confidentiality rules, which would generally be recommended to governments as part of the contract they use to retain attorneys. It is to be hoped that this matter will receive appropriate attention and the appropriate practices and documents will evolve.

III. Emerging Constitutional Problems of the WTO

Perhaps almost every human institution has to face the task of how to evolve and change in the face of conditions and circumstances not originally considered when the institution

---

[10] 'Japan Files Case with Trade Body in Fight with US over Auto Sanctions' (1995) 12 *International Trade Reporter* (BNA) 891; and 'Japan to Charge US in WTO with Violation of MFN, Bound Tariffs', *Inside US Trade*, 17 May 1995. See also the statement by Ambassador Mickey Kantor, 28 June 1995, <www.ustr.gov/releases/1995/06/95-45> announcing the settlement of the dispute.

[11] United States – Restrictions on Imports of Cotton and Man-Made Fibre Underwear, WT/DS24/AB/R, 25 February 1997.

[12] European Communities – Regime for the Importation, Sale and Distribution of Bananas, WT/DS27/AB/R, 9 September 1997, paras 4–12, 9 September 1997.

was set up. This is most certainly true of the original GATT, and now of the WTO. With the fast-paced change of a globalizing economy, the WTO will necessarily have to cope with new factors, new policies and new subject matters. If it fails to do that, it will, sooner or later, faster or more gradually, be 'marginalized'. This could be very detrimental to the broader multilateral approach to international economic relations, pushing nations to solve their problems through regional arrangements, bilateral arrangements and even unilateral actions. Although forms other than multilateral can have an appropriate role and can also be constructive innovators for the world trading system, they also run considerable additional risks of ignoring key components and the diversity of societies and societal policies that exist in the world. In other words, they run a high risk of generating significant disputes and rancour among nations, which can inhibit or debilitate the advantages of cooperation otherwise hoped for under the multilateral system.

In addition, also perhaps inevitable to human institutions and particularly to treaty negotiations involving over 130 participating nations or entities, is the fact that in many places in the Uruguay Round and WTO Agreement there are gaps, and considerable ambiguities. These are beginning to emerge in the discussions and dispute settlement proceedings of the new WTO. They seem to be particularly significant in the context of the new issue texts, namely GATS for services and TRIPS for intellectual property. However, even concerning the traditional GATT text itself, there are ongoing ambiguity problems that are calling for new approaches. We can see, for example, an evolution in thinking about the Article III national treatment obligations, as affected and perhaps embellished by other texts in the context of GATT in Annex IA, such as the Agreement on the Application of Sanitary and Phytosanitary Measures, the Agreement on Technical Barriers to Trade, etc.[13]

Already a number of other newer subjects have been suggested for allocation to cooperative mechanisms in the WTO context. These include questions about competition policy, investment rules, human rights issues, environment in trade, labour standards issues, sanctions (unilateral or otherwise) to enforce some of these policies and also questions of threats to peace and arms control. The inventory of potential new issues does not stop there.[14]

How will the WTO solve or attempt to solve some of these issues? The first ministerial meeting, held at Singapore in 1996, faced some of these questions. Many conclude that the results of that meeting did not suggest very innovative ways to cope with new issues. Obviously, the ministers felt both the legal constraints of the WTO 'charter', and political as well as economic constraints of attitudes of constituents in a number of different societies.

---

[13]   See, eg, Japan – Taxes on Alcoholic Beverages, WT/DS8, 10 and 11/AB/R, 4 October 1996; European Communities – Regime for the Importation, Sale and Distribution of Bananas, WT/DS27/AB/R, 9 September 1997; and European Communities – Measures Concerning Meat and Meat Products (Hormones), WT/DS26 and 48/AB/R, 16 January 1998.

[14]   See John H. Jackson, 'Global Economics and International Economic Law' (1998) 1 *Journal of International Economic Law* 1.

The issues needing resolution could be broadly grouped into two categories: (i) substantively new issues (such as some of those discussed or listed above) but also (ii) a number of procedural or arguably interstitial ('fine-tuning') issues for the WTO. It is clear, for example, that a variety of the procedures of the dispute settlement process (particularly relating to the text of the Dispute Settlement Understanding), as well as other procedures regarding decision-making, waivers and new accessions, are being scrutinized and various suggestions for improvement are being put on the table. With respect to dispute settlement, most readers will be aware that the treaty text itself calls for a review during the calendar year 1998, now ensuing.[15]

How can these many issues be considered and dealt with in the current WTO institutional framework? First of all, it has to be recognized that there is a delicate interplay between the dispute settlement process on the one hand, and the possibilities or difficulties of negotiating new treaty texts or making decisions by the organization that are authorized by the Uruguay Round treaty text, on the other hand.

What are the possibilities of negotiating new text or making decisions pursuant to explicit authority of the WTO 'charter'? Clearly these possibilities are quite constrained. In the last months of the Uruguay Round negotiations, the diplomatic representatives at the negotiation felt it was important to build a number of 'checks and balances' into the WTO charter, to constrain decision-making by the international institution which would be too 'intrusive on sovereignty'. Thus the decision-making clauses of Article IX and the amending clauses of Article X established a number of limitations on what the membership of the WTO can do. The amending procedures are probably at least as difficult as those that existed under GATT (largely copied from GATT, with the possible exception of certain non-substantive procedural amendments). Under GATT, it was perceived by the time of the Tokyo Round in the 1970s that amendment was virtually impossible, so the contracting parties developed the technique of 'side agreements'. The theory of the WTO was to avoid this 'GATT *à la carte*' approach and pursue a 'single agreement' approach. Various attitudes towards that approach persist in the WTO.

Apart from formal amendments, one can look at the powers concerning decisions, waivers and formal interpretations. But in each of these cases, there are very substantial constraints. Decision-making (at least as a fallback from attempts to achieve consensus) is generally ruled by a majority-vote system, but there is language in the WTO (Article IX(3)) as well as the long practice under GATT, that suggests that decisions cannot be used to impose new obligations on members.[16] Waivers were sometimes used in GATT as ways to innovate and adjust to new circumstances, but that process fell into disrepute and caused the negotiators to develop Uruguay Round texts that quite constrained the use of waivers, particularly as to the duration of waivers and also subjecting waivers to explicit

---

[15]   See note 18 below.

[16]   Final Act Embodying the Results of the Uruguay Round of Multilateral Trade Negotiations, opened for signature 15 April 1994, Marrakesh, Morocco, (1994) 33 ILM 1140–1272, Articles IX(2), X(3) and X(4), and Article 3(2) of Annex 2 of the Dispute Settlement Understanding.

revocation authorities. GATT had no formal provision regarding 'interpretations', and thus GATT panels probably had a bit more scope for setting forth interpretations that would ultimately become embedded in GATT practice and even subsequent negotiated treaty language. However, the WTO addresses this issue of formal interpretations directly, imposing a very stringent voting requirement of three-fourths of the total membership. Since many people observe that often one-quarter of the WTO membership is not present at key meetings, one can see that the formal interpretation process is not an easy one to achieve.

Some observers feel, however, that in some contexts the technical requirements of consensus (not unanimity)[17] may not always be so difficult to fulfil.

Given these various constraints, it would be understandable if there was a temptation to try to use the dispute settlement process and the general conclusions of the panel reports regarding interpretation of many of the treaty clauses which have ambiguity or gaps. However, the Dispute Settlement Understanding itself in Article 3(2) warns against proceeding in this direction too far, by providing: 'Recommendations and rulings of the DSB cannot add to or diminish the rights and obligations provided in the covered agreements.' As suggested in section II above, the emerging attitudes of the Appellate Body reports seem to reinforce a policy of considerable deference to national government decision-making, possibly as a matter of 'judicial restraint' ideas such as that quoted from Article 3 of the DSU, and otherwise expressed by various countries who fear too much intrusion on 'sovereignty' (whatever that means). The provision of an explicit power of 'formal interpretation' with a supermajority requirement in the WTO charter also arguably constrains how far the dispute settlement system can push the idea of its report rulings and recommendations becoming 'definitive'.

In short, there are indications that the dispute settlement system cannot and should not carry much of the weight of formulating new rules either by way of filling gaps in the existing agreements, or by setting forth norms which carry the organization into totally new territory such as competition policy or labour standards.

In addition, as noted above, there are many procedural questions. Some of the procedures under the Dispute Settlement Understanding are now being questioned. Various suggestions are coming forward, and some lists of proposals for change exceed 60 or 80 items or suggestions.[18] Many of these suggestions are reasonable 'fine-tuning', without dramatic consequence to the system, but even the fine-tuning can be difficult to

---

[17]   WTO Agreement, Article IX, footnote 1, defines consensus as follows: 'The body concerned shall be deemed to have decided by consensus on a matter submitted for consideration, if no Member, present at the meeting when the decision is taken, formally objects to the proposed decision.'

[18]   The Decision on the Application and Review of the Understanding on Rules and Procedures Governing the Settlement of Disputes, reprinted in John H. Jackson et al., *International Economic Relations Documents Supplement 956* (3rd edn, West Publishing Company, 1995), calls for a 'full review of the dispute settlement rules' of the WTO within four years of their entry into force, ie during 1998.

achieve given some of the constraints on decision-making. One of the geniuses of GATT and its history was its ability to evolve partly through trial and error and practice. Indeed the dispute settlement under GATT evolved over four decades quite dramatically – with such concepts as *'prima facie* nullification', or the use of 'panels' instead of 'working parties', becoming gradually embedded in the process – and under the Tokyo Round Understanding on Dispute Settlement became 'definitive' by consensus action of the contracting parties.

But the language of the DSU (as well as the WTO 'charter') seems greatly to constrain some of this approach compared to GATT. DSU Article 2(4) states: 'Where the rules and procedures of this understanding provide for the DSB to take a decision, it shall do so by consensus.' The definition of consensus is then supplied in a footnote, and although not identical with 'unanimity', provides that an objecting member can block consensus. Likewise, the WTO 'charter' itself provides a consensus requirement for amendments to Annexes 2 and 3 of the WTO. It will be recalled that Annex 2 is the DSU and the dispute settlement procedures. Thus the opportunity to evolve by experiment and trial and error, plus practice over time, seems considerably more constrained under the WTO than was the case under the very loose and ambiguous language of GATT, with its minimalist institutional language.

Thus we have a potential for stalemate, or potential for inability to cope with some of the problems that will be facing and are already facing the new WTO institution. That leads us to the final section of this paper.

IV. Exploring Possible Solutions and Developing Conclusions and a Prognosis for the Future

Perhaps the WTO can develop somewhat better opportunity for explicit amendment, using the two-thirds (and three-fourths in substance cases) power of amendment in the WTO charter. Perhaps also, some of the decisions that are possible by the WTO membership at its ministerial meeting or various council meetings can 'creep up on' some of the issues and decide them in a way that certain small steps of reform can be taken. These decisions will become part of the 'practice under the agreement' referred to in the Vienna Convention on the Law of Treaties. What are some other possibilities? With respect to the dispute settlement details and potential changes in procedures, it may be possible to work within the 'consensus rule' to make some changes in Annex 2 (the DSU). It at least appears that this does not require national government member approvals of treaty text amendments, and thus avoids some of the elaborate procedures of national government ratification of treaties, etc. The question of such consensus relates to at least two different kinds of decisions: changes in the text of the DSU; and decisions by the DSB which could involve incidental or interstitial and ancillary procedural rules, assuming that they are not inconsistent with treaty provisions of the DSU. Again of course, the consensus rule apparently applies. There may be a few situations where basic small and relatively unimportant decisions can be made as a matter of practice of the administration of the dispute settlement system, such as decisions about how to interpret time deadlines, or the form of complaints that should be filed, or the development of a relatively uniform set of procedural rules about activities of panels and panel members, translations, documentation, etc. Even then, there is at least some likelihood that an objecting member could force an issue to go to the DSB and that member could dare block consensus.

With respect to larger 'new subjects' for WTO additions, subjects as significant for example as rules on investment, competition policy or even environmental rules, it appears that matters will be somewhat more difficult even than the procedural changes. If amendment of the agreements is not feasible, one could look at the WTO Annex 4 'plurilateral' agreements which are optional, and thus in the drafting process do not necessarily need to be subject to 'consensus'. However, to add a negotiated plurilateral agreement to Annex 4 of the WTO does require so-called 'full consensus'. Thus once again, that could be blocked, and clearly that blocking opportunity will translate back into the negotiating process about what can be negotiated to be placed in such a new potential plurilateral agreement.

Other legal and procedural innovations to accomplish change may develop. For example, implementation of the results of both the telecommunication services negotiation and the financial service negotiation relies heavily upon insertions into the individual service schedules of commitments by members.[19]

Thus it may be that the critical development for the WTO is to address 'consensus' procedures and thus give attention to the meaning and practice of consensus.

It might be feasible to develop certain practices about consensus that would lead member nations of the WTO to 'self-restrain' themselves from blocking a consensus in certain circumstances and under certain conditions. In other words, the General Council, or the DSB (General Council acting with different hats), might develop a series of criteria about consensus concerning certain kinds of decisions, which would strongly suggest to member states that if these criteria are fulfilled, they would normally refrain from blocking the consensus. Perhaps this could develop a bit like the practice in the European Community history and jurisprudence of the 'Luxembourg Compromise', where it has been understood that governments would refrain from exercising their potential vote against a measure in certain circumstances, unless the measure involves something of 'vital interest' to the nation member involved. While not pursuing the analogy too far, one might see something similar develop in the context of the WTO. A 'vital national interest' declaration could be in practice a condition for blocking consensus, but a practice could develop to subject such declarations to inquiry, debate and criticism.

Let us by way of experiment consider what some of the conditions or circumstances might be to encourage nations to refrain from blocking a consensus on some of the more

---

[19] From discussions with WTO officials and from WTO documents, Successful Conclusion of the WTO's Financial Services Negotiation, 15 December 1997 <www.wto.org/wto/press/press86.htm>; and Basic Telecommunications – Schedules of Commitments and Lists of Article II Exemptions, April 1997 <www.wto.org/wto/press/gbtoff.htm>.

purely procedural reforms that might be desired, either in amending the DSU or in decisions of the DSB. The following might be considered:

(i) Clearly the major criterion is that a proposed measure be consistent with the fundamental principles of the WTO, including most-favoured-nation (MFN), and perhaps some of the substantive requirements of treaty texts such as national treatment, or restraints on border measures. Procedural changes ought not normally to challenge those particular rules anyway.

(ii) In addition, perhaps there should be a supermajority threshold such as 70 or 90 per cent of the members present, or some threshold percentage of total WTO membership trade represented by agreeing members (eg, 90 per cent of WTO trade). Some ideas about a 'critical mass' threshold have already been discussed.[20]

(iii) In addition, perhaps the consideration of any new procedural measure should first be examined in depth by a special expert group appointed by the DSB or the WTO membership, which group would consist of considerable expertise on legal procedures being considered, and which group would be recognized as impartial and not prone to be pushing one reform or another for particular advantage to the nation concerned. It might be preferable that the members of the expert group should be, like panels, working and discussing in their own right and judgment and not on the instruction of governments. Indeed, such an expert group might draw upon individuals who are not part of the diplomatic missions at Geneva, and in some cases not even government employees. The expert group could prepare certain recommendations or evaluate proposals that have otherwise been made, and then send them to the DSB, or to the WTO General Council, with a recommendation of adoption. Then, if the other criteria mentioned above were fulfilled, members would again be strongly encouraged to refrain from blocking consensus, partly with the notion that in the future they may be supporting some other measures which likewise would benefit from restraint in using consensus-blocking techniques.

Turning to more substantial reforms which might be developed through plurilateral agreements as candidates for Annex 4, one might also develop a set of criteria which would be used to persuade nations to refrain from exercising consensus-blocking techniques. For example, the criteria for a new plurilateral agreement that would benefit from such a developing practice over time (informal and not part of the treaty, of course) could include the following:

(i) The proposed agreement would not be inconsistent with any of the existing other rules of the WTO and its Annexes, especially Annex 1 (GATT, GATS and TRIPS). Thus MFN would be fulfilled where otherwise required by the rules of Annex 1. Other measures already embodied in the treaties would likewise be a requirement of consistency for the new treaty agreement. Of course the new plurilateral agreement

---

[20]   Address given by WTO Director General Renato Ruggiero at the 30 April 1998, 50th Anniversary Symposium, reproduced at pp. 1–3 above.

proposal would sometimes contain measures that would call for rules applying to those accepting the new protocol that differed from the other WTO rules. But there should be no impact on the non-members of the new protocol that would be considered detrimental.

(ii) The protocol or plurilateral agreement proposal should have among its proponents a 'substantial' number of members of the WTO. What is substantial? It should be relatively clear that bilateral agreements would not be good candidates. Beyond that how many should be required? Perhaps 10 or 20. Or perhaps the minimum number would be left ambiguous, as long as it was not just a few members. It could also be noted that smaller groups of members can enter into regional trading arrangements, provided that these are not inconsistent with the other rules of the WTO, particularly including Article XXIV of GATT.

(iii) The proposed plurilateral agreement should be open to accession by any WTO member. Possibly this ability to accede to the plurilateral agreement should be unconditional. That would mean that the proposal for a plurilateral agreement would have within its text all the measures to be required, leaving nothing further to be negotiated for accession. There might be some exception for a 'scheduling' type apparatus analogous to GATT tariff schedules or GATS service schedules.[21]

(iv) It could be required that a majority vote of the Council would recommend the addition of the plurilateral proposal to Annex 4. This majority vote could be something of a supermajority, such as two-thirds. Other formulas for the vote could be envisaged. Again, a vital national interest declaration could be used, however, to block consensus.

(v) Since bringing a new plurilateral agreement under the WTO 'umbrella' by adding it to Annex 4 might have some financial implications for the costs of secretariat and other assistance in enhancing and carrying out the plurilateral agreement, an additional principle to avoid consensus blocking could be that the financial costs of the additional activity created by the proposed plurilateral agreement would be carried entirely by the members who have acceded to the plurilateral agreement, under a special budget item in the WTO financial system.

Possibly with some approach like this to providing some constraint on blocking a developing consensus, the risk of the consensus requirement creating stalemate and inability to evolve and cope with new problems in the global economy could be minimized. These criteria could be developed through resolutions of the General Council or the DSB, in the form of 'recommendations to members' and might provide the relatively informal practice which nevertheless could be effective over time. If such practice was reasonably successful, it might achieve some of the best of several divergent policies, namely allowing measures to go forward short of unanimity or total consensus,

---

[21]   From discussions with WTO officials and from WTO documents, Successful Conclusion of the WTO's Financial Services Negotiation, 15 December 1997 <www.wto.org/wto/press/press86.htm>; and Basic Telecommunications – Schedules of Commitments and Lists of Article II Exemptions, April 1997 <www.wto.org/wto/press/gbtoff.htm>.

but at the same time protecting in some sort of ultimate and 'vital sense' the right and power of every member of the WTO to object in (it is hoped) only those very few cases where it felt it was so strongly important to its vital national interests that it would not refrain from blocking the consensus. Clearly this must develop as sort of a 'gentlemen's agreement' over time, and the practice of this procedure in its formative period (perhaps several years) would be extraordinarily important.

Chapter 8
The WTO's New Horizons

Patrick A. Messerlin

I. Introduction

Celebrating an anniversary is always a difficult balancing act: between being complimentary without being complacent, between recalling past successes without overlooking the difficulties of today or side-stepping the challenges of tomorrow. The present exercise is an even trickier one: the 50th anniversary of the General Agreement on Tariffs and Trade (GATT) must not overshadow the fourth anniversary of its infant successor, the World Trade Organization (WTO). And yet it is hard to imagine two more different 'personalities' than GATT, forceps-delivered and discreet-living, slowly building up its modest successes, and the WTO, born beneath the multicoloured salvoes of the Moroccan *fantasia*, quick to scoop up some major successes, and a media darling with its mixture of soap operas (headline-making negotiations) and boxing matches (settlement of disputes among members) involving 'goodies' and 'baddies' (differing, of course, over time and according to one's particular geographical standpoint).

In the space of 50 years, GATT has fostered international trading so intensively as to raise problems of 'world governance' that will become even more pressing in the future. These problems concern the impact of international trade on social cohesion, the environment, corruption or even the role of the state in WTO member countries. While these problems have little to do with the establishment of a world government (an idea at least as utopian today as a century ago), they share an essential feature: they are as much ethical problems as technical problems concerning the management of international trade rules. Hence, they are problems of governance.

Thus, willy-nilly and despite having inherited GATT's penchant for pragmatism, the WTO finds itself at the heart of these issues of world governance for one simple reason, which is that as the century draws to a close the WTO is the universal economic institution *par excellence*. In this paper we shall therefore focus on these issues. Besides, not to do so would be to turn a blind eye to the past. It would be to forget that GATT, while suffering from disadvantages in many respects, did have one great advantage in that it benefited from the attraction exerted by liberalization, both morally and in terms of economic dynamism, following two world conflagrations triggered by states that had no qualms about sacrificing their people to war. Protectionists then had to prove that states

© Kluwer Law International 2000. *From GATT to the WTO: The Multilateral Trading System in the New Millennium*, The WTO Secretariat (ed.), Kluwer Law International, London, 2000; ISBN 90–411–1253–7

which were closed in on themselves could offer the same degree of material and spiritual well-being as open countries. Nowadays those wars are a distant memory and there is a price to pay for GATT's very successes: questions are now being raised about the legitimacy of the present established order, seen as the result of multilateral liberalization, and about the dangers of social dislocation within countries. The WTO, like GATT, has to demonstrate the moral legitimacy of the economic principles on which it is based.

II.   Handling Unexpected Success

GATT was constantly surprising us with its unexpected successes. In fact, the first of these surprising successes was its birth, two years after World War II, when the big-hearted projects for the post-war period were being shattered by the Cold War and the colonial powers remained stubbornly blind to the emerging new world. Next came its steadfast advocacy of the principle of non-discrimination in all respects: as between foreign suppliers with the most-favoured-nation clause, and also as between foreign and domestic suppliers with the national treatment principle, as well as between industries, by setting its sights on tariff escalation and constantly stressing customs tariffs as the proper instrument of protection. And, lastly, round after round, it brought a reduction in those tariffs and other barriers on industrial products.

The Uruguay Round was true to this long tradition of unexpected successes. We can all remember the predictions of the period 1990–1993, each gloomier than the last, culminating in the caption 'GATT is dead'. And yet since 1994 each year has brought the establishment or signing of a major agreement: 1995 with the Uruguay Round, 1996 with information technology products, 1997 with basic telecommunications, and finally 1998 with financial services. In 1993, GATT disciplines covered only the 25–30 per cent of world GDP accounted for by manufacturing. Over the last five years, they have extended to another 15–20 per cent of world GDP with agriculture (4–5 per cent), telecommunications (2–3 per cent) and financial services (9–11 per cent).

This half-century of hard-won unexpected successes has not made for an easy relationship between GATT/WTO and the man in the street, who often sees the WTO as a machine for endless and pointless liberalization, each round of negotiations bringing the next in its wake. To the layman this routine is all the more bewildering as each round is preceded by doom-mongering and followed by boundless enthusiasm: each round is the 'round to end all rounds'. And so the man in the street, little inclined to take an interest in some distant GATT/WTO in the first place, is divided between worry, cynicism and fatigue: he is ready to ask for a 'time out' in globalization and insist on his own specific values, while at the same time proclaiming his daily solidarity with the whole of mankind (an inconsistency inherent in our media-driven societies).

Two rules of governance issue from this history. First, the WTO must not allow the man in the street to believe that the thrust of liberalization is imposed by outside forces external to his own country. As economic analysis shows, a country has to open up because it is in its own interest to do so and not in order to please its partners. And this has ethical implications: applying the principle of non-discrimination or using customs tariffs for protective purposes is not simply a question of economic optimization but also a guarantee of states' independence with respect to corruption, assuring them a real instrument of power. And, secondly, the WTO must not give the impression that 'as far as liberalization is concerned, everything has been done but everything remains to be done': it must make the layman understand the wisdom of the cautious pace of past liberalization and the ensuing need to pursue it over time.

These two rules are not easy to apply. Politicians tend to portray liberalization efforts as constraints imposed by partner countries. But at the same time they give their wholehearted backing to GATT/WTO, this wonderful success-producing machine. These tendencies are very clearly illustrated in the following extract, cited by Rodrik,[1] from the final communiqué of the G7 Summit in Lyons (1995):

> 'In an increasingly interdependent world, we must all recognize that we have an interest in spreading the benefits of economic growth as widely as possible and in diminishing the risk either of excluding individuals or groups in our own economies or of excluding certain countries or regions from the benefits of globalization.'

This passage raises the following questions: in what way does an increasingly interdependent world *increase* a government's interest in spreading the benefits of economic growth and diminishing exclusion within its *own* country? In what way is a government's interest in its own population not sufficient?

This emphasis on the domestic foundations of liberalization efforts has a corollary: these two rules of governance must be fulfilled above all by institutions existing within each WTO member country that are independent enough to present the man in the street with a clear explanation of his (and his country's) interest in joining in the liberalization efforts, together with a supportive but not biased analysis. Support of this kind is crucial for the WTO because it is the best way of ensuring that the man in the street does not view the WTO as imposing liberalization efforts.

III.   Governing Past Achievements

The man in the street is all the more bewildered because he has not the slightest idea of the genuine achievements of past liberalization. In the case of the WTO as well as GATT, successes are not achieved once and for all, and are sometimes even 'sold' twice, as in the case of the liberalization of the bulk of textile and clothing products with the Uruguay Round Agreements.

The WTO Secretariat reports on members' trade policies indicate how far from complete is the liberalization of manufacturing products launched 50 years ago, even in the case of the developed countries long engaged in the process. For example, the average

---

[1]   Dani Rodrik, *Has Globalization Gone Too Far?* (Institute for International Economics, Washington, DC, 1997).

(unweighted) tariff rate applied by the European Community (EC) to industrial goods has fallen from 7 to 6 per cent over ten years (1988–1997), and comparable figures could be given for the other industrialized countries.

Explaining this laggardly pace by the fact that current tariffs are so low that the costs of protection are small, thus removing interest in complete liberalization, is unconvincing. The average tariff rate is largely determined by a small number of high tariffs, for which the net cost of protection is therefore high (economic analysis shows that the cost of protection is the *square* of the rate of protection). Thus, the highest rate applied by the EC to manufactured goods is 23.8 per cent, comparable to that of the other developed countries.

These observations are much strengthened when non-tariff barriers are taken into account too – those resulting from a host of ways of providing protection or reprotection, from changing tariff headings for certain goods (under the pretext that they are based on new components or involve new production methods) to the imposition of anti-dumping duties. For the EC, these other trade barriers represent additional protection which alone may be estimated at an average rate of 3–5 per cent for industrial products in 1995.[2] And there is no reason to believe that the EC is an exception in this area.

Lastly, these protection rates, as unweighted averages of tariffs and equivalent barriers, underestimate the level of protection granted to domestic producers. All countries are readier to grant zero or low tariffs for goods that they do not produce rather than on the other goods. Consequently, if tariffs and other barriers are weighted by the relative weight of the industries concerned in domestic production, value added or employment, the existing level of protection today turns out to be even higher. Again taking the EC as representative, the aggregate level of protection is today around 11–13 per cent.[3]

What is true for the process of liberalization of manufactures that began 50 years ago is of course all the more true for the recent initiatives. Temperate-zone agricultural sectors are barely beginning to lower their scandalously high barriers. The agreements on telecommunications and financial services are merely first steps which dodge many essential issues, such as the desirable industry structure or desired 'universal service' obligations.

There is nothing shocking about any of this, and listing these limitations is in no way to denigrate the successes of GATT and the WTO. It is merely a reminder, and a necessary one for the man in the street to understand what is really going on, that GATT yesterday and the WTO today are institutions set up by sovereign states and largely dependent on them: time and boundless patience are needed to bring them into line and make them comply with the disciplines to which they had already committed themselves.

These comments lead us to another rule of governance. As the liberalization of international trade steadily expands, the WTO must acquire more efficient tools for

---

[2]   Patrick Messerlin, 'Trade Protection in the European Economy' (mimeo, Institute for International Economics, 1998).

[3]   Ibid.

'governing the achievements' of past liberalization. The Uruguay Round sought to attain this objective through the trade policy review procedure and by including notification procedures in the various parts of the Round. These procedures have to be strengthened, so that the wisdom of the cautious pace of liberalization efforts can be more readily understood.

Governing past achievements, however, also involves doing something that was carefully avoided in the Uruguay Round, namely the slow but steady elimination of anti-dumping procedures. The latter in fact play the role of a safeguard procedure, but they do so terribly badly, ie at a very high cost (in terms of level of protection and discrimination, as well as in terms of anti-competitive behaviour of the firms concerned) for the country imposing them, and also increasingly at a very high cost for the whole world since half of the WTO members are beginning to display a pronounced taste for anti-dumping actions. Insofar as they are opaque and confined to a small number of firms, these procedures tend towards what is eventually a dangerous takeover of the state by private interests.

IV.   Cultivating a New Art of Negotiation

The WTO is a negotiating forum. Over the last ten years, three problems have arisen in this area. How are negotiations to be conducted concerning future liberalization in the vast new field of services? How are negotiations to be conducted while similar negotiations are simultaneously taking place in the smaller framework of regional agreements? And, lastly, how are negotiations to be conducted on issues that do not concern only WTO member states but also subnational entities?

IV.1   Services

The problem of the negotiating procedures for liberalizing services has become a familiar one since the end of the Uruguay Round, but it appears to be growing increasingly thorny. At the end of the Uruguay Round, many observers took it for granted that the principle adopted for negotiating national commitments – namely a 'positive' schedule listing each country's liberalization commitments – was unsatisfactory. It seemed obvious that the grey areas left by these positive lists were too large: a country could freeze the actual effects of its scheduled commitments by maintaining a provision not included in its positive list. Accordingly, there seemed to be a clear need to move towards a system of 'negative' lists (where everything is liberalized aside from the exceptions scrupulously listed by member countries in their negative lists).

Since then, however, the negotiations on the Multilateral Investment Agreement (MIA) currently taking place in the OECD have also raised doubts about the value of negative lists. So far they have not produced much better results, as the lists of exceptions are excessively long and tend to break up the coalitions of interest groups supporting the MIA within certain key countries. However, final judgment should be withheld as these lists of exceptions have been the subject only of bilateral and not multilateral consultations.

Nevertheless, efficient negotiating mechanisms for services still seem to be lacking. An approach that to some extent supplements such mechanisms and to some extent replaces them is the adoption of 'mutual recognition' agreements. Agreements of this kind have speeded up the liberalization of services among EC member states. However, they are based on a legal system not yet available in the WTO: (i) the prohibition of any quantitative restriction or 'measure having equivalent effects'; (ii) exception for law-enforcement purposes; (iii) enforceable judgments (of the European Court of Justice) giving a very extensive interpretation of the above-mentioned prohibition; (iv) the possibility of avoiding this exception through the adoption by member states of common harmonization provisions; and, lastly, (v) grouping of these harmonization provisions in the form of a 'patrimony' (*acquis communautaire*) that is non-negotiable for countries subsequently joining the agreement. None of these points, except for point (ii) in part, exists in the WTO legal system. In this respect, the project of a 'New Transatlantic Market' (NTM) between the EC and the USA is interesting in that it raises all the issues involved in adapting this procedure of mutual recognition agreements to states that are not seeking to form an organic union (unlike the EC member states).

IV.2   Regional agreements

Of the three problems raised in this section, the most progress has been made on that of regional agreements. In recent years, economic analysis has brought a fuller understanding of the elements that have to be taken into account in order to balance the costs, where static effects are predominant (and it is more revealing to label these as economic), against the dynamic gains (which it is more revealing to call political). This analysis has shed increasingly strong light on the economic costs[4] while the political gains have appeared less and less convincing (although their list grows longer by the day). This development is partly due to the strengthening of the WTO disciplines. Thus, binding a country's trade reforms to a privileged partner by creating a regional union with the latter is claimed as one of the political gains mentioned above; but the force of this argument dwindles in view of the fact that the WTO dispute settlement mechanism places the reforms of the country in question under the surveillance of the world community.

As this balance between costs and gains is increasingly well understood, regional agreements should really only be of two kinds: either leaving the region as open as possible to the rest of the world, so that the economic costs have the smallest possible impact on limited political gains; or closing the region (or part of the region) in upon itself because the political gains are, rightly or wrongly, perceived as major. The first type of regional agreement is complementary to multilateral liberalization, and therefore only the second type poses serious problems for the WTO. And it would seem that the latter type of agreement is confined to Europe, because of the twin (and in my view mistaken) beliefs that European agreements have both small economic costs and major political gains. As a

---

[4]   Jagdish Bhagwati and Arvind Panagariya, *Preferential Trading Areas and Multilateralism: Strangers, Friends and Foes?* (Washington, DC, American Enterprise Institute, 1996).

matter of fact, Europe alone is involved in more than a third of the regional agreements notified to GATT and the WTO between 1947 and 1997.

IV.3 Subnational entities

These are member states of federations, the autonomous regions of centralized states and so forth. They are thus frequent among WTO members, present (Germany, Brazil, USA or India) or future (Russia or China). Awareness of the importance of this problem is relatively recent as it is linked to the 'new' WTO subjects, in particular services and government procurement.

If the undertakings entered into by WTO members are to have the force they are supposed to have, there appear to be only two solutions: either these subnational entities are implicitly present at the negotiating table where necessary, as occurred for the Uruguay Round agreement on government procurement in the case of the USA (as well as the EC); or else the undertakings given by WTO member states must compulsorily apply to their constituent parts. Here again, the NTM project between the EC and the USA is interesting in that it would provide a test of these approaches and their best possible variants.

V. Trade, Employment and Unemployment

This issue is the first to raise directly the problem of the impact of international trade liberalization on the 'social structure' of WTO member countries. However, it is by no means a new one. In the 1950s and 1960s it was used by developing countries which felt that they had to protect themselves against the 'unfair' competition of industrialized countries: the latter's productivity was so high that it seemed to deprive their own manufacturers of any chance of competing on their own domestic markets against the manufacturers of the North – from where the developing countries' protectionist policy during that period came. The argument was mistaken because it focused on only one side of the coin (productivity) while neglecting the other (low wages in developing countries). A wage of one franc together with productivity of one unit can perfectly well compete against a wage of ten francs with a productivity of ten units. What is important is the relationship between wages and productivity.

Thirty years later, in the 1990s, the argument has been taken up once again but the other way round, by some politicians or industrialists in developed countries, but this time it is only the wage side of the argument that is advanced: the countries of the North, it is claimed, cannot compete on their own markets with the low-wage competition from developing countries. Obviously, once again the other side of the coin has to be borne in mind: low wages imply low productivity of workers in developing countries, or of the latter's economies as a whole. Competition between 'low' and 'high' wages remains possible as long as the relationship between wages and productivity remains proportionately the same.

If this argument has raised its head 20 years after having been disproved for developing countries, it is because the successive rounds of liberalization of international trade have aroused fears in the industrialized countries, even though trade between industrialized and developing countries represents such a small part (a few per cent) of the OECD countries' huge economies that it is highly unlikely to have a big impact on the latter. The reason is that since the 1970s, the developed countries have undergone two adverse trends: a relative decline in wages of unskilled labour in OECD countries where wages are flexible, and a relative increase in unemployment among unskilled workers in OECD countries with downward wage rigidities (resulting from a legal minimum wage). Many empirical studies have had to be carried out to prove that these two trends were scarcely attributable to international trade, which can only 'explain' from 10–15 per cent at most of these two trends.

The factors responsible for the remaining 85–90 per cent are the rigidity of labour markets (which is sometimes very high) and surging technical progress over the last three decades. It is worth remembering in this connection that since 1950 maritime transport costs have fallen by 20 per cent, air transport costs by 60 per cent and telecommunication costs (crucial for transporting many services between countries) by 90 per cent (and this is a very provisional figure). All these causes combine to create a permanent and general feeling of concern that is amplified by 'globalization'.

VI. Liberalization and 'Globalization': An Ambiguous Relationship

Globalization – a term coined in the last decade – is already felt to have gone too far. What events caused this sudden strong shift in public sentiment? In his recent book,[5] Rodrik puts forward a list of such events, all of which share one remarkable feature: they have nothing whatsoever in common with the progressive liberalization of trade in goods or services, as can be shown by the two examples to which Rodrik attaches particular importance.

The first is the Maastricht Treaty which is not, in itself, remotely concerned with liberalization: it merely establishes a common currency. Pricing all goods in a single currency no doubt makes it easier for competition to prevail. But a number of economists have drawn attention to the costs of the macroeconomic policies associated with the creation of the common currency – among them the liberalization programmes undertaken by the EC within the framework of the Single Market, an enterprise *predating* the Maastricht Treaty. Not only does the latter add no liberalization scheme to the Single Market programme already established, it even expresses rather 'reactionary' attitudes towards past or ongoing liberalization – for example, by taking up the idea of discriminatory (sectoral) industrial policies, which is not found in the Treaty of Rome.

---

    5   Dani Rodrik, *Has Globalization Gone Too Far?* (Institute for International Economics, Washington, DC, 1997).

The second example is that of the French strike at the end of 1995, which was confined almost exclusively to the railways and the Paris underground and bus networks. This was enough to throw the entire French economy into utter chaos, but unlike many such events in the past, it failed to trigger off a general strike. It would be difficult to identify other sectors of the French economy so little concerned by opening up to the outside world, even in the long term. In fact, the issues involved in the strike were quite different: improved allocation of resources among these transport systems dominated by government monopolies; the halting of massive subsidies to certain coddled segments of those monopolies; and a comprehensive review of the idea of public service. With or without liberalization, these problems had to be tackled as they concerned *domestic* regulatory reforms.

Liberalization of goods and services and globalization are not, therefore, one and the same thing. What sets them apart is the liberalization of capital flows and the ensuing 'regulatory reforms' to attract such capital. However, these two factors have been determined more by the unilateral actions of countries than by a concerted or negotiated multilateral effort. In the circumstances, globalization and liberalization can be unconnected or even divergent: firms can combine the globalization of capital flows and regulatory reforms with the establishment or preservation of segmented world markets for goods and services by means of trade barriers between countries (which are not inconsiderable, as we have seen).

The fact remains that globalization has influenced liberalization efforts in two ways. First of all, capital flows accelerate the spread of technology and strengthen the force of 'kaleidoscopic' comparative advantages in the manner postulated by Bhagwati. Instead of being confined to a few well-defined industries (as in the 1960s and 1970s), competitive pressure is emerging in more sectors of industry, driven by more countries. Secondly, the dominant role of the state appears to be dwindling in favour of multinational companies, whether private or public (the latter are frequently overlooked, but the international activities of firms like Electricité de France or Deutsche Telekom should be remembered).

Globalization has therefore had a specific impact on labour markets. So far, most trade unions in the industrialized countries have not called for a return to national protectionism. And that is because they are clearly aware of the benefits of past liberalization, particularly for the lowest incomes. After all, customs duties often tend to be regressive, ie represent a greater burden for low-wage earners than high incomes; and foreign investors have often proved willing to invest in industries abandoned by domestic companies. It is also because the trade unions are aware that a tilt in favour of protectionist measures would expose their preferences for their own country's workers, to the detriment of workers in developing countries, even though the latter are less well off, thus infringing the universal values they claim to defend, including in particular the principle of fairness.

However, it was difficult for the trade unions to stay quiet, especially in countries where they were under pressure from 'rival' unions less anxious to cope with the real problems and more concerned with promoting 'turnover' (ie, increasing their membership). They therefore took up the idea of social standards in the emerging or developing countries. But this approach is neither reasonable nor appropriate. It calls for draconian measures if it is to have a rapid impact, with correspondingly disastrous results.

For example, banning child labour in developing countries would mean putting the children concerned on the streets, with all the extreme consequences that could entail. If rapid action is renounced, the establishment in emerging or developing countries of social standards comparable to those applied in the developed countries will take longer than is needed for wages in those countries to catch up with those in the industrialized world – ie for the fear of low wages to lose all justification. It need only be recalled that it took a mere 20 years for Japan's per capita gross national product (roughly equivalent to the average wage) to rise from 20 per cent of the American per capita GNP (in 1950) to 70 per cent (in 1973).

The only methods that are both economically appropriate and morally acceptable are those traditionally proposed within the framework of GATT and WTO. The first involves introducing the safeguard procedure (referred to above) which would make it easier to cope with the rapid restructuring requirements in certain areas of employment. However, care must be taken to ensure that the safeguards adopted are both transparent and transitional. For example, a scenario involving more than 30 years' protection (of the kind granted to the clothing industry in some developed countries) should not be re-enacted, if only because the fact of protecting an industry for longer than a full generation shows that something other than workers is being protected. The second method is to address the structural aspects of labour supply in the developing countries: for example, trade unions in the industrialized countries could contribute funds (or more funds, if they are already doing so) to establish morning or evening classes for children to attend before or after work, thereby enabling them to improve their knowledge, even to a modest extent. As is emphasized in the following section, free trade does not mean *laissez faire* and is fully compatible with appropriate responses to specific challenges.

VII. Has Globalization Gone Too Far?

In recent years, some criticisms have gone beyond calling for just a breathing space: globalization has been accused of threatening the 'social cohesion' of countries. Even allowing for the broad differences between globalization and liberalization programmes, which were emphasized in the previous section, it is clear that the shift in the WTO's focus from frontier barriers (such as tariffs on industrial products) to internal trade barriers (such as regulations affecting services) can only place the WTO under growing fire.

It is important, then, to examine these criticisms, and this section offers a brief overview. First, though, a preliminary comment. Even when such criticisms relate to new topics, they do not require the WTO to deploy new arguments: the Organization can rely on two traditional arguments used by GATT, which need merely be adapted to each of the criticisms in question. The first argument is that the WTO is a member-driven organization and that every WTO member therefore exercises ultimate control over its own decisions: the further pursuance of liberalization programmes depends on the capacity of a country's leaders to understand that such programmes redound to the public good and to persuade their compatriots that this is so. The second argument is that trade liberalization, including even free trade, is not synonymous with *laissez faire*: in order to produce the benefits it promises, free trade may even require appropriate measures in other fields. The following three examples lead to the same conclusion, in accordance with economic analysis: threats to social cohesion exist only to the extent that appropriate measures are not taken to complement trade liberalization.

VII.1   Trade and fiscal competition between countries

A first criticism alleges that globalization leads states to compete among themselves, thereby limiting their capacity for initiative. It is true that WTO is involved in a global process which treats states as producers of laws and regulations and ensures that, as such, they are as efficient as possible. To achieve that objective, it is desirable to encourage emulation or 'competition' between states. All too often, however, this approach is subject to a one-dimensional criticism alleging that competition compels states which produce too much legislation to produce less. In fact, there is a second dimension to this approach: competition has the further effect of impelling states which do not produce enough appropriate legislation to produce more.

Taxation policy provides an example of competition between states. Such competition is said to reduce some states' ability to collect taxes and ensure social cohesion by means of fiscal transfers. For example, the social cohesion between workers and retired people is allegedly imperilled in countries which rely exclusively on pay-as-you-go pension schemes (where the working population pays for pensioners). This criticism (which was put forward during the French strikes in 1995) overlooks a number of facts. In the case of France, for instance, it overlooks the fact that, during the last 20 years, pensions have grown faster than wages, so much so that on current trends the per capita income of the elderly non-working population will be Ffr265 000 per year in 2020, compared with Ffr172 000 for employed persons, an utterly untenable situation in the light of the proportion that pensioners will represent within the total population then.[6] In fact, the problem raised is not one of taxation but one of funding, which includes but is not confined to a taxation component; the solution could well be facilitated by the higher growth and broader financial markets associated with greater worldwide liberalization.

This tax-related criticism is only the latest version (to date) of a criticism levelled in 1860 against the free trade agreement between the United Kingdom and France (which is, moreover, repeated ad infinitum by the developing countries in an attempt to invoke loss of customs revenue as justification for their protectionist policy). It might be worth recalling what happened in 1860. Gladstone, the British Chancellor of the Exchequer, laid a finance Bill before Parliament which included both the free trade agreement and a fiscal reform package. The latter involved the substitution, on an even greater scale than before, of a more modern and fairer taxation scheme (income tax) for a more archaic scheme (indirect taxes on imports). In so doing, Gladstone provided one

---

[6]   Jean Peyrelevade, 'Economie: le poids du vieillissement' (Notes de la Fondation Saint-Simon, 1996).

of the most brilliant illustrations to date of a free trade policy in its purest form of unilateral liberalization, accompanied by firm government action to strengthen social cohesion.

VII.2   Trade and environment

Another criticism links trade liberalization schemes to environmental degradation. We could merely repeat what was said above, emphasizing the extent to which the appropriate measures decided at the recent Kyoto Summit are compatible with trade liberalization. But it is more relevant to review the development, over the last ten years, of the relations between environmentalists and GATT/WTO: these trends are instructive because the environmentalists were among the first to take an interest in GATT/WTO.

Initially, most environmentalists saw GATT as both the cause and the cure for the problems that preoccupied them: the cause, because economic growth perceived as giving rise to pollution is accelerated by international free trade; the cure, because halting such trade appeared to be the key to reducing pollution – GATT/WTO as the policeman's truncheon. Subsequently, however, the environmentalists came to regard themselves as 'hostages' to GATT/WTO: they observed that in the negotiations conducted in that forum all governments expressed preferences which were far removed from those they proclaimed back in their capitals. In other words, GATT/WTO reflected the 'real' policies of their countries – and this led many environmentalists to refocus their activity on their own countries. A third stage has perhaps been initiated by the debate arising from the dispute over turtles and shrimps between the USA, on the one hand, and India, Malaysia, Pakistan and Thailand, on the other. The debate split the environmental movement because fishing conditions are not the same in the Caribbean as in the Pacific or in the Atlantic. It also pitted ecologists against champions of national values because nature (the life of turtles) is not assigned equal 'value' in the USA and in Asia. This case merely illustrates a long tradition in GATT (and among economists): the most appropriate measure is the one taken at the level closest to the problem faced. The problem raised by the dispute is a regional, not a global one: regional measures should therefore be taken.

Another case involving the environment – in the broad sense of the term – deserves careful attention, as it raises fundamental moral issues and shows that 'obvious' solutions can have many hidden ethical aspects, while the principles of GATT/WTO highlight those aspects – or at least require them to be studied. 'Mad cow disease' is a bovine disease associated with industrial methods of livestock farming and capable of being communicated to humans. Based on the current state of knowledge, the risk of dying from this disease is estimated, at worst, to be of the order of one in a million. This risk led to an immediate ban on meat imports involving several countries, a solution which seems 'obvious'. However, it raises questions which can best be illustrated by the following observation: every year 10 000 people die on the roads of France (many of them victims of bad driving for which they bear no responsibility), giving a probability of one in a million (since there are roughly 10 million cars on French roads). Up to now, however, no one has ever thought of banning the car trade. Why such different solutions for two such similar risks? Why was the solution based on individual freedom – ie labelling the meat concerned in order to warn consumers of the potential danger – rejected without discussion? This is an extreme example, but it does raise questions encountered in many other cases, fortunately in less dramatic form, which ought to be tackled in their full complexity, a complexity concealed by the trade-ban solution.

VII.3   Trade and corruption

A last criticism is that globalization is supposedly a major cause of corruption. The distinction between globalization and liberalization is important in this context. Without that distinction, it is difficult to understand that the liberalization principles on which the WTO relies provide the best possible protection against incitements to corruption. For example, non-discrimination prevents the arbitrary decision-making which favours certain parties and gives them artificial rents. Moreover, the incentive to adopt low or moderate customs duties as an instrument of protection reduces the incentive of bribery as a means of evading high barriers.

Whenever GATT/WTO members fail to abide by these principles, as when they agreed to accept textile, clothing or audiovisual quotas, voluntary restraints on steel or automotive exports, anti-dumping measures based on minimum prices or maximum quantities, the risk of bribery and corruption makes its appearance. And whenever GATT/WTO calls for the elimination of such discriminatory measures of protection, as in the recent settlement of the disputes over the European banana regime, major areas of corruption can be eliminated. One of the vital benefits of the WTO dispute settlement mechanism certainly lies in the fact that it opens up to public debate, in the country concerned, systems of protection so deeply rooted in custom that their cost, however high, is no longer even regarded as outrageous.

VIII.   The WTO, the State, National Identity and 'Values'

The man in the street tends to imagine GATT/WTO as a supranational institution. If this view merely amounted to ignorance of the extent to which the daily life of GATT/ WTO is dominated and driven by member countries, it would hardly be harmful. However, it leaves the average person with the impression that GATT/WTO undermines states – and this is more serious. In fact, the principles of GATT/WTO make it the guarantor of the integrity of states: by encouraging non-discrimination, non-use of quotas and other grey-area protective measures, GATT/WTO is fighting to maintain customs revenues and limit the surrender of state powers to private interests.

The fact remains that past liberalization programmes have tended to bring about a significant reduction not in national identity but in some of its most common manifestations: products no longer originate in a country except by virtue of consistently complex and frequently arbitrary rules of origin; the only trace of national origin maintained by firms is the facade of headquarters location; under some regional agreements (the EC), firms on a given territory may be subject to the laws of the country of origin. A comprehensive review of WTO relationships and national realities would call for a number of pertinent questions to be asked about the relations between state and nation, which go beyond the scope of this paper. It should perhaps merely be recalled that the experience of this relationship is recent (barely 100 years), that its benefits have been earned through two major world wars, and that the large-scale migrations of the years 1950–1970 transformed those countries which most closely identified state with nation into much more diverse communities, no doubt for a long time to come. If the WTO places national identity in doubt, it is certainly not the only factor involved, nor even the most important.

A problem closely related to national identity is the problem of 'values': 'Western' or 'Asian' values, French or Canadian 'cultural exception'. The full list would doubtless be lengthy. This approach seems terribly narrow-minded (or indeed quite incoherent, as is illustrated by the case of those 'intellectuals' who passionately defend their cultural exception and, in the same breath and with equal conviction, affirm the oneness of mankind). For proof, we need only look back at the 50-year interval between the 1860 free trade agreement between Great Britain and France and World War I in 1914. This was a period which saw greater liberalization of trade in goods and services than we are seeing now (even though transport costs were much higher than they are nowadays), and which, at the same time, produced much more violent conflicts between the main trading partners than those taking place today: 'British', 'French' and 'German' values were characterized by a force and a violence difficult to conceive of in this day and age. However, 100 years (and of course, two world wars) later, what remains of those oppositions other than the pleasure of being different and a taste for reaping the fruits of those differences?

As an institution at the service of its members, GATT/WTO makes no claim to uniqueness. In fact, what was said above about free trade and *laissez faire* suggests that world governance would be improved if GATT/WTO was one of a cluster of institutions which would focus on some of the quite specific problems considered above, such as labour or the environment, institutions which already exist in some cases (eg, the International Labour Office), but not in others (eg, an environment forum). 'Cluster' does not mean that a large number of such institutions is needed – quite the contrary. This word is simply used to draw attention to the fact that there is no need to impose global 'coherence' by establishing a single institution, which is hardly the case at national level. WTO cannot do everything, nor is that its role.

Chapter 9
Looking Back to Look Forward: The Multilateral Trading System after 50 years

Sylvia Ostry

I. Introduction

In celebrating the 50th anniversary of GATT, a look back at 'the creation' provides some useful guidelines for assessing the future of the multilateral rules-based universe. GATT was but one building – undoubtedly the least impressive – in the post-war architecture of international economic cooperation. In contrast the WTO is the first post-Cold War institution, its creation a tribute to the resilience of the liberal trading order. But there are profound differences between the challenges which faced GATT in the post-war decades and the role of the WTO in today's global economy. It is these contrasts between the mandates and capabilities of these two institutions which are the subject of this essay.

II. The Creation of GATT

The USA took the leading role in building a new trading system. Memories of the protectionist battles of the 1930s, initiated by the notorious 1930 Smoot Hawley tariff, were still vivid. Cordell Hull, Roosevelt's Secretary of State, had reversed the long-standing protectionist policy of the USA in 1934 by the passage of the Reciprocal Trade Agreements Act (RTAA) which authorized the President to negotiate tariff reductions with foreign states on a non-discriminatory basis (the Constitution of the USA gives Congress exclusive power 'to regulate commerce with foreign nations' but Congress may delegate trade policy powers to the executive branch). Hull was convinced that freer international trade was essential to USA prosperity, to world recovery and to the maintenance of world peace. From 1934 on, Hull's vision became 'the core mythology' of American foreign policy.[1]

The other major actor in the design of the post-war institutions, the UK, was also strongly influenced by the memory of the 1930s. British Lord Keynes and American Harry Dexter White, the fathers of Bretton Woods, saw the beggar-thy-neighbour

---

[1]   John A.C. Conybeare, *Trade Wars: The Theory and Practice of International Commercial Rivalry* (New York, 1987), p. 251.

©   Kluwer Law International 2000. *From GATT to the WTO: The Multilateral Trading System in the New Millennium*, The WTO Secretariat (ed.), Kluwer Law International, London, 2000; ISBN 90–411–1253–7

devaluations as pernicious as the tariff war of the 1930s. They agreed that a stable rule-based payments system required a stable rule-based trading system, and vice versa. But they were unable to agree on the norms and principles to construct such a system. It is of interest to note that it was easier for these macroeconomists to deal with monetary issues involving exchange rates, capital flows and the like. They shared a convenient kind of macromyopia that allowed them to delegate the detailed, messy, 'political' micro issues to people in other government departments, not in treasuries. Thus only the broadest generalities on trade were included in the International Monetary Fund's Articles of Agreement. The trade negotiations followed a separate track.

The disagreement between the British and Americans concerned two fundamental issues: non-discrimination, or the most-favoured-nation (MFN) rule; and the extent and nature of 'escape clauses' to permit temporary import barriers for protection of the domestic economy. The British wanted to maintain their system of preferential treatment of Commonwealth countries for political reasons. And, as stated in their 1944 White Paper on Employment Policy, they regarded the maintenance of full employment and the creation of the welfare state as more important than free trade. Even the *Economist*, the traditional champion of *laissez faire* and free trade, declared:

> 'that it did not challenge the old principle that international exchange and division of labour leads to the highest possible national income, but modifications were necessary, because the modern community had acquired economic needs other than maximum wealth.'[2]

While there were some Americans, especially Keynesian academics, who shared that view, it was not the prevailing view of the elites. As Jacob Viner noted:

> 'the zeal of the USA for the elimination of special and flexible controls over foreign trade is in large part explained by the absence of any prospect that the USA will in the near future devise or accept a significant program for stabilization of employment or for the planning of investment, the confidence prevailing in this country that our competitive position in foreign trade and the exchange position in foreign trade and the exchange position of the American dollar will continue to be strong, and the availability of the cache of gold at Fort Knox to tide us over even a prolonged and substantial adverse balance of payments if perchance it should occur.'[3]

The depth of this transatlantic divide on the crucial issue of the role of government deserves underlining. There was no government-constructed post-war 'social contract' in the USA. While an Employment Act was passed in 1946 (and the Council of Economic

---

[2]   Karin Kock, *International Trade and Policy and GATT, 1947–1967* (Almquist and Wiksell, Stockholm, 1969), p. 9. The desired 'modification' was the right to take temporary trade restrictive measures when faced with balance-of- payments difficulties.

[3]   Jacob Viner, 'Conflicts of Principle in Drafting a Trade Charter' (1947) *Foreign Affairs*, issue 4, 621–622.

Advisers created as an instrument of the Keynesian policy approach), after the 1946 elections the Republicans dominated Congress and the role of the Council in this respect was somewhat limited (most of the American social contract was negotiated by the mass production unions in the golden age of growth, in other words it was largely privatized). Furthermore, the European social contract involved more than Keynesian demand management: it included a commitment to income redistribution involving an expanded role of the state in both taxation and expenditure, alien to the historical and deeply embedded USA conception of the government's role. The New Deal represented a departure dictated by changed circumstances but not a fundamental transformation of the vision of the Founding Fathers. Thus the romantic ideal of the Hull vision was undergirded not by a widely held international consensus shared by Americans and Europeans about the nature of the relationship between the trading system and domestic policy. Rather, as Jacob Viner noted, American support for GATT stemmed primarily from trade and investment opportunities abroad because of America's lead in the world economy.

The separate trade negotiations between the USA and the UK began in 1943. It was not until the end of 1945 – well after Bretton Woods – that a document was released in Washington which included, among a number of proposals, a Charter for an International Trade Organization (ITO) and GATT, a subset of the broader institution. After several preparatory meetings and extensive negotiations, the ITO Charter was presented in 1948 to a meeting in Havana.

The Charter of the ITO reflected the many compromises negotiated during the preparatory process. In contrast to the Bretton Woods institutions, weighted voting (according to economic clout) was dropped for a 'one country, one vote' rule. Chapters on employment, development, anti-trust, investment, agriculture and a number of exceptions to liberal trade rules were included. The battles among both developed and developing countries were over exceptions and exceptions to exceptions. Even Commonwealth preference was included under a 'grandfathering' of existing preferential arrangements.

But all the compromise and difficult negotiations leading to agreement in Havana were overtaken by events. At the time of the Havana meeting the Marshall Plan was launched. The trade and payments liberalization of the Marshall Plan institution, the Organization for European Economic Cooperation (OEEC), based on discrimination against the USA, settled the issue of non-discrimination without debate. The ITO was not ratified after Havana by any country because all were waiting for the leader to ratify first. The President required another extension of negotiating authority in 1949 so decided not to send the ITO to Congress that year. However, opposition was building from many quarters – and support from few. As well, the Korean War had started. Interest in global cooperation had waned. Truman judged there was virtually no chance of approval of the Havana Charter and so decided not to seek Congressional approval.

The basis for the judgment seems pretty plausible: no strong support (except among academics and some bureaucrats) but lots of strong opposition. Why did Bretton Woods get by Congress? And the Marshall Plan? 'No strong opposition', seems to be the answer. Bretton Woods was about money and the dollar. Americans were not worried about the dollar – as Viner noted, they knew there was lots of gold in Fort Knox. The Marshall Plan was about the Cold War. There was little opposition to the Cold War. But the domestic coalition for the ITO was too weak. There were too many loopholes, far too much government intervention for free traders, and too much free trade for protectionists, especially labour unions who formed a National Labour Management Council on Foreign Trade with some import sensitive industries. But the most effective business opposition was not based on fear of import penetration. As Diebold explains:

> 'Their objection was that the Charter would do little to remove the trade barriers set up by foreign countries and might even strengthen some of them … Moreover, the businessmen who took this view usually believed that the Charter went too far in subordinating the international commitments of signatory countries to the requirements – real or imagined – of national economic plans and policies.'[4]

What lay at the heart of the opposition of powerful business lobbies was a rejection of the idea that there can be many variants of market systems, with different institutional arrangements including different mixes of government and business roles. And where such differences existed, they were, in the view of American business, probably unfairly protectionist. The support for trade liberalization by many USA business groups was based on support for access to foreign markets which were seen as less open than those of the USA, in large part because of government intrusiveness.

Despite this opposition, American leadership in the trade arena did not fail with the death of the ITO. It was an American initiative that launched GATT in Geneva in 1947 as a prelude to Havana. GATT, signed by 23 'contracting parties', was never put to Congress. But GATT was much narrower in coverage and because the commitments contained in the Agreement were less binding, it did not elicit the widespread opposition of the ITO. Its weakness was its strength – at least at the outset.

Successive rounds of negotiations in the 1950s and 1960s reduced the tariffs erected in the disastrous 1930s. This was the 'golden age' of trade liberalization, defined in terms of the reduction of border barriers. But over time the essential compromises embedded in GATT came to erode the structure – like termites in the basement.

The onset of a different mode of trade liberalization began in the 1970s with the Tokyo Round. The mid-decade OPEC oil shock had produced a new economic malady termed 'stagflation' and a marked increase in so-called 'new protectionism', including voluntary export restraints (VERs), quasi-legal market-sharing agreements (orderly marketing arrangements or OMAs), and an explosion of subsidies to support declining industries, especially in Europe, adding to the enormous subsidy support in the Common Agriculture Policy (CAP). GATT system was not equipped to handle either non-transparent measures such as VERs and OMAs or domestic declining industry strategies. The weak dispute settlement mechanism added to American frustration with the system.

---

[4]   William Diebold, Jr, 'The End of the ITO' (Essays in International Finance, No. 16, Princeton University, 1952), p. 14.

The USA administration's response to the rise of the new protectionism was to begin the move of the trade policy agenda inside the border. The Tokyo Round included negotiations on trade-impeding barriers arising from domestic policies such as industrial and agricultural subsidies, government procurement and regulation of product standards, as well as a strengthening of anti-dumping rules to facilitate the use by business of their favourite remedy against 'unfair' trade. Thus the focus of the Tokyo Round was, for the first time in GATT experience, no longer simply on reducing border barriers to trade. Rules governing domestic policy with trade spillover were now on the table, highlighting differences in the extent and nature of government intervention in different counties.

The Tokyo Round also launched another fundamental change: the legalization of the trading system. Perhaps increased legalization was inherent in the shift from reciprocal bargaining over tariffs to rule-making. But arguably more important was the changing nature of American trade policy. There was growing conviction among business groups and labour unions that other countries were engaged in unfair trade practices and that the 'free ride' of the 1950s and 1960s had to stop. For the Administration, the best option seemed to be a strengthening of the trade remedy laws. Congress demanded detailed legalistic prescriptions to prevent circumvention by any future administration unwilling to defend 'national interests'. One notable result of the Tokyo Round was the enormous increase in the use of anti-dumping provisions by both the USA and the EU (and an equally impressive rise in American countervailing actions against 'unfair subsidies') that marked the onset of the 1980s. This rise in the use of trade remedy laws was dubbed 'administered protectionism'.

III.   The Creation of the WTO

The Tokyo Round legacy – and the shift of policy focus inside the border and the legalization of the system – were vastly expanded by the Uruguay Round. Indeed one could argue that the change was qualitative not quantitative. The reasons for this transformation of the system are worth spelling out.

The negotiation to launch the Uruguay Round negotiation took almost as long as the entire Tokyo Round of the 1970s. The Americans had been trying to launch a new round since the early 1980s because of dissatisfaction with the results of the Tokyo Round and rising protectionist fury in Congress (mainly because of the over-valued dollar). After a number of near-failures, the Uruguay Round was launched in Punta del Este in September 1986 and formally concluded in Marrakesh, Morocco in April 1994, several years later than the target completion date originally announced.

The extraordinary difficulty in both initiating and completing the Round stemmed essentially from two fundamental factors: the nearly insuperable problem of finishing the unfinished business of past negotiations, in particular agriculture; and the equally contentious issue of introducing quite new agenda items, notably trade in services and intellectual property and, though in a more limited way, investment. The Europeans blocked the launch to avoid coming to grips with the Common Agricultural Policy (CAP) and a number of developing countries were bitterly opposed to including non-traditional issues such as services and intellectual property because they involved negotiation of *domestic policies and institutions* such as regulation and legal systems, alien to the GATT world of shallow integration and considered a direct challenge to national sovereignty.

Yet, however difficult were the 'traditional negotiations' concerned with the 'leftovers' of previous rounds – the potholes and roadblocks such as agriculture, textiles, some sensitive tariffs and non-tariff barriers – the direction was clear. The objective was the original GATT objective, the liberalization of trade by reducing or eliminating border barriers or their close domestic proxies.

But the other part of the Uruguay Round, the so-called new issues of services, intellectual property and investment, was anything but traditional. The inclusion of the new issues was demanded by the Americans to correct the basic structural asymmetry of the original GATT. In the post-war era the term 'trade in services' would have been an oxymoron and intellectual property was covered by the World Intellectual Property Organization (WIPO) and its predecessor agreements. For the 'new issues', barriers to access are not at the border and are not necessarily transparent but mainly involved domestic regulatory and legal systems. This is hardly a GATT world of shallow integration but a different world of ever-deepening integration which has generated and will generate a new form of trade dispute – system friction.

Trade in services grew much more rapidly over the 1980s than did merchandise trade, and the USA was the leading exporter by a considerable margin. The same lead status was evident in investment and technology. USA multinationals controlled 43 per cent of the world stock of foreign investment at the outset of the 1980s and the American technology balance-of-payments surplus was well over US$6 billion while every other OECD country was in deficit. Without a fundamental rebalancing of GATT, it seems highly improbable that the American business community or politicians would have continued to support the multilateral system for much longer.[5] Indeed by the mid-1980s American trade policy was multi-track: unilateralism in the form of section 301 of the 1974 Trade Act; bilateralism exemplified by the Canada–USA Free Trade Agreement; and multilateralism via the Uruguay Round. So there were other options available.

But the new issues must be seen in a broader context than the rebalancing of the GATT structure to ensure American support for the multilateral system. In the second half of the 1980s, an unprecedented surge in foreign direct investment (FDI) ushered in a new phase of interdependence sometimes termed globalization. While the bulge of the 1980s was partly due to one-off factors there were and are underlying forces generating globalization especially the revolution in information and communication technology. Thus the multinational enterprises (MNEs) have become dominant global actors – the main channels for trade, finance and technology, the engines of growth. For the MNE, border barriers are less important than domestic 'structural impediments' which are barriers to effective market access by trade or effective presence by investment, which is also a two-way funnel for technology flows. These impediments can arise (often

---

    5   Sylvia Ostry, *The Post-Cold War Trading System: Who's on First?* (University of Chicago Press, 1997), pp. 105–108.

unintentionally) from regulatory policies, legal cultures or the behaviour of private actors – in other words, from differences in systems among countries. GATT agenda implied a primacy of trade and a preservation of system *diversity*, a diversity which was evident 'at the creation'. The agenda of deeper integration covers trade, investment and technology and is far more intrusive and erosive of national sovereignty as it incorporates an intrinsic pressure for *harmonization* of diverse systems. This pressure is reinforced by locational competition for investment which facilitates regulatory arbitrage by the MNE. The Uruguay Round marked the transition to the new agenda. All future negotiations, whether multilateral, regional or bilateral, will involve a move inside the border because the main forces of globalization, FDI and the information and communication technology revolution, will not abate. Since the frontier between the state and the market is not clear and immutable, but varies over time and geography, the deeper integration agenda will be far more contentious than the negotiation of lower border barriers.

In a sense the Uruguay Round launched the first small step on the long and difficult path to a single global market. The term 'contestability'[6] blessed by OECD ministers in 1995 as the overall objective of trade policy, remains vague and undefined in terms of practical policy guidelines but could be interpreted to ensure that a firm in any country should be able to satisfy demand in any other country by either trade and/or investment, unimpeded by significant 'structural impediments' to effective access and presence. This sounds pretty much like the notion of a single market in the only example known to the post-war world, the European Union. While full regulatory convergence need not be required – for example mutual recognition agreements could 'satisfice' as second best in the realm of technical and regulatory standards – regulation in many service sectors would probably require a commitment to a specified regulatory model as in the agreement on telecommunications.

But it must be stressed that the Uruguay Round was only the first small step in the road to a global market and indeed the Round is not over. The 'built-in' agenda left over from the negotiations involves the launch of new services negotiations in 2000 and also the remit from the 1996 WTO ministerial meeting in Singapore adds consideration of competition policy, investment and environment to the WTO's mandate. This will entrench and extend the deeper integration policy focus. A fundamental but little understood part of this new policy template relates to the legal system. A few examples are worth describing to illustrate this point, especially because there is far greater diversity of legal systems among present and potential member countries today than in 1948, at the creation of GATT.

The first example concerns *transparency*, now regarded as a pillar of the multilateral trading system. Yet while it is today considered one of the basic rules governing

---

[6]   See, for example, Edward M. Graham and Robert Z. Lawrence, 'Measuring the International Contestability of Markets' (1996) 30 *Journal of World Trade*, issue 5, 5–20; and Americo Beviglia Zampetti and Pierre Sauvé, 'Onwards to Singapore: The International Contestability of Markets and the New Trade Agenda' (1996) 19 *World Economy* 333–334.

that system, its genesis, captured in Article X of the 1947 GATT, was based on American administrative law and was of little import at the time of the creation of GATT.[7]

In 1946, while the negotiations for the new trading system were underway, the USA Congress passed the Administrative Procedure Act (APA). In the September 1946 State Department document, *Suggested Charter for an International Trade Organization of the United Nations*, Article 15, entitled 'Publication and Administration of Trade Regulations – Advance Notice of Restrictive Regulations', becomes Article 38 in the Havana Charter for the International Trade Organization (ITO) and Article X of GATT which survived the death of the ITO.[8] In Article X the title does not include 'advance notice of restrictive regulations', but otherwise there is no significant difference from the State Department drafting. By way of contrast most other Articles of the original American proposals involved considerable haggling and compromise, especially with the British. The Canadians, who participated in the negotiations from their launch in London in October 1946 to their conclusion in Havana in November 1947, in a memorandum to the Secretary of State for External Affairs, which tracks the negotiating process and the changes in each Article at each stage, note that Article 38 'was not altered nor were any interpretive notes required'. The memo goes on to state: 'This article imposes no obligations upon Canada not already complied with, and the general benefit to international trade needs no elaboration.'[9] Evidently each of the 56 delegations at Havana felt exactly the same! Why this indifference and/or endorsement of the American position as a pillar of the new international trading system? There obviously is no way of definitively answering this question but a look at the nature and origins of administrative law is suggestive.

Administrative law is not substantive but procedural. It establishes norms to control what government bureaucrats do and how they do it. It arose essentially because of the delegation of power from legislators to administrative bodies propelled by the expanded role of government in the industrialized countries that began in the 1920s and 1930s. While all Western countries developed administrative law regimes in the period after World War I, the American system has some characteristics which distinguish it from continental European regimes and also from the English common law legal family. The American system reflects not only its common law roots but also its origins in the American Revolution which created a unique diffusion of power among the three branches of government and a system of checks and balances intended to ensure against any accretion of power. This is significantly different from common law parliamentary systems in the UK, Canada or Australia which rest on legislative primacy and a strong

---

[7]   This discussion on transparency is based on Sylvia Ostry, 'China and the WTO: The Transparency Issue' 3 (1998) *UCLA Journal of International Law and Foreign Affairs*.

[8]   World Trade Organization, *Guide to GATT Law and Practice* (Geneva, 1995), vol. I, p. 309.

[9]   Canadian Legation, 'Report of the Canadian Delegation to the United Nations Conference on Trade and Employment at Havana' (mimeo, Berne, 13 July 1948), p. 32.

executive. Among the more important distinguishing characteristics of the American system are greater use of independent regulatory agencies, often with quasi-judicial as well as quasi-legislative functions; greater emphasis on notice and comment and freedom of information laws; and a greater reliance on judicial review of the rule-making activity of administrative agencies or departments. By and large the American system is more litigious and adversarial and hence more fact- or evidence-intensive. It is designed to limit the room for administrative discretion.

Article X of GATT replicates most of the American approach. The word 'transparency' does not appear but the Article spells out in detail the rules for 'publication and administration' of trade regulations with the latter emphasizing the *desirability* (rather than the *necessity*) of independent tribunals and judicial review (although the Protocol for Chinese accession requires independent tribunals and judicial review). Perhaps this 'dilution' reflected a compromise with the UK in earlier negotiations or a recognition by the State Department that some of the participating countries had not yet fully established their legal infrastructure. Be that as it may, the inclusion of Article X on transparency at the time of GATT's origin appeared to be non-controversial to the drafters of the new system, because it mainly involved reporting tariff schedules. It was non-controversial because it was insignificant.

The Tokyo Round nudged transparency a bit further. An 'Understanding Regarding Notification, Consultation, Dispute Settlement and Surveillance' was adopted at the close of the Round. Paragraph 3 of the Understanding[10] introduces a modified version of surveillance and underlines the desirability of advance notice. But the really significant changes take place in the Uruguay Round. The concept of surveillance is greatly expanded in the new WTO Trade Policy Review Mechanism (TPRM) which was promoted by the FOGS (Functioning of the GATT System) negotiating group in the Uruguay Round. The TPRM was based on the OECD 'country studies' designed to enhance the effectiveness of the policy-making process through informed public understanding – ie transparency.

More importantly, the new issues give transparency a radically different meaning. It requires publication of laws and regulations and the mode of administration in services or, to a more limited extent, investment regimes. The agreement on TRIPS (trade-related intellectual property) included detailed enforcement procedures which mirror step-by-step the administrative and judicial mechanisms in the USA. Finally, the TRIPS

---

[10]   'Contracting parties moreover undertake, to the maximum extent possible, to notify the CONTRACTING PARTIES of their adoption of trade measures affecting the operation of the General Agreement, it being understood that such notification would be without prejudice to views on the consistency of measures with or their relevance to obligations under the General Agreement. Contracting parties should endeavour to notify such measures in advance of implementation. In other cases, where prior notification has not been possible, such measures should be notified promptly *ex post facto*. Contracting parties which have reason to believe that such trade measures have been adopted by another contracting party may seek information on such measures bilaterally, from the contracting party concerned.' World Trade Organization, *Guide to GATT Law and Practice* (Geneva, 1995), vol. I, p. 300.

agreement underlines the transparency issue – the word is used as a heading in the relevant Article. A separate council is established to which notification of regulations and administrative arrangements must be made and this council is mandated to monitor compliance. Disputes will come under the new dispute settlement arrangements.

Implementing these vastly expanded transparency requirements will present formidable difficulty among countries with systems that differ markedly from the 'Western' legal families. For example, since the origin of administrative law in Western countries was the growth of government and the *raison d'être* of the law was to constrain this expanding administrative power – to control the bureaucrats – this is hardly a trivial point. More significantly, in the present context, effectively *monitoring* that implementation would require a significant improvement in the capability of the WTO.[11] But before turning to that subject another example of the legalization of the trading system illustrates how contentious this aspect of the new agenda can be.

The second example of the trend to legalization, the protection of investment, is taken from a regional agreement – the North American Free Trade Agreement (NAFTA). The investment provisions of NAFTA included procedures for resolving disputes by which private parties as well as governments could take action and adopted a very broad definition of investment expropriation, so broad that it could lead to investor claims against government regulation in, say, environmental or cultural or health areas which negatively affect the value of investment.[12]

In the USA property rights are protected by the Constitution and this meaning of expropriation is quite common in jurisprudence concerning 'takings'. In international law the 'taking' versus 'regulation' distinction exists but the jurisprudence mainly covers conventional expropriation and not the question of where a 'state action implemented for clear public policy purposes crosses over the line from non-compensable regulation to compensable taking'.[13] In Canada, where constitutionally entrenched property rights do not exist, the extent of judicial control over government action is far less stringent than in the USA and jurisprudence in the area of 'takings' is quite different from that in the USA. This has led to a situation by which a foreign firm could sue for compensation (say, because of a federal or provincial environment regulation) but a domestic firm could not – a vastly inflated definition of 'national treatment' and one which is unlikely to be politically acceptable. Indeed, it was the adoption of the NAFTA language on expropriation in the MAI which provided a powerful rallying point for opponents of the negotiations.

---

[11]   See below.

[12]   However some form of investment protection has to be included in WTO negotiations on investment (as it was in the OECD's negotiations on a Multilateral Agreement on Investment (MAI)) because there would be little business support for an agreement without it. For a discussion of the 'takings' issue, see David Schneiderman, 'NAFTA's Takings Rule: American Constitutionalism Comes to Canada' (1996) *University of Toronto Law Journal*, 500–537; and Jon Johnson, *The North American Free Trade Agreement: A comprehensive Guide* (Canada Law Book, Aurora, 1994), pp. 289–333.

[13]   Jon Johnson, *The North American Free Trade Agreement: A comprehensive Guide* (Canada Law Book, Aurora, 1994), p. 290.

In Canada a case concerning the expropriation provisions is now pending[14] and the outcome will be of considerable interest, not only in the NAFTA countries. If the case is won by the plaintiff the restoration of a more acceptable version of 'national treatment' would necessitate either amendment of the relevant NAFTA provisions or a significant change in Canada's legal system which would have long-run implications for the role of government in that country (even if the case is lost it need not deter skilled lawyers from pursuing other such litigation to induce policy settlements). This example of the influence of lawyers on seemingly reasonable policy norms and principles suggests that the most significant import and export of trade agreements may well be legal systems! Indeed one could argue that legalization creates its own built-in reinforcement – an endogenous growth process is launched (see dispute settlement below) – hardly an outcome intended at the creation of GATT, 50 years ago but very much a part of the WTO mandate. Which brings us to the most important issue: is that mandate congruent with the WTO's capabilities?

IV.   Conclusions: The WTO and Globalization

In the launch of the Uruguay Round there was recognition that GATT would not provide an adequate foundation for the much more ambitious and comprehensive trading system embedded in the negotiating agenda. Thus the Punta del Este Declaration established the FOGS negotiating group. FOGS was promoted by a coalition of middle powers, both developed and developing, since institutional issues were not a priority for either the USA or the EU. The middle powers recognized that the alternative to a rule-based system would be a power-based system, and, lacking power, they had the most to lose.

None the less, the goals of FOGS were relatively modest: to improve the adaptability of GATT in order to respond to accelerating change in the global economy; to improve the 'coherence' of international policies by establishing better linkages between GATT and the Bretton Woods institutions; and most importantly to strengthen the enforcement of the trading system's rules of the road by improving dispute settlement arrangements. The creation of a new institution was not included among these objectives, and the proposal by Canada for a new institution – the World Trade Organization – was not put forward until April 1990. It was soon endorsed by the EU. The main reason for this change was growing concern about American unilateralism. The EU, which had opposed a strengthening of dispute settlement in the Tokyo Round, and took a position of benign neglect with respect to FOGS, became an active supporter of a new institution which could house a single, strong dispute settlement mechanism.

The Canadian proposal was couched in terms of the substantive aspects of the Uruguay Round negotiations. As the press release announcing the Canadian proposal stated:

---

[14]   'Ethyl Sues Canadian Government for $250 Million over MMT Ban', *Chemical Market Reporter* (New York), 21 April 1997.

'Developments in the substantive negotiations are now demonstrating that the Uruguay Round results cannot be effectively housed in a provisional shelter. It is also becoming clear that the post-Uruguay trade policy agenda will be complex and may not be adequately managed within the confines of GATT system as it now exists.'[15]

The World Trade Organization turns GATT from a trade agreement into a membership organization. But it is a minimalist institution forged solely on legal principles. It establishes a legal framework that brings together all the various pacts and codes and other arrangements that were negotiated under GATT. Members of the WTO must abide by the rules of all these agreements as well as the rules of GATT as a 'single undertaking'. The most important element of the WTO – the jewel in the crown – is the greatly strengthened dispute settlement mechanism.[16] The WTO also includes two institutional innovations proposed under FOGS: a trade policy review body, as mentioned above, designed to highlight changes in the policies of member countries through published analytical studies; and a bi-annual ministerial conference, designed to raise the public and political profile of trade policy. As to the objective of greater coherence, the Final Act included only a hortatory declaration encouraging the Director General of the WTO to review possible cooperative mechanisms with the heads of the International Monetary Fund (IMF) and the World Bank. Formal agreements specifying cooperation modalities between the WTO and the IMF and the World Bank were concluded in November 1996. They carefully detail who can attend which meeting and what information can be exchanged, and provide for the possibility of consultation between secretariats on trade-policy-related issues.

This minimalist-legal template for the WTO was probably the most that could have been achieved at the time. The premise of increasing substantive complexity on which the WTO was agreed was correct but seriously underestimated. As this paper has tried to demonstrate, the agenda of deeper integration is profoundly different in scope, complexity and contentiousness than the trade policy agenda of the post-war world. Yet the WTO is not significantly different in *capabilities* than GATT.

Two other differences between the two 'institutions', which also heighten the capability deficit, also deserve mention. First, despite its weakness GATT has been termed a bicycle that kept rolling along through successive negotiations. GATT bicycle hogged the road – there weren't any others in the way. Today, of course, there is plenty of traffic, some of it very speedy: regional limos; bilateral trucks and occasional unilateral tanks!

Finally, and over the longer term most fundamentally, the new dispute settlement system involves a supranational encroachment on sovereign terrain. For many who worked hard for a successful conclusion of the Uruguay Round the dispute settlement mechanism was *a* if not *the* major achievement of the negotiations. After all, what is the point of having new rules if they cannot be enforced? In choosing to strengthen greatly

---

[15]   Ottawa, April 1990.
[16]   See below.

the dispute settlement system they were right: there was no acceptable alternative. But not many understood the full implications of the new system. For example, the juridification of the process creates a built-in reinforcement of legalization. The tendency to appeal rulings already seems a part of the system and one would expect that more and more panel reports would be written for the Appellate Body rather than the parties. In turn this should shift the selection panels from trade-types to lawyers. And so on. Further, under GATT when the negotiated norms or rules were less binding the decisions on disputes were less significant in the political domain. The binding nature of the WTO arrangement can catapult the decisions right into the centre of domestic politics. This greater power inevitably shines a spotlight not just on the WTO dispute body *decisions* but also on the *process* of decision-making – there are increasingly frequent demands for more 'transparency' and 'democratization'.

These tensions between the polity and the economics of deepening integration has been well put in a recent paper on the current problems of defining European citizenship: 'In Western liberal democracies public authority requires legitimation through one principal source: the citizens of the polity.'[17] The comparison of the WTO with the European Union is not entirely over-stretched. The danger of the EU 'democratic deficit' is that you cannot throw the scoundrels out so you target the whole institution. There are some who might argue the same case against the WTO: if they will not 'democratize' the system, tear up the contract. In sum, it is difficult to disagree that the WTO needs strengthening and I will conclude with some suggestions for institutional reinforcement.

IV.1   Reinforcing the WTO

The WTO is *au fond* like GATT in being a member-driven organization without a significant knowledge infrastructure, ie a secretariat of highly qualified experts able to undertake research directed at policy analysis as in the OECD, the IMF and the World Bank. This analytic deficit virtually precludes policy discussion, and the important peer-group pressure it generates, on the issues described above such as regulatory convergence, the role of legal systems, the trade-off between domestic and international objectives and the crucial issue of the state-market frontier, ie all the basic aspects of the new agenda. Further, without the instrument of peer-group pressure the transaction costs of achieving consensus in the WTO can be so high that more flexible and therefore speedier alternatives will be desirable. Moreover, in addition to the complexity and contentiousness of the issues and the high transactions costs of policy momentum, the size and disparate interests of the membership greatly add to the difficulty of achieving consensus. Equally important, with the entry of new members such as China and Russia, the lack of 'transparency' threatens a serious overload of the already stretched and evidentiary-intensive dispute settlement system.

Although the notion of a shared vision of the post-war trading system is partly a romantic myth, the post-war elites did share enough basic ideas to serve as a context for

---

[17]   Joseph Weiler, 'To be a European Citizen – Eros and Civilization' (mimeo, Faculty of Law, University of Toronto, 1 April 1998), p. 12.

policy dialogue and, of course, the Cold War was a powerful fount for cohesive purpose. While some may argue that there is far greater support for trade liberalization today than in 1948, as always the devil is in the details – what do we mean by 'trade liberalization'? The most basic issues facing democratic countries – the domestic balance between market efficiency and other social and political objectives and the balance between these domestic objectives and international rules – were hardly a matter of vital concern in the border barrier liberalization after the war. Further, while the deeper integration policy agenda was and will continue to be determined not only by governments but also by MNEs, other actors are now increasingly visible on the global stage, ie the international non-governmental organizations among which the environmentalists are the most prominent. The traditional politics of trade in GATT-land involved the Olsonian distributional coalitions concerned with the division of the pie. Some of the international non-governmental organizations may have similar objectives but their message today is more easily sold either on TV or by e-mail, pitched to an audience sensitive to the globalization issue. And, more importantly, where there are genuine and significant *systemic* differences in a global optic based on ecology and one based on efficiency, consensus will require difficult debate and dialogue. The ecology message is especially attractive to a younger generation searching for a worthy cause. The point of all this is not to discuss trade and the environment but to illustrate the radically changed politics of trade policy in WTO land.

So what reforms would be necessary to strengthen the WTO and ensure the sustainability of the multilateral rules-based system? There will be a wide range of views on this matter and my suggestions are not intended to be exhaustive, but perhaps may stimulate discussion.

The first requirement to enhance the flexibility and adaptability of the WTO is to establish a smaller body or executive committee akin to the IMF Interim Committee or the World Bank's Development Committee. A Uruguay Round attempt to establish a successor to the 1975 Consultative Group of Eighteen (CG18) unfortunately failed, mainly because of opposition from a number of developing countries who feared exclusion. But, given the change in atmospherics since the late 1980s, in particular the much more widespread appreciation of the need for a global rules-based system, the time is now ripe for another effort.

The next WTO ministerial meeting should propose that an Executive Committee of Ministers be established to provide overall guidance to the WTO in promoting the ongoing liberalization of the world trading system. The Executive Committee would be able to meet on a regular basis and, with the assistance of the Director General and the secretariat, review current and prospective policy issues in order to advise the biennial ministerial conference which would retain full decision-making authority. With such a forum, at both a ministerial and senior official level, the *norms* and *principles* of liberalization rather than the *specifics of legalistic detail* could be discussed and debated. It is essential to underline that forging a consensus in a smaller group aided by expert policy-analytic information is facilitated by peer-group pressure. The Executive Committee can then play a role in promoting the extension of the consensus to the entire membership.

In establishing such a Committee, the most difficult problem, of course, is membership and the various formulae tried out in the Uruguay Round failed to secure agreement. But in establishing the TPRM, the FOGS Committee created a precedent for a possible formula. Thus different countries were subject to different review schedules on the basis of the member's share of world trade. This same formula could be used for establishing a committee of reasonable size and rotating membership which would ensure that all countries and regions would be represented within a given time frame.[18]

Another function of the Executive Committee supported by a high-quality (although not necessarily large) expert secretariat would be the diffusion of knowledge in national capitals, another essential ingredient of consensus-building. Further, in order to keep up to date and remain reasonably small in size, the WTO could not possibly generate all its policy analysis in-house. Like most research bodies today, the WTO secretariat would have to establish a research network linked to other institutions such as the OECD, the Bretton Woods institutions, private think-tanks, universities and the like. Knowledge networks are key elements in promoting cooperation and coordination. This networking should also include other international non-governmental organizations such as business groups (the International Chamber of Commerce, for example), transnational environmental groups, international labour associations and intergovernmental organizations such as the ILO. Cooperative programmes involving technical assistance in trade, legal and environmental issues could be launched with business and other organizations. This would enhance the possibility of achieving agreement on the 'linkage issues' (environment and labour) to reduce the negative impact on trade policy and to generate mutually agreed proposals for improved transparency of the WTO policy process.

Issues like regulatory reform, competition policy, effective and transparent administrative law regimes and other institutional issues will require substantial administrative and legal adaptation in many member countries, especially because of the wide system diversity among current and prospective members. Thus the WTO will also have to strengthen greatly its currently minimal facilities for technical training in a wide range of areas. But even under the most optimistic scenario of enhanced resources, the WTO capabilities in training would be dwarfed by the technical assistance resources of the World Bank and, increasingly, the IMF. So some cooperative arrangement would be required – a good and practical example of coherence, but hardly sufficient.

Because of recent changes in the policy orientation of the IMF and the World Bank, the problem of improved policy coherence has taken on very different dimensions. Both institutions (albeit for different reasons and not entirely in harmony) are shifting policy focus to issues of institutional infrastructure – domestic regulatory policies, 'transparency', the role of government, trade policies – essentially the same broad range of issues as the WTO. It is probably not an exaggeration to assert that:

---

[18]   Robert Wolfe, 'Global Trade as a Single Undertaking: The Role of Ministers in the WTO' (1996) 51 *International Journal*.

'IMF and … World Bank programs not just in East Asia but in India, Latin America, Central Europe and Africa, have led to more systematic trade liberalization than … bilateral or multilateral negotiations have ever achieved.'[19]

In the light of these developments the coherence agreements of 1996 would require significant changes to be meaningful. But real cooperation between the WTO and its sister agencies would require the upgrading of the WTO's strategic knowledge assets. Which brings us back to the main point: the basic mismatch between the WTO's capabilities and its mandate.

It is difficult to predict whether the political leaders of WTO member countries will recognize the need for significant reinforcement of the institution created to replace the ITO, the third pillar of the post-war architecture of international cooperation. A more likely scenario is minor incremental change. If that is so, it will constitute the greatest threat to the rules-based multilateral system in the past 50 years.

---

[19]   Lawrence Summers, 'Why America Needs the IMF', *Wall Street Journal*, 27 March 1998, p. A22. This is hardly the best route, since none of the measures are bound in the WTO.

Chapter 10

Low-Income Developing Countries in the GATT/WTO Framework: The First Fifty Years and Beyond

T. Ademola Oyejide

I. Introduction

Even before the birth of the General Agreement on Tariffs and Trade (GATT), developing countries were concerned with three important issues: what should be their relationship with the more developed countries in the context of the global trading system? How can their trade policies be used to promote their economic growth and development? And how do the global economy and developments therein impinge on their prospects for growth and development? These three key concerns have become even more pressing in today's rapidly globalizing world economy in which integration into international markets has become an important (and perhaps indispensable) source of growth which can no longer be ignored by any country, developed or developing.

The overriding consideration which ties these concerns together is that trade has been closely associated with economic growth and development over the last half-century or so. In broad terms, most of the countries that have been successful in achieving significant rates of economic growth over this period appear to be the ones that have utilized available trade opportunities, while those countries that have erected barriers against trade appear to have fallen behind in terms of economic growth and development. A strand of the literature pushes this point further to suggest that the developing countries which achieved spectacular growth, particularly since the 1960s, are those that adopted outward-oriented development strategies focusing specifically on the promotion of exports. Implicit in this claim is the idea that openness – defined broadly as the free flow of goods, people, capital and knowledge across national frontiers – transmits technology and generates economic growth virtually worldwide. It is an idea that has apparently found favour even in the developing countries that had hitherto been wedded to trade restrictions. Thus, many of the countries of sub-Saharan Africa started to open their economies to trade in a much more concerted way than ever before from the early 1980s.

This widespread movement towards greater openness notwithstanding, considerable tension continues to exist between, on the one hand, what the initial conditions and the

© Kluwer Law International 2000. *From GATT to the WTO: The Multilateral Trading System in the New Millennium*, The WTO Secretariat (ed.), Kluwer Law International, London, 2000; ISBN 90–411–1253–7

developments needs of the low-income countries appear to demand in the area of trade policy and, on the other hand, the trends towards a convergence of policies implicit in globalization. This tension raises the question whether openness is equally important at all levels of development. It also suggests the need for a careful analysis of the extent to which the multilateral trading system is driven by this globalizing trend and whether the system accommodates (or can be made to accommodate) the development needs of the low-income developing countries.

This paper pursues these questions in stages. First, it briefly reviews the theoretical basis of the relationship between trade, trade policies and growth, as well as the broad lessons that development experience offers with respect to this relationship in section II. Secondly, section III examines the experience of low-income developing countries in GATT, focusing in particular on the extent to which GATT framework took account of their initial conditions and development needs. In section IV, the paper reviews the broad 'policy convergence' implications of the Uruguay Round agreements (and the new framework of the World Trade Organization (WTO)) for the low-income developing countries. In articulating what the WTO can do for this category of countries, this section offers specific suggestions aimed at bringing about a fuller integration of the low-income developing countries into the multilateral trading system at reasonable costs to them and the system. The paper concludes in section V.

II.   Partnership for Development Through Trade

A key rationale of the multilateral trading system is to promote the growth of the economies of all participating countries through the freer (and hence, expanded) flow of goods and services across national borders. In this sense, the multilateral trading system can be thought of as a partnership development through trade implicit in which is the expectation that participation will be mutually rewarding to all parties. The intellectual support for this proposition derives largely from theories of trade and development and also from accumulated practical development experience. It is therefore not out of place, at this point, to ask what these theories and experiences teach us about trade and development as well as the policies that promote them.

Traditional theories of international trade offer explanations of actual trade in terms of comparative advantage. These theories are based on key assumptions such as constant returns to scale, perfect competition, no significant externalities, and virtually costless knowledge of technologies and markets. In general, these theories generate the policy prescription that free trade is the best of all possible policies. New theories and models of trade recognize the pervasiveness of learning effects and external economies, particularly in manufacturing production and exporting activities, as well as market imperfections. This recognition radically changes the trade policy prescription associated with traditional trade theories. As Krugman puts it, 'if increasing returns and imperfect competition are necessary parts of the explanation of international trade, however, we are living in a second-best world where government intervention can in principle improve on market outcomes'.[1] In other words, the new trade theories suggest that there may be room for a degree of selectivity in trade policy. It follows that, subject to rational policy articulation and implementation strategies, low-income developing countries may find sound intellectual support for conducting active trade and industrial policies targeted at ameliorating the effects of market failures, to maintain fiscal and payments balance and to build competitive supply capabilities.[2] It should be emphasized, of course, that while theoretical support can be found for a limited 'window of opportunity' for carefully constructed government intervention, the new theories by no means provide 'an open season' and unqualified support for all manner of trade restrictions.

The development experience of a set of developing countries that achieved rapid and sustained economic growth rates since the 1960s provides us with a broad profile of what type of trade and associated policies could be appropriate for the present-day low-income developing countries. This experience can be summarized in the form of the following stylized facts:

(i)   the countries that have grown rapidly have adopted an export-led growth strategy that has relied on selective trade and industrial policies, rather than purely market-oriented policies characterized by incentive neutrality;

(ii) in the typical two-track policy menu of these countries, deep import liberalization follows the consolidation of export-oriented industrialization in the context of a scheme where strong export-support mechanisms (including capacity-enhancing industrial policy measures) co-exist side by side with protection for import-substituting activities;

(iii) interventionist measures were associated with objective performance requirements and were quickly terminated for lack of adequate performance;

(iv) export and global market orientation provided an external check on interventionist measures and induced beneficiaries to aspire to and maintain international competitiveness.

Based both on theoretical analysis and a review of accumulated development experience, it may be concluded that reliance on an outward-oriented policy stance which increasingly integrates the domestic with the global economy would be a critical component of an appropriate development strategy for today's low-income developing countries. This conclusion should, however, recognize a transitional stage that would occur as the economy moves from inward orientation to an outward one during which a two-track approach could be the most feasible. More specifically, the anti-export bias that is inherent in the protective trade regime would need to be offset by export incentives and other capacity-enhancing industrial policies during this inevitable transitional phase. Thus, it is to be expected that, during this transitional phase, the low-income developing countries

[1]   P.R. Krugman, 'Is Free Trade Passé?' (1987) 1 *Economic Perspective* 131–144 at 134.

[2]   D. Rodrik, 'Conceptual Issues in the Design of Trade Policy for Industrialization' (1992) 20 *World Development* 309–320; and J.E. Stiglitz, 'Some Lessons from the East Asian Miracle' (1996) 11 *World Bank Research Observer* 151–177.

will maintain trade restrictions and industrial/export support measures that are higher and which have wider sectoral dispersion than those prevailing in the developed countries.

In this regard, the concept of partnership for development through trade has a number of implications. First, the norms and rules of the multilateral trading system should explicitly recognize and permit this transitional asymmetry of obligations between the low-income developing countries and other participants in the system. Secondly, the developed country members should be willing to accept this asymmetry as an element of the necessary cost of inducing reforming low-income developing countries to prepare themselves for fully integrating their economies into the global trading system after establishing their capacity to participate effectively and in a mutually rewarding way. Thirdly, the low-income developing countries should be willing to accept greater and more transparent international discipline on their trade policies and other capacity-building support measures.

III. What Did GATT Do for the Low-Income Developing Countries?

Until the early 1960s, most of the present-day low-income developing countries were not members of GATT in their own right, since they were still European colonies. But even after they achieved political independence and became a significant proportion of the contracting parties to GATT, they remained passive bystanders in the early rounds of multilateral trade negotiations. During this period, the interests of the low-income developing countries were neither specifically and directly articulated by them nor were these interests explicitly taken into account in the negotiations. Two common explanations have been offered for this behaviour. One was that since they benefited through the most-favoured-nation (MFN) principle which extended to them reciprocal tariff reductions negotiated between the developed countries, the low-income developing countries were content to 'free-ride' on those reductions rather than directly engage in reciprocal negotiations themselves. A second common explanation is that the low-income developing countries relied on the 'special and differential' treatment granted to them which made it unnecessary to offer specific concessions that would be required in the give-and-take process of reciprocal negotiations.

Both of these reasons are facile and appear to ignore the more fundamental considerations that guided the behaviour of low-income developing countries. These include three significant disabilities which made more active participation in the GATT process virtually impossible for the low-income developing countries. First, since they were not 'principal suppliers' with respect to any of the trade sectors in which the developed countries chose to negotiate, the low-income developing countries lacked the 'right' to negotiate. Secondly, they also lacked the 'power' or leverage to negotiate since they were usually not major markets, individually or collectively, of significant developed country exports. Thirdly, the low-income developing countries lacked the human and institutional capacity to participate effectively in the GATT process, both in terms of the capability in state capitals to articulate their trade interests and in terms of adequate permanent representation at GATT to assert their membership rights and negotiate those interests.

To the extent that these disabilities constituted binding constraints, the only ways through which the low-income countries could obtain relatively free access to developed country markets were by relying on the extension to them via MFN of whatever tariff reductions were negotiated by the developed countries and by accepting whatever was offered in the form of special trade preferences.

In any case, for the large majority of these countries, their economies were so small that it was virtually impossible for them to integrate the domestic politics of trade liberalization into the reciprocal negotiation process of GATT, there being no strong export lobbies around which to build support for seeking concessions abroad in return for giving some at home.

It can be argued that the inherent asymmetry that characterized GATT process was largely responsible for the enduring relative protectionism against exports from low-income developing countries in the markets of the developed countries. This has often been cited as an important factor for the failure of developing countries to increase their exports. The impact of the asymmetrical process was reflected in several forms. First, the developed countries were on average more protectionist towards developing countries than towards themselves. Secondly, several of the trade restrictions applied by the developed countries were specifically targeted at exports of the developing countries. Thirdly, the most serious trade restrictions were placed on precisely those goods in which the low-income developing countries typically had comparative advantage in producing and exporting. Thus, developed country trade barriers were typically high for such items as agricultural commodities, as well as labour-intensive and technologically unsophisticated consumer goods, including textiles and apparel. It is instructive to note, in particular, that under the Multi-Fibre Arrangement (MFA), developed countries do not impose quotas on exports from one another but do so only on exports from the developing countries.

Participation without obligation is, in a sense, a term that perhaps best approximates the residual role of the developing countries in the GATT framework, if one bears in mind the exemptions from certain GATT disciplines which they were granted. Key among these were that they were not required to offer reciprocal concessions or bind their tariffs, they were permitted temporary use of trade restrictions, under specified conditions, for protecting infant industries and combating balance-of-payments problems, and they were allowed to use subsidies. But clearly the most significant attempt, in the GATT framework, to accommodate the needs of developing countries was the establishment of special trade preference schemes (the so-called generalized system of preferences (GSPs)) in their favour. Taken together, these initiatives implied that, without placing developing countries under any substantive obligation, the GATT framework bent over backwards to provide them with special access to the markets of the developed countries.

While the GSPs have not been entirely without value to the recipients, they suffer from severe limitations which significantly diminish their intrinsic worth and turn them into a doubtful basis upon which low-income developing countries could reasonably be expected to build more permanent comparative advantage. Key among these limitations are their unilateral rather than contractual basis, their restricted product coverage, and built-in quotas as well as restrictive rules of origin.

In practice, therefore, the preferential trade arrangements have neither helped the low-income developing countries to expand and diversify their exports nor have they been sufficient to enable them to maintain (far less expand) their share of world markets. The benefits derived from the GSPs have accrued largely to the top layer of developing countries which had, prior to the grant of trade preferences, established the domestic capacity to take effective advantage of the special export opportunities that the schemes offered. This suggests that while the creation of preferential trade schemes may be a necessary condition for the expansion of exports of developing countries, it is by no means sufficient; the potential beneficiaries must also have the capacity to respond effectively. Where the domestic response capacity has been lacking – as is obviously the case with respect to many of the low-income developing countries – trade preferences cannot be expected to generate significant export-enhancing benefits.

When the low-income developing countries eventually began their trade-liberalization process in the early 1980s, it had virtually nothing to do with GATT and its rules. In other words, rather than continuing to rely on derogations from GATT rules under the 'special and differential' treatment rubric and the GSPs, many of the low-income developing countries started undertaking the fundamental change of direction towards a greater degree of openness for reasons completely outside GATT framework.

IV. What Can the WTO Do for Low-Income Developing Countries?

Both domestic and external pressures induced the more developed of the developing countries, especially those whose growth was export-led, to be more actively involved in the GATT process from the late 1970s and early 1980s. The rapidly increasing share of these countries in the world trade in manufactures enhanced both their 'right' and 'leverage' to engage in the GATT negotiation process. Corresponding to their enhanced right to negotiate was the need for this upper layer of developing countries to participate more fully in the Uruguay Round as a means of protecting and enhancing the trade interests represented by this right. Similarly, their increased leverage induced the developed countries to bring this set of 'advanced' developing countries more fully into the Uruguay Round negotiations and thus under greater GATT discipline. Viewed from this perspective, a significant part of what the Uruguay Round achieved was to reflect explicitly the marked differences between the upper layer of developing countries which had acquired a certain degree of industrial development and capacity for competing effectively in the world market for manufactures and were therefore in a position to enter the GATT negotiating process, and the low-income developing countries which have not built an industrial base that is internationally competitive.

The question here is whether the WTO can help this lower layer of developing countries to integrate themselves into the global economy, and, if so, how. This question derives its primary relevance from the premise that the recent success of the more developed developing countries derives, at least in part, from their integration into the world economy. An important part of the answer probably lies in the extent to which the WTO framework can provide special market access to these countries which are, almost by definition, not in a position to bargain for lower tariffs on their exports in return for offers of appropriate concessions in their own markets. A second part of the answer would depend on the extent to which they can use the multilateral framework to support their own policy reforms. In other words, these countries could strengthen their reform by using the WTO as leverage against domestic anti-reform forces by accepting tariff bindings and other trade policy commitments. This is particularly desirable since the policy regimes of low-income developing countries are often characterized by a high degree of uncertainty and lack of credibility fed by excessive discretion and absence of transparency. Acceptance of and strict adherence to WTO discipline in appropriate policy areas could enhance the effectiveness of their policies by rendering them more certain and more credible.

One may review the key provisions of the Uruguay Round agreements against the background of the likely areas, identified above, in which the WTO can help the low-income developing countries. In broad terms, these provisions call for actions on the part of these countries that will inevitably result in their deeper integration into the world economy. But one must wonder whether this category of country is capable of doing so as quickly as the Uruguay Round agreements seem to expect.

Those elements of 'special and differential' (S&D) treatment that survived the Uruguay Round have become more targeted and made specific to each agreement. In addition, these provisions are time-bound. In some areas (eg, agriculture, subsidies and safeguards), provisions have been made for thresholds for undertaking certain commitments and for preserving market access that are more favourable to developing countries. But the nature of the provisions in respect of the last three dimensions of the S&D treatment remains rather haphazard and confusing. First, the category of countries to which various requirements of fewer obligations apply is not clear. Thus, in some cases reference is made to 'smaller producers', in others the reference is to 'poorer countries' (ie, those with per capita income below US$1 000); while in another set, 'least developed countries' are focused upon. Secondly, the transitional time-frame varies considerably between different Uruguay Round agreements, and it is not clear why. For instance, least developed countries are allowed 11 years (or more) to meet their TRIPs obligations, seven years for TRIMs and five years for sanitary and phytosanitary measures. Thirdly, the offer of technical assistance is targeted in some parts of the agreements at 'developing countries', while in others, the beneficiaries are the 'least developed countries'.

It seems reasonable to expect that the rapidly unfolding process of globalization will continue to push in the direction of a widening of WTO's mandate over various policy areas. The low-income countries cannot escape being drawn into this process. But, as Krueger argues: 'if developed countries should decide upon deeper integration in some facets of economic activity, they could provide time-phased "concession" of different lengths to different groups of developing countries.'[3] The rationale for a time-phased transition is to take into account the speed with which low-income developing countries

---

[3]   A.O. Krueger, *Trade Policies and Developing Nations* (Bookings Institution, Washington, DC, 1995), p. 63.

can alter their trade and payments regimes and build the necessary institutional framework. In other words, there is need to relate the time-bound phasing to differences in initial conditions and to accommodate differences in the capacity for adjustment.

The case being made for time-phasing in the process of accepting full WTO obligations applies also to the question regarding whether trade preferences for low-income developing countries should be abolished, given the many limitations of the existing preferential schemes. In other words, are these countries likely to be better served by a world trading system that is based on full reciprocity in making concessions and complete symmetry with regard to rights and obligations among all participants? The arguments against this idea are implicit in the discussion above and can be restated very briefly as follows. The low-income developing countries are without the negotiating leverage necessary for active participation in the WTO process; the preferential trade arrangement is probably the only effective mechanism through which they can continue to maintain some access to the markets of the developed world. The significant diversity that exists in the initial conditions as well as the marked differences in levels of development among countries imply that adjustment is likely to be asymmetrical as the ability of countries to adopt trade-liberalizing measures varies considerably.

The Uruguay Round agreements do not include a multilaterally negotiated and comprehensive framework from which can be derived both the special market access rights and time-phased derogation from appropriate WTO disciplines for low-income developing countries that would meet the needs specified above. To be effective, such a framework would have to be contractually binding on all the contracting parties to the WTO, cover all trade and trade-related issues, adopt commonly agreed criteria for the special market access and derogation from relevant rules, set agreed time limits on derogation, and establish agreed criteria for, as well as a system of, international review to determine graduation from both special market access and derogation from rules. In more specific terms and with particular reference to the special market access component of this proposal, it would be necessary to reach agreement on the criteria for classifying countries into the beneficiary (ie, low-income developing) category. Included in the criteria might be objective indicators such as per capita income and exported manufactured goods as a proportion of total exports (to measure income level and the degree of industrialization). To eliminate the deficiencies of the existing GSPs and similar trade preferences, it would be necessary to grant contractual zero-tariff treatment to *all* exports of *all* qualified beneficiary countries. In the case of derogation from WTO rules, a multilaterally negotiated list of WTO disciplines should be the basis with respect to which an agreed time-phased transition is granted to qualified beneficiaries (based on the same criteria used for the trade preference scheme) for up to 25 years, subject to periodic review at ten-year intervals.

In partial exchange and to ensure that the beneficiaries do not become permanent 'free-riders', they should be subject to the following conditions. First, they would have to agree to bind their tariffs at multilaterally agreed levels (perhaps not above 50 per cent). Secondly, they would also agree to a negotiated schedule of tariff reductions over the transition period that should bring their bound tariffs to reasonable levels (such as 10–15 per cent).

This proposal combines the provision of secure preferential market access and transitional derogation from selected WTO disciplines with the requirements that recipients should pursue stable, credible and transparent outward-oriented development strategies and trade policies that would enhance their export supply response capacity and promote their integration into the global economy.

V.   Concluding Comments

The Uruguay Round agreements and subsequent decisions of the WTO recognize that the low-income developing countries are not able to participate effectively in the WTO process because of acute limitations arising from inadequate human and institutional capacity. The WTO has focused on two kinds of initiatives to deal with this problem. One is to offer technical assistance in the area of training and capacity building. The other is to lighten the burden of low-income developing countries in meeting the requirements of WTO membership by permitting them to use streamlined procedures in satisfying certain obligations, to carry lighter notification burdens, and undergo simplified consultations on balance-of-payments restrictions, etc.

While these special provisions address some of the limitations faced by the low-income developing countries, they do not exhaust them. There remain the huge costs, in terms of human and institutional capacity, of participating fully and effectively in the full range of WTO activities. Both human and institutional capacity will clearly benefit, eventually, from the technical assistance that is currently being offered. This will contribute to a solution only in the longer term. Taking care of the immediate needs of representation may require that elements of the WTO governance and management structures be altered. Perhaps an executive directorate system or a similar arrangement could be an appropriate way of ensuring that low-income developing countries which cannot afford to maintain requisite permanent delegations at the WTO would have their interests watched over by 'group' executive directors who constitute an integral part of the regular staff of the institution.

VI.   Bibliography

Blackhurst, R. (1998), 'The Capacity of the WTO to fulfil its Mandate' in A. Krueger (ed.), *The WTO As An International Organization* (University of Chicago Press).
Krueger, A.O. (1995), *Trade Policies and Developing Nations* (The Bookings Institution, Washington, D.C.).
Krugman, P.R., 'Is Free Trade Passé?' (1987) 1 *Economic Perspective*, 131–144.
Rodrik, D., 'Conceptual Issues in the Design of Trade Policy for Industrialization' (1992) 20 *World Development* 309–320.
Stiglitz, J.E., 'Some Lessons from the East Asian Miracle', (1996) 11 *The World Bank Research Observer* 151–177.

Chapter 11
Regionalism and the WTO

*Jaime Serra Puche**

I. Introduction

Over the last three decades, regional trade agreements (RTAs)[1] have proliferated to the point that, by 1995, virtually all the members of the newly formed World Trade Organization (WTO) belonged to an RTA of some kind – in most cases a customs union, a free trade agreement (FTA), or an interim agreement leading to one or the other (see Figure 1). This development has greatly changed the world trade scene and represents both an important challenge and a unique opportunity for the new WTO: a challenge because RTAs can result in trade and investment diversion leading to high welfare costs for non-participants; an opportunity because RTAs may create regional dynamic forces in favour of freer trade which, in turn, can generate important welfare benefits for the rest of the world.

The phenomenon of 'regionalism' has emerged in the context of very rapid growth in world trade. Over the past 50 years, while world income has risen six-fold, real world trade has increased twelve-fold. Over the last 20 years, foreign direct investment has multiplied twelve-fold. Among the causes of these developments, trade and investment liberalization policies have played a very significant role. Trade liberalization has taken place at both the unilateral and multilateral levels. Market-oriented economic national reforms have consistently encompassed ambitious unilateral programmes to eliminate trade and investment barriers; these have facilitated the access of goods, services, and new foreign investment, leading in turn to new trade and investment flows. At the multilateral level, further trade liberalization measures have been introduced after the conclusion of each of four rounds of trade negotiations under the General Agreement on Tariffs and Trade (GATT), which have also generated additional trade flows.

---

* This paper is based on the Summary Overview and section VI of J. Serra et al., *Reflections on Regionalism* (Carnegie Endowment for International Peace, 1997).

[1] 'RTAs' refers to all preferential trade agreements – whether or not their member countries are geographically proximate. It also refers only to RTAs that have been notified to GATT.

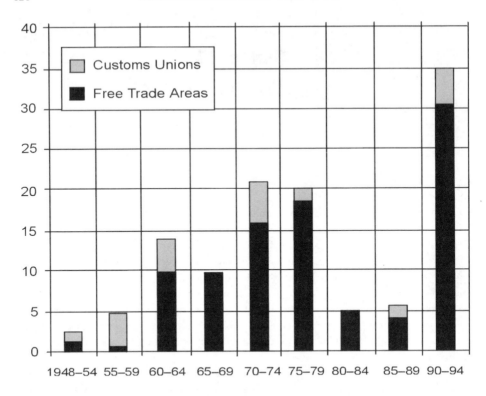

Figure 1   Number of Regional Trade Agreements notified to GATT

Source: World Trade Organization, *Regionalism and the World of Trading Systems* (Geneva, 1995)

While the recent creation of many RTAs marks progress on liberalization policies within particular regions, it can constrain potentially broader benefits from liberalization under multilateral arrangements. In the early 1990s, RTA formation gained momentum for a variety of economic and institutional reasons. On the economic front, many of the smaller, more protectionist countries took it upon themselves to implement comprehensive trade liberalization reform programmes. Unilateral liberalization became relevant in RTA creation to the extent that the smaller countries needed to complement internal efficiency gains from trade with external market access. Trade among 'natural', already firmly established, trading partners intensified dramatically. On the institutional front, unilateral liberalization was taking place concurrently with the launching of the Uruguay Round of GATT negotiations (1986–1994). Early on, that round was held up in extremely complicated negotiations, in part because of the ambitious agenda defined from the outset; reaching consensus on many of the issues became a cumbersome exercise with numerous political obstacles. Regional initiatives emerged from the midst of this political quagmire as 'safe havens' for many smaller countries that could not afford a 'wait and see' strategy in the multilateral arena. By 1995, more than 50 per cent of world trade was estimated to take place within RTAs (see Figure 2).

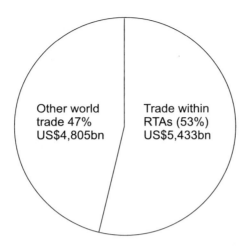

Figure 2   Estimate of World Trade within Regional Trade Agreements, 1995

Source: IMF (1995) and World Trade Organization, *Regionalism and the World of Trading Systems* (Geneva, 1995)

Note: [a] In the absence of detailed information, these figures were estimated by subtracting from total world trade the trade of all countries that do not belong to RTAs or WTO. Total trade within RTAs was then calculated as the product of intra-regional trade shares (World Trade Organization, *Regionalism and the World Trading Systems* (Geneva, 1995)) and the total RTAs trade. It is assumed here that all intra-RTA trade is conducted on preferential terms.

Analysts are divided about the effects of these RTAs. Some believe that taking further steps in the direction of trade and investment liberalization – even when restricted to a particular region – contributes to the creation of world trade and investment. Others believe that the implicit discrimination that these agreements embody diverts rather than creates worldwide trade and investment. Both sides of the debate have legitimate arguments.

Existing *theoretical* analysis leads to ambiguous conclusions. Economic theory alone cannot tell us whether RTAs are likely to increase or reduce distortions in the world trading system. From a static perspective, RTAs are more likely to enhance than to reduce world efficiency if their primary effect is to create new investment and trade rather than to divert existing investment and trade. The prospects for this depend upon existing trading patterns among would-be RTA members and the way in which the agreement is structured.

From a dynamic perspective, the key question is whether RTAs promote or retard further liberalization at the multilateral level, where it generates efficiency and other benefits for many more countries. Not much is yet known about which outcome is more likely, but the WTO must be ever vigilant that RTAs are not used in a discriminatory way, as substitutes for global agreements.

The empirical analysis available also leads to ambiguous results. Most studies suggest the same conclusions as the theory: RTAs do not necessarily bring harm to non-member countries, but they are not necessarily benign.

Since neither trade theory nor empirical analysis demonstrates conclusively what the trade- and investment-diverting effects of RTAs will be, the possibility remains that RTA proliferation may generate trade and investment diversion.

II.   Recommendations in regard to Article XXIV

The WTO should be better equipped to prevent trade and investment distortions that might constrain the emergence of a more efficient liberal multilateral trading system. Existing multilateral trade rules, under the WTO umbrella, and rules on investment, under various agreements and WTO codes, are either incomplete or dispersed and overlapping. In principle, the WTO addresses the formation of RTAs through Article XXIV and other enabling mechanisms, but analysis and experience demonstrate the inadequacy of these clauses. In addition, regional or bilateral investment agreements are outside the WTO's sphere of influence. As a result, trade- and investment-diverting effects of RTAs and other investment agreements have not been sufficiently constrained. The following policy recommendations address this issue.

II.1   Precise compliance criteria

Recommendation 1: The WTO should strengthen Article XXIV to provide precise compliance criteria for RTAs, specifically on the following three topics:

(i)   MFN tariffs;
(ii)   rules of origin; and
(iii) transparency and enforcement.

II.1.a   Tariff levels and MFN bindings

The Understanding on Article XXIV that resulted from the Uruguay Round of negotiations and the strengthened dispute settlement provisions accorded in that Round have only to some extent reduced the problem of ambiguity. Now there is an explicit, although still arbitrary, method for comparing pre-agreement and post-agreement tariff levels; time limits for transitions are defined; there are rules for ex ante compensation for movements towards a common external tariff that raises protection in one or several countries; there are compulsory working party reviews; and there are automatic dispute settlement procedures. Nonetheless, basic uncertainties persist, since the principles of 'substantially all trade' and 'not on the whole higher or more restrictive' are not yet precisely bound.

Article XXIV must be viewed as a process. Some steps in this direction already have been taken with the establishment of the WTO Special Committee on Regionalism for the purpose of overviewing RTA compliance with Article XXIV. The Committee should organize working parties prior to the negotiation of an RTA, since WTO input may be helpful in shaping an agreement to make it compatible with the multilateral trading system. Probably more important, early engagement can influence the negotiating parties' objectives and strategies. Similarly, WTO involvement should continue well *after* the creation of an RTA. The implementation of an RTA, whether in its complete or interim form, can be just as critical as its textual foundation. The Trade Policy Review Mechanism (TPRM) now in place could be extended to include review of contracting parties' RTA trade.

The current Understanding of Article XXIV places emphasis on specific criteria to quantify tariff compliance. Leaving aside the issue of the analytical pertinence of the new criteria, these guidelines are still insufficient, and stricter controls on *MFN bindings* should be introduced. For example, if a country's bound tariffs are higher than the tariffs it applies before it becomes a member of an RTA, then, once the RTA enters into force, the MFN tariff structure can be subject to protectionist pressures. One solution to this problem, based upon applied MFN tariff rates, would be to have the Article state that the tariff bindings in an RTA become MFN bindings, with possible allowance for a transition period. With respect to customs unions, experience has shown (particularly in Latin America) that negotiating this type of agreement from scratch can lead to common external tariffs, that are higher than the set of minimum tariffs among the partner countries. This result can be interpreted as a violation of the 'shall not on the whole be higher or more restrictive' principle. Therefore, in the case of customs unions, Article XXIV should provide stricter guidelines for common external tariff determination. An ideal outcome would be to bind each member's pre-agreement applied tariff levels and allow for a transition towards a minimum common external tariff.

II.1.b Rules of origin

This section focuses on preferential rules of origin – those used to grant preferential access within an FTA. One simple procedure that avoids trade diversion reasonably well is to define preferential rules of origin that reflect to the greatest extent possible the ex ante observed regional content of regional exports. If rules of origin are set more restrictively, so that they require more regional integration than that observed prior to the establishment of the FTA, trade diversion is likely to result: in this case, the rules of origin are restrictive. Inefficient regional industries have an incentive to lobby for highly restrictive rules of origin. Since consumers and efficient producers from the rest of the world are under-represented, the governments' concern should be to press for non-distorting rules of origin. If negotiators believe it is necessary to grant some protection in specific cases, it is preferable to define a more gradual phase-in of tariff preferences than to introduce permanent distortions through restrictive rules of origin.

If countries that negotiate an FTA have sectors with very similar protection with respect to the rest of the world, it is unnecessary to embark on a cumbersome and complex definition of rules of origin for goods produced in such sectors. In these cases, trade deflection – to avoid entry through the country with the highest tariff – will not initially be significant. Adopting a region-wide external tariff (a 'sectoral' customs union) is a superior option provided that a minimum tariff is adopted. For sector-specific common tariffs to work, however, protection with respect to third countries has to be very similar for both final goods and the most important intermediate goods used in the production process.[2]

At present the WTO does not provide any guideline on how to evaluate the effects of rules of origin on the patterns of trade; moreover, there is no legal basis for initiating formal discussions of such effects, since preferential rules of origin are not mentioned explicitly in Article XXIV and are not considered to be a trade policy instrument. The first step towards remedying this situation should be to adopt a new formal understanding of Article XXIV whereby rules of origin used to determine preferential access within FTAs are considered 'other regulations of commerce', as defined in paragraph 5(b) of that Article. The understanding should also establish that rules of origin will not be more restrictive than the status quo ex ante regional content of exports.[3] This would preclude a comprehensive harmonization of preferential rules of origin, and different agreements could have different rules.[4] The understanding would imply that, when a given FTA is enlarged, the rules of origin will be redefined so as to accommodate, industry by industry, the smaller regional content observed ex ante.

The implementation of such an understanding might not be especially difficult. First, its very existence would imply an increased discipline for countries negotiating an FTA, and flagrant violations would thereby be discouraged. Secondly, as in the case of customs unions with distorting common external tariffs, transition periods could be established to phase out restrictive rules of origin. Finally, rules for compensation in the case of severely restrictive rules of origin could be introduced; third parties hurt by rules of origin could initiate a dispute and prove that, in the special case being considered, a 'more restrictive' regime had been established and damage had occurred because products previously incorporating third-country intermediate goods do not benefit from regional preferences.

II.1.c   Transparency and enforcement

Perhaps the most serious problem with Article XXIV is that it is weakest where it should be strongest. Article XXIV should generate strict and transparent rules-based RTAs. But

---

[2]   Wonnacot suggests this hybrid approach for the NAFTA enlargement: P. Wonnacot, 'Beyond NAFTA – The Design of a Free Trade Agreement of the Americas' in J. Bhagwati and A. Panagariya (eds), *The Economics of Preferential Trade Agreements* (American Enterprise Institute, Washington, DC, 1996), pp. 79–107.

[3]   For a formalization of this argument, see P. Rodriguez, 'Rules of Origin with Multistage Production' (mimeo, Princeton University, Princeton, NJ, 1996).

[4]   The economic distortions created by preferential rules of origin could be reduced, but the diversity observed today would not be eliminated. For instance, E. Vermulst, P. Waer and J. Bourgeois (eds), *Rules of Origin in International Trade: A Comparative Study* (University of Michigan Press, Ann Arbor, MI, 1994) noted that the European Union has 14 different sets of preferential rules of origin, the USA and Canada six each; and Australia five.

it is loosely worded. In today's most important RTAs, tariff-based trade diversion seems to be less of a concern than non-tariff-based diversion. Article XXIV could be improved substantially to address this important issue in a constructive and practical way.

One avenue to explore is to hook up Article XXIV with the improved codes and rules that resulted from the Uruguay Round negotiations. To assure greater transparency, the hook-up with other WTO rules and procedures would give the Article objective criteria for evaluation. One alternative would be to word the Article so that all WTO disciplines on non-tariff barriers are observed (especially with respect to procedures). This approach would integrate Article XXIV with the multilateral agenda contained in the WTO codes and give the global institution a pivotal role in the process of convergence through an explicit mandate to the Special Committee on Regionalism. It would then be possible to establish compatibility criteria based on the set of rules and procedures followed by RTAs (in the case of non-tariff barriers), as well as on quantitative criteria (in the case of tariff barriers). This would not only greatly facilitate convergence on issues such as harmonization of standards (or mutual recognition) but also significantly enhance the role of the WTO as the overseer of RTA convergence.

Article XXIV needs to induce adequate compliance. The WTO's mandate needs to be strong enough to enforce a stricter Article XXIV. One aspect that should be strengthened is the TPRM. Ex ante, compulsory working party evaluations under Article XXIV – which allow the WTO to make recommendations regarding inconsistent provisions in an RTA, and which link the recommendations to the automatic dispute settlement provisions agreed to in the Uruguay Round – would give the review process substance and credibility. Ex post, for the purposes of RTA evaluation, the TPRM should be regional in scope, and the principal conclusions of the review process should be made public.

II.2   Convergence to common trade rules

Recommendation 2: As an RTA matures, trade rules employed by the member countries should be required to converge to a common set of rules. In addition, non-preferential rules of origin should not become more restrictive during the transition period to harmonization.

Trade deflection may occur – even with a common external tariff in a customs union – when member countries maintain different national trade rules, such as anti-dumping and countervailing-duty codes or technical, health and safety standards. To avoid deflection, member countries apply national 'non-preferential' rules of origin. As an RTA moves towards harmonization of trade rules, the need for non-preferential rules of origin vanishes, minimizing trade distortions.

Two examples of how trade rules among RTA members have evolved in this direction relate to anti-dumping policy. In one case (an FTA), New Zealand and Australia have substituted their national anti-dumping codes with regional anti-trust legislation. Similarly, in another case (a customs union), the EU applies a regional competition policy. Moreover, a common anti-dumping law is applied by the EU. In the case of NAFTA, the three partners decided to maintain their national legislation and to develop a regional review procedure that assures exporters due process.[5] The future of NAFTA's approach to contingent protection, beyond the protectionist pressures that impeded further progress during the negotiations, depends on the region's ability to develop a common competition policy.[6]

Although the harmonization of trade rules within RTAs would provide the most benefits, the prospects for immediate harmonization are poor. The proliferation of free-trade agreements, each of which maintains distinct trade rules, suggests that countries place a value on maintaining their own trade rules, or that harmonization is too troublesome or difficult a task to undertake. Since it appears that harmonization is too ambitious at the present time, the best approach for addressing potential conflicts may be to pursue a middle course. Such a course would call for a gradual harmonization. During the transition, domestic trade rules would be enforced by applying non-preferential rules of origin. The EU provides a good model for such an approach.

With respect to non-preferential rules of origin in particular, the Uruguay Round Agreement on Rules of Origin established the goal that all non-preferential rules of origin should be harmonized by 1998. These rules should be clear and predictable and should not create unnecessary obstacles to trade. The work programme calls upon the Technical Committee to develop harmonized definitions and methodologies for determining the country of origin of a good. The attainment of the Agreement's objective of harmonization of non-preferential rules of origin should result in more efficient world trade flows by creating one standard set of methodologies and definitions. However, the agreement does not call upon the Technical Committee to ensure that the definitions and methodologies agreed upon are, by some measure, less stringent than those used in different countries before the negotiations.

II.3   Accessibility for aspiring RTA members

Recommendation 3: The WTO should require that the architecture and accession conditions of RTAs do not prevent other countries from becoming members.

The WTO should develop a model accession clause to be included in all RTAs. Such a clause should articulate the set of WTO disciplines that a potential new member must meet prior to entering into accession negotiations (eg, the binding of an effective tariff schedule, compliance with the final WTO panel reports against it). Compliance with these conditions should entitle the aspiring members to initiate negotiations.

II.4   Development of a legal framework for foreign direct investment

Recommendation 4: The WTO should develop rules to ensure that RTA investment provisions and other investment treaties do not divert investment.

The diversity of rules and the differing scope for their application in areas such as liberalization, protection, insurance and dispute settlement may lead to uncertainty and

---

[5]   NAFTA, Chapter XIX.
[6]   NAFTA, Chapter XV.

distortion in the flows of capital. It is necessary to develop a more structured and uniform legal framework applicable to foreign direct investment. A WTO multilateral agreement on investment would provide the crucial benefit of harmonizing investment standards, thereby lowering information costs for potential investors.

Such a multilateral agreement on investment should have three basic building blocks: market access (eg, MFN status and national treatment); protection (eg, rules for expropriation of investments, intellectual property rights) and dispute settlement (eg, arbitration rules).

II.4.a   Market access

With regard to market access, trade liberalization programmes frequently have been accompanied by concomitant direct foreign investment deregulation. This has been accomplished through the elimination of barriers to entry and performance requirements. In particular, the national treatment principle guarantees foreign investors sector access similar to the most favourable treatment accorded domestic investors. Similarly, the MFN principle guarantees all foreign investors the same treatment.[7]

Appropriate definitions of 'investment' and 'investor' are essential for they limit the scope and sectoral coverage of the foreign direct investment (FDI) regime. With respect to the definition of investment, since FDI projects generally involve more that the simple transfer of equity from an external to an internal asset (eg, such projects often involve complex financing mechanisms, or technology transfer), investment should be defined broadly, so that the disciplines accorded apply to the different ways in which FDI can materialize. As for the definition of investor, given the mobility of international capital and the virtually global nationality of foreign investors, any person who carries on substantial business activity in one or more of the partner countries should be treated as a regional investor, regardless of nationality. The last point is important, since it resolves the issue of 'inwardness' with a straightforward and non-discriminatory solution: any foreign investor who locates investment in one of the RTA's partner countries is automatically considered a regional investor.

With respect to performance requirements and incentives, RTAs should prohibit their use to promote or regulate FDI flows, since they are a source of distortion and resource misallocation. Performance requirements can also generate non-tariff barriers to trade (eg, if an external balance condition is imposed on FDI or, more indirectly, if domestic content is imposed on government procurement) and performance incentives can generate 'actionable' subsidies (ie, ones against which formal proceedings may be initiated).

II.4.b   Protection

With regard to investment protection, the basic issues involve compensation rules in case of expropriation and the protection of intellectual property rights. Expropriation rules

---

[7]   Many countries still apply exceptions to non-discrimination principles on performance requirements.

should include due process and should guarantee prompt, adequate, effective and freely transferable compensation at fair market value. In addition, a WTO multilateral agreement on investment should build on existing international instruments for the protection of intellectual property rights (including TRIPS). Particular emphasis should be given to enforcement issues.[8]

II.4.c   Dispute settlement

With regard to dispute settlement, foreign investors should be granted access to investor-state arbitration to resolve treaty-related disputes with host governments.[9] However, the effectiveness of arbitration, whether between private parties or with the state, greatly depends on the international instruments that govern its practice and on national attitudes towards the non-judicial settlement of disputes. Although many countries have recently modified their legislation to favour private commercial arbitration, the non-judicial resolution of 'treaty-related' controversies between investors and a state is still controversial in some parts of the world (for example, in Latin American countries that endorse the Calvo Doctrine).

The OECD's experience with investment-related issues and current progress in the negotiations would seem to favour it as the preferred negotiating forum for a Multilateral Agreement on Investment (MAI). One important advantage of initiating MAI negotiations within the OECD might be – as the organization itself argues – that the nature of present investment instruments also gives a certain guarantee against discriminatory provisions and against the reintroduction of restrictions. Such pressures would probably arise in a start-from-scratch effort within the WTO. This consideration nonetheless must be balanced against the risk of alienating non-OECD nations, which ex ante might feel that their concerns are better represented in other fora, such as the United Nations Conference on Trade and Development (UNCTAD).

The first item on an *investment rules policy road-map* for the WTO should build on the OECD MAI. The WTO should borrow from the OECD's 'open-accession' concept; given the extraordinary difficulties inherent in forging consensus among all WTO members, the broader new multilateral agreement should be instituted as a WTO non-compulsory code with open accession. This might facilitate the necessary consensus for its adoption. Ideally, members could reach broad consensus during negotiations, and a large proportion of WTO members would then become charter members of the new accord.

---

[8]   E. Mansfield, 'Intellectual Property Protection, Direct Investment, and Technology Transfer: Germany, Japan and the United States' (Discussion Paper No. 27, International Finance Corporation, 1995) surveyed USA executives and found that the level of intellectual property protection in source countries substantially affects the willingness to make more technologically advanced investments as opposed to building low-tech production facilities or simple distribution networks. The logic is that such protection corrects any free-rider problem.

[9]   Investor-to-investor controversies can of course always be resolved through arbitration by contractual agreement.

A second component of the investment rules policy road-map should be WTO implementation, for all of its members, of an Investment Policy Review Mechanism (IPRM), as part of the TPRM. This would serve two main purposes: monitoring actual investment performance; and promoting accession to the MAI. Both goals would entail considerable effort and might not be feasible initially, but the administrative burden would diminish as additional nations acceded to the investment code as a result of the incentives created by a peer-pressure system of reviews.

The investment policy road-map should also contribute to the multilateral negotiations on the liberalization of trade in services. A service provider with a permanent commercial presence in a country other than his or her own becomes, for all practical purposes, an investor in that country. Accordingly, the investment should be protected as such by the MAI, rather than by the GATS. This is a point that the WTO will have to come to grips with in assuming a leading role in the field of investment.[10]

II.5   Promoting compatibility between RTAs and the WTO

Recommendation 5: The WTO should use its institutional structure and procedures actively to promote compatibility between RTAs and the WTO itself.

The problems facing the multilateral system cannot be resolved by creating additional institutions and procedures for the settlement of trade disputes. Policy-makers – whether they are at the domestic, the regional or the multilateral level – generally dread the implications of new international bureaucracies. Existing international institutions (like the WTO) and procedures (like the WTO's Dispute Settlement Body (DSB)) embody decades of evolution in the direction of a rules-based trading system. More effective than their predecessors, the WTO and the DSB show promising potential in the quest to harmonize RTAs and the multilateral system.

Nonetheless, there are now several regional trade arrangements with institutions, dispute settlement procedures, secretariats, committees and working groups that potentially duplicate the work of the WTO. For instance, of the 24 regional trade authorities that the WTO has started analyzing, 22 have their own anti-dumping rules, 18 have regulations governing the use of subsidies, 19 have provisions on competition policy, and 12 incorporate dispute settlement procedures. RTA institutions may threaten the authority of the WTO if they direct member countries to follow the regional rules to the exclusion of the multilateral GATT/WTO structure. The risk of weakening WTO principles is particularly great if RTAs do not follow GATT/WTO guidelines at the time of their inception (eg, Article XXIV).

The recently created WTO Special Committee on Regionalism should play a pivotal role in *monitoring* the compliance of RTAs with the provisions of Article XXIV. Such

---

[10]   Article I (2-c) of the GATS Agreement still considers commercial presence to be one of the four modes of delivery of services. Under the NAFTA, for example, that logic is eliminated: any form of establishment is entitled to protection pursuant to the investment chapter (Chapter 11).

scrutiny should go beyond a mere examination of the original text of an RTA to careful consideration of its negotiating and implementation stages. As suggested earlier, the Special Committee on Regionalism could borrow from the procedures of the TPRM and the IPRM to closely follow RTA implementation and possible amendment.

The WTO should discourage RTA members from adopting closed *forum selection* provisions in their agreement: countries that enter into an RTA should always be free to take to the WTO any dispute that calls into question both WTO and RTA rules.[11]

The adoption of specific rules for the selection of arbitrators in regional disputes can greatly contribute to harmonizing the operation of the WTO and RTAs. For example, RTAs could either grant a WTO institution (eg, the Special Committee on Regionalism) the right to designate a limited number of the panellists to be included in the RTA roster; or require that the members of the RTA select a panellist for a particular dispute directly from the WTO roster.

In many instances, RTAs either incorporate by reference or entirely copy GATT principles. For example, Article 301 of NAFTA states that national treatment for trade in goods shall be granted in accordance with Article III of GATT; and Article 309 of NAFTA expressly refers to Article XI of GATT on import and export restrictions. For practical purposes, this means that disputes under Articles 301 or 309 of NAFTA require an understanding of the GATT body of precedents on Articles III or XI, respectively. In any such instance, an RTA panel should be allowed to consult WTO (eg, the Appellate Body), or the WTO could decide to submit an opinion to that RTA panel regarding the interpretation and application of the relevant RTA provision. This would promote the formation of a *uniform body of precedents* on such fundamental WTO principles as national and MFN treatment.

Finally, the Understanding on Article XXIV has made it clear that the WTO dispute settlement provisions 'may be invoked with respect to any matters arising from the application of Article XXIV'. In addition, new WTO–DSB rules regarding the constitution of a panel, the adoption of its report, and the application of compensatory measures would contribute to overcoming any stalemate resulting from possible blocking of the operation of dispute settlement procedures under GATT. Together, these changes in scope and operation would greatly enhance the legal prospects for the enforcement of Article XXIV.

---

[11]   For example, Mexico, Canada and the USA adopted both open and closed forum-selection clauses in their recent RTA. Pursuant to Article 1005(1) of the NAFTA, disputes arising under both the NAFTA and GATT, or its successor, may be settled in either forum, at the discretion of the complaining party. However, in the case of disputes concerning certain measures related to the protection of human, animal, or plant life or health, or the environment, the defending party can block recourse to GATT.

III. Summary

These recommendations provide an ambitious agenda. They are offered as guidelines for future WTO decisions and actions. Clearly not all of them can be implemented immediately. But unless changes of this nature are initiated very soon, preferential regional trade, investment liberalization and the establishment of regional monitoring institutions will continue to pose a serious challenge to the WTO's ability to protect and advance the interests of all participants in world trade. This is why – 50 years after the creation of GATT – it is important that the WTO oversee the formation of these alliances to ensure that the agreements are structured in ways consistent with the broader goals of the world trading community. The trends towards regional integration need to be harnessed as a force for global liberalization.

Chapter 12
What Does Globalization Mean for the World Trading System?

*Horst Siebert**

I. Introduction

Institutions matter. They define how things are being done. In the world economy, as in national economies, a set of norms, rules and informal procedures serve to reduce transactions costs, most prominently to diminish uncertainty arising from the behaviour of market participants or originating from the non-cooperative conduct of sovereign nation states. The basic idea of such a world economic order for the trading system is to provide an institutional framework that allows the participating economies to capture the potential welfare gains from the international division of labour.

An international order[1] which develops in the course of time[2] represents a public good being used in equal amounts by all. It provides a skeleton of an international economic constitution for sovereign nation states in the area of international exchange. A rule system for the behaviour of governments takes the place of ad hoc negotiations between governments. A central element of such a rule-based institutional framework for the world economy is that sovereign states voluntarily commit themselves to respect rules which prevent strategic, ie uncooperative, behaviour by individual countries. The contractually binding commitments, undertaken freely by governments, are ratified through domestic legislative processes.[3] Strategic behaviour of national governments would destroy the public good of the international order, representing a negative

---

*   I appreciate the critical comments of Rolf J. Langhammer, Oliver Lorz and Daniel Piazolo.

[1]   On the relevance of establishing an institutional order (*Ordnungspolitik*) compare the Freiburg school of economics in Germany, especially W. Eucken, *Die Grundlagen der Nationalökonomie* (Berlin, 1940), translated as *The Foundations of Economics: History and Theory in the Analysis of Economic Reality* (Berlin, 1992).

[2]   R. Axelrod, 'An Evolutionary Approach to Norms' (1986) 80 *American Political Science Review* 1095–1111; and D. North, *Institutions, Institutional Change and Economic Performance* (Cambridge, 1990).

[3]   R. Ruggiero, 'From Vision to Reality: The Multilateral Trading System at Fifty' (Brookings Institution Forum on 'The Global Trading System: A GATT 50th Anniversary Forum', 4 March 1998).

externality for the rule system. The rules must prevent such strategic behaviour. Self-commitment by states limits national governments' choice of actions in the future and in this sense represents a negative catalogue. It protects the international division of labour against national governments.[4] The self-commitment of states is also a shelter from the power of protectionist groups in the individual economies. Moreover, the rules must induce nation states to act cooperatively in certain areas[5] and to develop the system further. The WTO is not only about respecting rules but also about rule-making.

The contents of the institutional arrangement for the world economy depend on the types of interdependence among countries. The rules follow changes and trends in global interdependence. When traditional areas in the international division of labour vary in their character, rules have to adjust. When new areas of international exchange are opened up, new rules have to be worked out. When the rule system itself leads to liberalization, new rules have to be developed for a more liberalized world.[6] Traditionally, rules for the exchange of goods are at the core of the world trade order. Recently, other policy aspects and their relation to trade such as national competition policies, national regulations and social norms were discussed. Moreover, other areas of exchange have come to the foreground such as the trade of services and the international exchange in information technology and information services. Also rules for the mobility of production factors – labour, investment (capital) and technology, most prominently property rights – as well as conditions for the international division of labour in the financial and monetary area are receiving increased attention in the economic policy discussion. Finally, norms for the use of the environment will acquire greater significance in the future.

Our issue is how the policy of establishing, securing and extending a world trading order is affected by a globalizing international economy. Globalization means that the interdependencies among countries in the world economy are becoming more intense. Transport costs and communication costs are drastically decreasing, other impediments to international exchange such as tariffs and political barriers lose importance, the economic distance shrinks:

(i)   In the goods market, segmentations are reduced, markets are more contestable, competition becomes fiercer.

(ii) New regions like Eastern Europe and China, so far more or less excluded from the international economy, are now being fully integrated into the international division of labour. Since these countries have an abundant labour supply, the world experiences an increase in the supply of labour. At the same time, the world market is widening to an unprecedented extent.

(iii) New products such as services are gaining more relevance in the international division of labour.

---

[4]   J. Tumlir, 'International Economic Order and Democratic Constitutionalism' (1983) 34 ORDO 71–83 at 72.

[5]   S. Haggard and B. Simmons, 'Theories of International Regimes' (1987) 41 *International Organization* 491–517 at 513.

[6]   A.O. Krueger (ed.), *The WTO as an International Organization* (Chicago, 1998), p. 3.

(iv) Capital and technical knowledge become more mobile, locational competition among states for mobile capital and mobile technical knowledge is intensified.

(v) There is a greater awareness of global phenomena, an important area being global environmental goods.

II. Challenges in the Traditional Area of the Exchange of Goods

The aim of the trading system is to allow the international division of labour to occur as smoothly as possible. For this task, quite a few challenges exist in the traditional area of trade.

II.1 Adding missing pieces to the free trade system

One line of strengthening the WTO system is to continue the liberalization efforts in the traditional areas of merchandise trade and to add some missing pieces to the institutional arrangement for free trade.[7] This means pushing the results of the Uruguay Round further. First, there is room for further tariff reductions. Even though average tariffs rates of the OECD countries are low, peak tariffs are still relatively high for some consumer goods. Average industrial tariff rates of developing countries are in the range of 10–20 per cent.[8] Secondly, all voluntary export restraints which were used to circumvent tariff liberalization should be eliminated by the year 2000. No new forms of quantitative restrictions should be allowed. Thirdly, the two sectoral exemptions from the non-discrimination principle and from the most-favoured-nation treatment in the domains of agriculture and textiles represent quite a challenge. It is important to stick to the phase-out until 2005 in textiles, and not to delay the bulk of liberalization to the latest possible deadline.[9] In agriculture, where tariffs have become more important with the tariffication of quantitative restraints, new negotiations have to be launched.

II.2 Subsidies and strategic trade policy

When tariffs and quantitative restraints lose importance in the future, governments may be tempted to use subsidies in order to lower their producers' production costs, thus establishing an artificial price advantage and distorting the international division of labour. One conceivable response to this would be simply to ignore and tolerate domestic subsidies, especially for old industries like coal, since a subsidizing country does not

---

[7]   R.J. Langhammer, 'Die Weiterentwicklung der WTO: Wegbereiter einer weltumfassenden Harmonisierung von Regelwerken?' (1998) 27 WiST 121–126.

[8]   J.M. Finger, M.D. Ingco and U. Reincke, *The Uruguay Round – Statistics on Tariff Concessions Given and Received* (World Bank, Washington, DC, 1996).

[9]   Richard Blackhurst, 'The WTO and the Global Economy' (1997) 20 *World Economy* 527–544; and D. Spinanger, 'The WTO after the Singapore Ministerial: Much to Do about What?' (Kieler Diskussionsbeiträge 304, Institut für Weltwirtschaft, Kiel, 1997).

employ its resources optimally, and thereby accepts a loss of its own welfare. One cannot, however, be too complacent about domestic subsidies because strategic trade theory could, in the future, become more appealing to practical politics and provide a rationale for subsidizing 'new' sectors, albeit on the basis of rather naive models. We may see more of this interventionistic approach in some European countries as a reaction to globalization with subsidies by one country being used to take market shares away from the corresponding sectors of other countries. This may lead to political demands for retaliation. Thus, the effect of subsidies may be as detrimental to international trade as traditional protectionist measures; they may also be part of an aggressive bilateralism. According to the WTO rules, trade-distorting subsidies for export goods and import substitutes are forbidden and product- and industry-specific subsidies are inadmissible if they harm the trade prospects of other members. Even so it is difficult to demarcate subsidy practices from other admissible policies such as research assistance and aid in adapting to new environmental technologies. It is likewise difficult to penalize and stop violations in the framework of monitoring processes. Furthermore, important sectors such as agriculture and the aviation industry either implicitly or explicitly still enjoy special treatment. Therefore, the existing subsidy code, of which the core is present in the world trade order, must be further developed in order to prevent subsidy competition between governments.[10]

National technology policy should be dealt with in the same way as national subsidies. Thus, the international subsidy code must set limits for industry-specific research subsidies. In contrast, there is no need for international institutional regulations concerning the improvement of the general conditions for research and development, for example, when countries generally improve the tax framework or the conditions for research and development, innovation, investment and entrepreneurial activity as well as organize basic research and further technology transfer so that their countries can be internationally competitive.

II.3   Administered protection

Anti-dumping and countervailing duty measures, though elegantly defensible on a theoretical level, can easily develop into a severe impediment for trade. They are defined by national legislation and can be captured by national interest groups. They represent a way around bound tariffs and (now) forbidden quantitative restraints. Even if they are not actually applied, the threat of using them entails uncertainty and may already lead to the 'appropriate' export behaviour. In economic categories, contingent protection represents effective protection. This 'administered protection'[11] seems to have become more important as an instrument of USA trade policy as a protectionist device in the course of time. The task for the WTO will be to contain the protectionist impact of this approach; standards have to be defined which must be respected by national anti-dumping laws.

---

[10]   On the difficulty of subsidy control, compare the EU experience.

[11]   A.O. Krueger (ed.), *The WTO as an International Organization* (Chicago, 1998), p. 8.

II.4   A new form of protectionism?

With the integration of the world economy due to globalization, single sectors, individual regions or specific groups may lose, most prominently, low-skilled labour in the industrialized countries. Although the academic debate is still unresolved with respect to the question whether the need for wage differentiation in industrial countries is due to labour-saving technological progress or due to intensified trade,[12] political pressure in industrialized countries may increase to take refuge in protectionist devices, especially in continental Europe where unemployment is high. This is a severe threat to the world trading system. Moreover, some developing countries fear becoming marginalized in a globalized world. The international community has to withstand these political pressures for more protectionism. The main response to this backlash of globalization must be to point out that each individual country will gain from an intensified international division of labour than under fragmented markets. It is the task of each country to find national measures to compensate the potential losers of globalization.

II.5   Social standards

As a response to globalization there have increasingly been calls to harmonize social norms internationally or to introduce worldwide minimum standards.[13] Several arguments are put forward. One is that it is ethically unacceptable to have workers in developing countries work under dramatically diverging conditions from those in the developed world. The other is that workers in industrialized countries cannot possibly compete against the low wages in the developing countries and that 'reasonable' social norms in industrial countries cannot be enforced if imports enter markets under 'substandard' norms. The harmonization of social norms is supposed to be accomplished by using trade policy measures as a threat. Countries which do not apply these standards would be denied access to markets elsewhere. Above all, the developing countries would be negatively affected by such an approach. These countries have a lower labour productivity and are thus unable to pay the same wages that industrialized countries can pay. For similar reasons neither can they be expected to adopt the industrialized countries' social security systems. Therefore, a worldwide harmonization of social standards should be avoided.

II.6   Free market access

The world trade order is essentially oriented to denying governments (or integrated regions) tariff and non-tariff instruments with which the governments could directly intervene in trade flows at their borders. Such instruments have been outlawed through a

---

[12]   R.B. Freeman, 'Are Your Wages Set in Beijing?' (1995) 9 *Journal of Economic Perspectives* 15–32; and R. Baldwin, 'Trade and Wages' (Symposium on 'Challenges for Highly Developed Countries in the Global Economy' of the Kiel Institute of World Economics, 20 March 1998).

[13]   On environmental norms see below.

negative catalogue. However, this does not guarantee that there will be free access to markets. Quite in contrast, national legislation has recently become more important as a market entry barrier than impediments at the border. Such barriers, arising from national legislation or informal practices, can include economic policy measures in the broadest sense, such as licensing procedures for economic activities, ie for facilities and for products, technical standards, arrangements for public procurement and interlocking ties between firms (as with Keiretsu in Japan) on the same or different levels of the vertical production structure, thereby discriminating against outsiders.[14]

Recently the tendency has become apparent to link market access more strongly to national regulations of the country of destination. Such conditions set up additional barriers to the international division of labour. The country-of-destination principle leaves it to the importing country to set the domestic standard as the yardstick for its imports. The result would be a potpourri of diverging standards representing barriers to trade; moreover, such regulations can easily be captured by interest groups. The attempt of GATT has been – and the aim of the WTO must be – to push back the role of the country-of-destination principle. Which regulations are set for the production of goods should be left to the discretion of the country of origin. The different regulations of national countries of origin should rather have equal standing competing with each other. A weakening of the country-of-origin principle and a strengthening of the country-of-destination principle will inevitably harm the multilateral order.[15] The goal of the world trade order is therefore that countries mutually accept the regulations of the country of origin for product quality and production processes in order to minimize transaction costs. Thus, competition among rules can thrive. Only in precisely demarcated cases, for example in public health protection, should the country of destination and its standards take precedence over the norms of the country of origin. But even then the measures adopted should involve neither discrimination nor protection.

II.7 Competition policy

In an international economic order, markets must not be closed or distorted through the market power of firms. The globalization of world markets makes markets more contestable, and in this sense free trade is the best competition policy; all measures which increase market access support competition policy. However, globalization also enables enterprises to orient their policies with the aim of creating international monopolistic positions and to exploit them in controlling prices to the disadvantage of buyers. Two issues arise in this respect: One is that national competition policies should not be oriented towards the advantage of domestic enterprises or home-based multinationals and should not permit firms to build up or exploit monopolistic positions internationally. The other is that (national or international) competition policy should counteract

---

[14]   S. Ostry, 'New Dimensions of Market Access: Challenges for the Trading System' in OECD, *New Dimensions of Market Access in a Globalizing World Economy* (Paris, 1995).

[15]   R.J. Langhammer, 'Die Weiterentwicklung der WTO: Wegbereiter einer weltumfassenden Harmonisierung von Regelwerken?' (1998) 27 WiST 121–126.

business practices intended to reduce competition, prevent the exploitation of market power, and help to improve the contestability of the world product markets.

An international institutional framework in which competition policy effectively restricts the misuse of monopolistic market positions and discourages competition-limiting mergers is not presently foreseeable. Currently, the international community does not appear close to an agreement on a right of complaint which parties injured by anti-competitive practices or policies could employ before an international court or an international competition authority empowered to enforce competition rules.[16] Thus, at present we can only expect to establish a few minimal competition policy rules for countries or integrated regions (such as the EU), either in the framework of the WTO[17] or the OECD. We must also consider the option that initially only some of the rules would be agreed upon by the most important OECD countries, because there are fundamental differences in their legal systems, as between Anglo-Saxon and continental European law. What will be necessary is to change the orientation of national competition policies. Restrictions on competition which domestic enterprises impose abroad will have to be taken into account so that a country harmed by another country's competition policy will have the right to obtain changes in the objectionable competition policy. An institutional consultation and sanctioning mechanism must be created.[18] The details of how a framework for competition policy can be achieved is currently being intensively discussed in the literature.[19] Under consideration are the effects doctrine with an international right to extraterritorial legal application,[20] treaty agreements – including bilateral treaties between the USA and Europe – on the concession of mutual competencies,[21] the harmonization of international competition law on the basis of national legal system[22] and the competition of institutional rules through mutual recognition, thus a *Cassis de Dijon* approach with an international interpretation.[23]

---

[16]   F.M. Scherer, *Competition Policies for an Integrated World Economy* (Washington, DC, 1994).

[17]   U. Immenga, 'Konzepte einer grenzüberschreitenden und international koordinierten Wettbewerbspolitik' (Kiel Working Paper 692, Institut für Weltwirtschaft, Kiel, 1995).

[18]   E.M. Graham, 'Competition Policy and the New Trade Agenda' in OECD, *New Dimensions of Market Access in a Globalizing World Economy* (Paris, 1995).

[19]   World Trade Organization, *Annual Report 1997* (Geneva, 1997), vol. I, *Specific Topic: Trade and Competition Policy.*

[20]   U. Immenga, 'Konzepte einer grenzüberschreitenden und international koordinierten Wettbewerbspolitik' (Kiel Working Paper 692, Institut für Weltwirtschaft, Kiel, 1995).

[21]   C.D. Ehlermann, 'The Role of Competition Policy in a Global Economy' in OECD, *New Dimensions of Market Access in a Globalizing World Economy* (Paris, 1995).

[22]   W. Fikentscher and U. Immenga (eds), 'Draft International Antitrust Code' in *Kommentierter Entwurf eines internationalen Wettbewerbsrechts mit ergänzenden Beiträgen* (Baden-Baden, 1995).

[23]   P. Nicolaides, 'Towards Multilateral Rules on Competition. The Problems in Mutual Recognition of National Rules' (1994) 17 *World Competition*, issue 3, 5–48.

II.8   Multilateral trading system and bilateralism

The multilateral trading system is not effectively protected against aggressive bilateral trade policy. The USA and the EU have set up new arsenals of trade policy instruments. These can be employed as retaliatory measures or market openers without regard for the mechanisms of the world trade order. Thus, with its instrument 'Super 301' the USA can react within the shortest period against trade policy measures of other countries. It can independently introduce trade-limiting measures against individual states. Agreed-on preferential trade treatment can be cancelled, import restrictions can be imposed and bilateral export limitation agreements can be arranged. With the so-called 'Trade Defense Instruments' the EU has created a similar apparatus. With these trade policy weapons, in the sense of result-oriented bilaterally conceived systems,[24] the two trading blocs have introduced the option to exempt themselves from the rules of the multilateral world trade order.[25] The danger exists that bilateral measures will escalate and that the multilateral order will thereby degenerate. The additional risk is that a large player like the USA receives preferential treatment by exerting a country-specific market access. Moreover, export interests can reach their targets outside the WTO; they no longer are a counterweight to the protectionist forces.[26] This weakens the WTO. An aggressive market-opening policy must be integrated into the rules of the world trade order. It is desirable to limit bilateralism.

II.9   Multilateral trading system versus regionalism

The territorial exception from the principle of most-favoured-nation treatment which holds for regional integration schemes (free trade areas, custom unions, preference zones) conjures up the fundamental danger that the multilateral order will disintegrate into regional blocs.[27] It is true that past experience suggests that regional integration has not led to significant segmentation.[28] The regional integration efforts in Latin America have so far tended to remain weak; the new regional integration in East Asia (the Asia–Pacific Economic Cooperation Council) is geared to market integration and is not set to create external barriers. European integration has had attractive power – it has not closed itself to the possibility of accepting additional members. Through the growth of regional integration, cum grano salis, the trade diversion effects at the expense of third parties were, despite protectionistic interventions, probably over-compensated, except for agriculture. The North American Free Trade Area (NAFTA) lacks the internal coherence

---

[24]   R. Dornbusch, 'Policy Options for Freer Trade: The Case of Bilateralism' in R.Z. Lawrence and C.L. Schultze (eds), *An American Trade Strategy: Options for the 1990s* (Washington, DC, 1990).

[25]   H. Klodt et al., 'Standort Deutschland: Strukturelle Herausforderungen im neuen Europa' (Kieler Studien, 265, Tübingen, 1994), p. 119.

[26]   A.O. Krueger (ed.), *The WTO as an International Organization* (Chicago, 1998), p. 9.

[27]   J. Bhagwati, 'Regionalism and Multilateralism' (1992) *World Economy* 535–555.

[28]   World Trade Organization, *Regionalism and the World of Trading System* (Geneva, 1995).

found in the EU. In spite of all this, the danger cannot be dismissed that regional blocs could become entangled in an escalating trade war. Thus, in the case of a conflict between the blocs, NAFTA could, even without a de jure common trade policy, tend to reinforce a possible aggressive trade policy on the part of the USA. Moreover, an extended regionalism in Europe, the Americas and Asia could divert interest away from the WTO and weaken the multilateral trade system. It is therefore important to find mechanisms which multilateralize regional integrations.

III.   Rules for New Areas of International Exchange

Besides the trade of traditional goods, new forms of international interdependence have come to the fore in the international division of labour, among them services and the exchange of factors of production, ie of technical knowledge, capital and labour. The movement of factors of production plays an important role in a new paradigm, namely in the context of locational competition among governments.

III.1   Services

Manufacturing accounts for 33 per cent of the world GDP; in the industrialized countries the share of manufacturing in GDP is much lower, 25 per cent in European countries and below 20 per cent in the USA.[29] Services make up 63 per cent of world GDP; compared to this, exports of services add up to 18–20 per cent (1993–1995) of total world exports (merchandise plus service trade). They have grown at a higher rate than traditional trade in the 1970s.

The international division of labour in the area of services relates to diverse phenomena: a service like an international telephone call may actually cross the border ('cross-border supply'), consumers or firms of one country may use the service in another country ('consumption abroad'), a service may be supplied in another country ('commercial presence') or individuals may travel to supply their service in another country ('presence of natural persons'). The diversity of services becomes apparent by GATT classification list with seven main categories (and 62 subcategories), namely distribution services, education services, communication services (including telecommunication services, audiovisual services such as motion picture production and distribution, radio and television services), health care services, professional services (including legal services, accounting services, advertising services, architecture, engineering), transportation services and travel and tourism services. In addition other areas and aspects have to be taken into consideration, as in the annexes, such as the movement of natural persons (temporary stay) and financial services.

---

[29]   H. Siebert, *Weltwirtschaft* (Stuttgart, 1997).

A rule system for the international exchange of services should hold for the whole variety of services. Since the phenomena to which rules are to be applied are so divergent, it is difficult to establish an all-encompassing international rule system. A major distinction is between border-crossing and local services analogous to tradeable and non-tradeable goods. For this classification, another distinction becomes relevant, namely between 'person-disembodied' and 'person-embodied' services.[30] Disembodied services are not 'embodied' in persons, for example, detail engineering using computer-supported programs, the development of software and the adoption of accounting systems. For the international trading order, these services (cross-border supply) are not very different from material goods. Just as commodities are carried by the transport system, disembodied services cross national borders by means of communication media. As a consequence, markets must be open for them just as they must be for commodities. Border-crossing disembodied services should be treated like commodities.

In the case of person-embodied services (consumption abroad, commercial presence, presence of natural persons), non-discrimination can be obtained through national treatment, ie equal treatment for foreigners and one's own nationals. With person-embodied services two cases are to be systematically distinguished. First, foreign enterprises may have a competitive advantage relative to domestic enterprises as a result of their organization, technical knowledge or other factors, without lower labour costs being the decisive factor. For example, a foreign insurance company may have a more favourable risk structure. Secondly, with person-embodied services the competitive advantages may be based on the low costs for labour alone, in which case national treatment of foreign suppliers is especially controversial. But even in this case it accords with the basic concept of the international division of labour that market access must be free. It must be permitted to suppliers from other countries to offer their services at the prices prevailing in the country of origin. In both cases, national treatment opens up market access.

The General Agreement on Trade in Services (GATS) established for the first time a framework for notification of existing rules, but it has a long way to go before a rule system for all forms of international services with free market access is fully developed.[31] Markets are yet to be opened in many respects, barriers discriminating against foreigners or non-discriminatory barriers erected by competition policy will have to be torn down and the product coverage must be extended. So far, these are exemptions to the most-favoured-nation (MFN) treatment (favour one, favour all); the conditionality of the most-favoured-nation clause prevalent in services must be extended to an unconditional use. National treatment as a central principle only applies to services where a country has made a specific commitment, exemptions are allowed. Moreover, the present approach is

---

[30]   J. Bhagwati, 'Splintering and Disembodiment of Services and Developing Nations' (1984) 7 *World Economy* 133–143; and H. Klodt et al., 'Standort Deutschland: Strukturelle Herausforderungen im neuen Europa' (Kieler Studien, 265, Tübingen, 1994), p. 128.

[31]   R.H. Snape, 'Reading Effective Agreements Covering Services' in A.O. Krueger (ed.), *The WTO as an International Organization* (Chicago, 1998), pp. 279–295.

to find agreements for specific services.[32] This sector-by-sector approach raises the risk that sector-specific aspects dominate; it has the disadvantage that it does not sufficiently harness the export interests of the economy as a whole in order to dismantle barriers of trade.[33]

III.2   Rules for the internationally mobile factors

Besides the exchange of goods and services, factor migrations are a further important form of interdependence between economies. Countries compete for mobile technical knowledge and mobile capital. Factor migrations are interlinked with the exchange of goods in various ways. In the case of technology and non-financial capital, factor migrations can occur through trade in goods or they even themselves represent trade in goods, as with the purchase or sale of user rights, for example patents. They may, in a comparative-static sense, take the place of movements of goods and thus serve as a substitute to commodity flows, but in a dynamic perspective they can, in the sense of acquired comparative advantage, also decisively influence future comparative advantages and thereby be forerunners for the trade of goods in the future.[34]

In contrast to the somewhat esoteric strategic trade literature, locational competition (*Standortwettbewerb*) may be a more relevant concept explaining the behaviour of governments in the global economy. According to this approach, governments compete for the mobile factors of production, namely mobile technical knowledge and mobile capital. The policy instruments governments can use in order to attract these mobile factors are institutional arrangements, taxes and infrastructure in the widest sense, including the educational and the university systems. If a country succeeds in attracting mobile production factors or in keeping them from leaving the country, the real income for the immobile production factors increases, especially for labour.

Some fear that competition among states will represent a downward spiral in the provision of public goods and that this race to the bottom will degenerate; this fear is unfounded.[35] Even with high taxation rates, capital will not emigrate if infrastructure is adequate and if the immobile labour supply possesses suitable qualifications, ie if human capital is well developed. Capital taxation can thus be compensated for (within limits), through the quality of public production factors, especially if these are financed in the

---

[32]   In financial services a multilateral agreement was reached in December 1997 with 70 WTO members; other sector agreements relate to telecommunication and information technology.

[33]   A.O. Krueger (ed.), *The WTO as an International Organization* (Chicago, 1998), p. 405.

[34]   H. Siebert, 'An Institutional Order for a Globalizing World Economy' in Klaus Jaeger and Karl-Josef Koch (eds), *Trade, Growth, and Economic Policy in Open Economies – Essays in Honour of Hans-Jürgen Vosgerau* (Heidelberg, 1998), pp. 331–349.

[35]   H. Siebert, 'On the Concept of Locational Competition' (Kiel Working Paper 731, Institut für Weltwirtschaft, Kiel, 1996); and H. Siebert, *Disziplinierung der nationalen Wirtschaftspolitik durch die internationale Kapitalmobilität. Zeitschrift für Wirtschafts- und Sozialwissenschaften des Vereins für Socialpolitik* (forthcoming, 1998).

sense of the principle of equivalence (or benefit taxation) from taxes or user prices. Rising marginal costs of production with lower human capital and poorer physical infrastructure ensure that locational competition for mobile capital finds a self-imposed lower limit. The better a country's provision of human and infrastructure capital, the less a country needs to permit locational competition. Consequently, an appropriate reaction is to allow locational competition among governments. Nevertheless, locational competition may be a new area of interest for the economic world order. Some aspects are discussed below.

III.3   Property rights

When countries compete for mobile technical knowledge, property rights become important. These relate to all sorts of intellectual property, copyright and associated rights, trademarks, industrial design, patents, the layout designs of integrated circuits and geographical indications (like appellations of origin). Issues to be solved (and already included in the Agreement on Trade-Related Aspects of Intellectual Property Rights (TRIPS)) are minimum standards of protection to be provided by the individual countries, enforcement of intellectual property rights and dispute settlements.

With respect to patents an institutional arrangement must be found which, by respecting property rights, offers sufficient incentives for individual economies to search for new knowledge, but simultaneously does not in the long term block possible diffusion of new knowledge throughout the world. Thus, a similar problem must be solved to that of a national patent system. On the one hand, user rights to new technical knowledge must be secure, since otherwise there will be insufficient incentives to search for and adopt new technical knowledge. This means that property rights to new knowledge must be respected throughout the world. On the other hand, this property protection must not create permanently exclusive positions and make markets uncompetitive. Rather, the diffusion of new knowledge must be possible after a certain passage of time; accordingly time limits should be set on the protective effect of user rights. The optimal duration of protective rights depends among other things on product life cycles and the time frame of research and development phases; this can differ greatly from product to product. Since countries may have an interest in protecting their firms' technological knowledge for as long as possible (although this reduces the incentives for their own technological dynamics), the solution cannot consist simply in mutually recognizing national patent laws. Rather, it may be desirable to set time limits on the validity of national patents. With respect to the other types of property right such as trademarks and geographical indications there is no necessity to let protection run out.

III.4   Rules for capital

International capital mobility limits national governments' freedom of action and changes the opportunity costs of economic policy decisions. This holds not only for the case when capital should be attracted, but also when its emigration should be prevented. For each economic policy consideration, for instance about the tax system, about infrastructure and about regulations, the cost–benefit calculus is affected by a higher capital mobility; the opportunity costs of economic decisions are raised if capital can choose between various locations.

One position for the rules on capital mobility is to assume that it is in the best interest of each country to keep capital at home and attract more capital from outside. Each country should structure its institutional framework accordingly, providing for the security of property rights, avoiding uncertainty about corporate taxes, developing a tax system and a general economic framework and supplying an efficient infrastructure, which all make the country attractive as a location. An important condition for an efficient international division of labour is therefore that capital should not be prevented from seeking better opportunities abroad. Otherwise countries would force their savers to invest solely at home. The allocation of savings would then be inefficient. An explicit exit right for savings is thereby a decisive element of the international division of labour. But an exit right is not a sufficient incentive if we consider physical capital which is locked in. Of course one can argue that we can leave capital mobility to the locational competition of governments. But even if in the end it is the host country's responsibility to enhance its own attractiveness, multilateral agreements can make the direct investments of the sending country more secure for its companies, and multilateral agreements may make potential recipient countries appear less risky for direct investments.[36] Moreover, uncertainty for investment may be a cause for uncertainty in trade. Consequently, an investment code is required which surpasses the trade-related investment measures (TRIMs). It is an open question whether a two-speed approach should be recommended for an investment code with the OECD countries going ahead and the WTO following or whether an investment code has better chances of being accepted if it is initiated by the WTO (Krueger 1998: 408).[37] Eventually, an investment code should include the developing countries; it should be administered by the WTO.

III.5   Rules for immigration

In all countries citizens should be guaranteed an exit option as a civil liberty. The right of individuals to leave a country, ie the exit option, can be interpreted as an important element of a liberal order. The individual should have the opportunity to choose to leave, given life conditions which he or she finds unacceptable. A credible right to exit which is respected by the government of the potential country of emigration is, as a rule, a limit on the actions of that government; it represents an implicit control of governmental actions and reduces the incentive for individuals to emigrate.

The exit option does not, however, imply the right to immigrate into any given country. States define their identity by setting their immigration policy.[38] This creates

---

[36]   The argument is analogous to subsidies to old industries which hurt the subsidizing country but cannot be ignored in the world trading order.

[37]   On WTO-Plus, see below.

[38]   A.L. Hillman, 'The Political Economy of Migration Policy' in H. Siebert (ed.), *Migration: A Challenge to Europe* (Tübingen, 1994), pp. 263–282.

difficult ethical questions which can be more easily resolved if potential countries of immigration – beyond the duty to accept the politically persecuted – are sufficiently open and if regional integrations such as the EU, although only spatially limited from an international economic perspective, guarantee freedom of movement within their territory. For many reasons labour migration should be replaced by the movement of goods and capital mobility. If a country finds open markets for its goods elsewhere and attracts capital, its citizens have less need to emigrate for economic reasons. The strengthening of an international economic order for the international exchange of goods and the openness of markets reduces the necessity of migration.

III.6   Stability in other areas, especially in the financial markets

A rule system for the exchange of goods and services and for the free movement of factors of production requires stability in other areas of international interdependence. The rule system of a trading order is not sustainable if other important areas of international interdependence are unstable. Obviously, political stability is a necessary condition for the WTO system (which itself contributes to international political stability). This can be discussed under the heading of interdependence of orders in the sense of Eucken;[39] it also has been addressed in a more technical sense as the issue of 'coherence' among international organizations.

Another condition discussed the absence of excessive exchange rate volatility and of instability in the financial markets. Exchange rate volatility leads time and again to demands for greater stability in the international currency system. It cannot be denied that nominal exchange rates are greatly influenced by financial flows and that they can overshoot and thus distort trade flows. No doubt, there can be speculative bubbles. However, the following points have to be taken into consideration.

First, currency convertibility is a very important ingredient of the world trading systems. Restricting the convertibility of currency for foreigners or citizens, setting different exchange rates for different transaction purposes, for example, for goods considered more or less important or for movements of goods and capital, granting privileged access to better exchange rates as in a system of import licences, and exchange rate protectionism all have negative consequences for the exchange of goods and the efficient allocation of capital. It is hard to profit from the international division of labour if currency convertibility is limited by different countries' political decisions. Especially after the experience of the 1930s, countries made efforts during the period of reconstruction following World War II to ensure convertibility and liberalize capital movements. Therefore, as a rule the need for currency convertibility is accepted today.

Secondly, the problem of excessive volatility in exchange rates can be solved by small countries with an exchange-rate-oriented monetary policy (the Netherlands, Austria in the D-Mark zone) or a currency board (Argentina, Estonia). These countries attach

---

[39]   W. Eucken, *Die Grundlagen der Nationalökonomie* (Berlin, 1940), translated as *The Foundations of Economics: History and Theory in the Analysis of Economic Reality* (Berlin, 1992).

themselves to a country with a stable price level. This has often been successful in the short term, but in the medium term it entails great pressure towards monetary, fiscal and wage policy adaptation to the situation in the anchor country. For large countries this solution is, as a rule, politically unacceptable. In addition, at least one larger country must be the stability leader. A solution for larger countries would be to submit to a system which guarantees stability. Historically the gold standard has been such a system. Countries refrained from employing a national stabilization policy. They accepted fluctuations in output and employment in order to maintain exchange rate stability. Such an approach is not internationally practical today: for one thing, no anchor is visible on the horizon (gold can hardly serve as such an anchor); for another, a readiness to submit to an international rule system is lacking.

Thirdly, other approaches for limiting the volatility of exchange rates must be regarded sceptically:

(i)   It will not prove possible to set up reference zones for exchange rates,[40] if the conditions for stability are not fulfilled in the individual countries.
(ii) The idea of a return to a system analogous to that of Bretton Woods ignores the fact that financial markets are now globalized.
(iii) Throwing sand into the gears of international financial markets[41] works against the aim of reducing transaction costs.

Fourthly, too often – if not always – the triggers for exchange rate volatility are political ones reflecting economic policy conditions, above all failed stabilization policy, fiscal disorder, misguided monetary policy and also real economic changes. Exchange rate movements thus represent a barometer of fundamental disturbances.

Under these conditions a solution can only consist in each individual country keeping its own house in order and maintaining a stable domestic price level. Then exchange rates will generally remain stable. This approach should be complemented by some minimum agreement on prudential rules for the financial sector in order to shield the overall system against instability.

IV.   Rules for the Use of the Environment

Globalization also means that awareness of global interdependence increases. This is especially relevant in the use of nature and the environment. Countries are not only interdependent in terms of goods, production factors and monetary transactions; they also influence each other through the use of nature and the environment as receptacles for wastes and emissions. However, a distinction should be made between whether national

---

[40]   Williamson 1983.

[41]   The 'Tobin tax': see J. Tobin, 'A Proposal for International Monetary Reform' (1978) *Eastern Journal* 153–159.

usage rights are definable for nature and the environment or whether global environmental goods are at stake.[42]

IV.1 The environment as a factor of national endowment

Just as countries are differently endowed with capital and labour, there are also territorial differences in the capacity of nature for absorbing emissions. The absorptive and regenerative capacities of regional environments vary. In addition, heavy population density makes it more difficult to separate spatially residential and recreational areas from environmentally degrading transport and production activities. The preferences of countries for environmental quality can differ as well. If the environment is an immobile resource factor, the prices for environmental services – as a receptacle of emissions – must also differ between countries. Different environmental scarcities will thus be signalled by different prices. A market economy approach to environmental policy which taxes emissions or establishes prices for environmental services through emission trading is consistent with an institutional framework for the international division of labour. Insofar as the environment is a national endowment factor, prices can express the different environmental scarcities of countries. The environment is then fundamentally not the object of an international rule system.

IV.2 Protecting health and conserving natural resources

If prices for environmental use are not (or cannot be) applied and other measures such as administrative approaches, emission norms or product standards are employed by countries to protect their citizens' health and life and to conserve natural resources (Article XX of GATT Treaty), those measures must be non-discriminatory. Non-discrimination requires that in the case of market entry restrictions, regulations through production permits, facility permits and product norms must not give preference to domestic producers and domestic goods. Thus, it should not be permissible, for example, with the aim of reducing health hazards, as in the Thailand cigarette case (1990),[43] to restrict the import of goods or to tax them unless the same measures are simultaneously taken against similar domestic goods.

The similarity of the goods plays a crucial role in non-discrimination. Similarity of products should be defined from the demand side, for example, in terms of possible harmful effects, and not from the production side, ie from the production technology. As in the Mexican–American tuna fish case (1991),[44] the principle of similarity should not be applied to the production methods (in the tuna fish case methods of fishing which do not sufficiently protect dolphins). This means that the country-of-origin principle should apply.

---

[42] H. Siebert, *Economics of the Environment. Theory and Policy* (5th revised edn, Heidelberg, 1998). Border-crossing environmental problems (transfrontier pollution) require a specific solution. The upstream country should compensate the downstream country with the prices for emissions used in the upstream country; they reveal its willingness to pay.

[43] Thailand – Restrictions on importation of and external taxes on cigarettes, DS10.

[44] United States – Restrictions on imports of tuna, DS21.

Non-discrimination should also satisfy the condition that measures taken are in accordance with the proportionality principle. Measures must accordingly be necessary in the sense that environmental policy aims or the protection of natural resources cannot otherwise be achieved. As a rule, these aims are, however, better achieved through specific environmental policy measures rather than through trade policy. Thus, if environmental policy employs a regulatory approach to national environments, the non-discrimination and country-of-origin principles should apply.

IV.3   The territorial principle as a restraint for national measures

Since countries have different amounts of environmental resources and also different environmental preferences, those with stronger environmental preferences should not be entitled to impose their environmental preferences on other countries by means of trade-restricting measures.[45] The thesis that the country-of-origin principle should be fundamentally recognized for national environments is generalizable. If harmful effects appear outside a country's territorial area, countries should not have the right to use trade policy to influence the production methods of a country of origin. Also, the protective clauses for health, life and exhaustible resources of Article XX should in the case of national environmental goods be applied only within a country's own territorial area. Countries should thus not have the right to employ unilateral measures to protect the environment in other countries. Thus, trade policy must not be employed to force national preferences on other countries. Any country's environmental policy should not apply to external effects outside its own territorial area.

In the technical terms of the economist, environmental quality in a foreign country may well be an element in the utility functions of the home country's citizens. And if they are willing to compensate the foreign country for undertaking environment policy, that is just fine. The concept of externality cannot go as far as to extend to emotional externalities which then would legitimate a right of the home country against the foreign country to become active.[46]

IV.4   The environment as a global public good

In contrast to national environmental goods, global environmental goods are public goods with a worldwide spatial dimension. In what amount and with what quality these public goods should be produced requires the agreement of all countries. What must be

---

[45]   H. Siebert, *Trade Policy and Environmental Protection. The World Economy, Global Trade Policy 1996* (Cambridge, MA, 1996), pp. 183–194.

[46]   The territorial principle in this interpretation finds its limit when a country does damage to another country (or violates its rights) as in the case of transfrontier pollution. Then international public law even allows reprisal under specific condition (E. Mohr and J. Thomas, 'Are Legality Constraints on International Sanctions a Codification of Economic Optimality?' (mimeo, 1998)). Compare also the effects doctrine in competition policy which is a way to acknowledge an interdependence.

decided on is not just the extent to which emissions should be reduced, but also the proper distribution of costs among individual countries. It is difficult to reach international consensus, because countries have different preferences and because they have different per capita incomes and thus a different willingness to pay. In addition, the cost functions for disposal differ from country to country. Moreover, nations can behave as a free-rider. Thus, implementing the polluter-pays principle for global goods runs into difficulties. To what extent a stable international environmental framework with voluntary commitments by states can be created under these conditions using compensatory payments is a complex issue and has been the subject of numerous studies.

IV.5 The consistency of the international trade order and the international environmental order

Environmental policy aims at protecting the natural conditions for life; ie, it deals with scarcity. An institutional order for the international division of labour attempts to make it possible to increase the prosperity of all countries through exchange, ie it also deals with scarcity. Both orders attempt to do away with distortions. Since environmental policy and international trade intersect at many points, the rules of both frameworks should not conflict. The aims are not in principle contradictory, since scarcity must be defined by taking the natural conditions for life into account. If we start from the premise that the valuation of the goods on which affluence is based as well as the valuation of environmental quality must depend on the formation of the national will, a contradiction between both regimes can be avoided.

In the past international arrangements for environmental questions and the world trade order were developed separately and independently. In the future it will be important to pay more attention to the consistency of both orders. The more successfully the environment as a scarce good is integrated into the economic orders of individual countries and the more affluence is defined by taking into account nature and the environment as well as economic conditions, the sooner congruence of targets will be achieved between both orders. Compared to the administrative approach using regulations, the market economy approach to environmental policy provides more congruence between both sets of rules. The sooner the polluter-pays principle is accepted as a guideline by all countries, the easier it will be to achieve consistency of the two orders in the case of global environmental concerns. This clearly holds for national environmental goods. For global goods, implementing the polluter-pays principle has to overcome the difficulties mentioned above like the differences in preferences, in willingness-to-pay and free-rider behaviour. What would be needed is a consensus on the conditions under which the polluter-pays principle can be applied to global goods; this is equivalent to a consensus under which conditions compensations must be used.[47]

---

[47] We could also consider a minimal solution which would define improvements in environmental quality (or reduction of emissions) relative to the current state. Since, however, the costs of improving a given state of the environment differ from country to country, acceptance is doubtful. Cf. the discussion on the victim-pays principle for cases of border-crossing environmental problems: H. Siebert, *Economics of the Environment. Theory and Policy* (5th revised edn, Heidelberg, 1998).

Inconsistencies between the WTO system and environmental agreements should be prevented.[48] The world trading order and groups of countries signing international environmental agreements should not be too divergent.

IV.6   Consistency on the operational level

Even if the international environmental order and the international trade order must have consistent aims, the rules of both orders must, however, not be contingent upon each other (see below). The set of instruments of both orders must be kept separate. The following orientational points could minimize aim conflicts:

(i)   The rules in the world environmental order and the world trade order should not be mutually conditional. This would cause considerable uncertainty not only in the international division of labour, but also in the production of environmental goods. Institutional orders should not be uncertain.

(ii)   Judging from past experience it appears ill-advised to create a temporary waiver for environmental issues as an exception to the world trade order. One reason is that the previously created exemptions for the agricultural and textile sectors have become resistant to change and have led to a permanent infringement of the most-favoured-nation principle. If an exceptional regulation is questionable even in the case of internationally declining sectors, then a similar procedure appears still less desirable for an area that will be increasingly important in the future.

(iii) Trade policy instruments should not be employed for environmental policy purposes. Countries should not have the right to apply their environmental policy outside their own territory. Non-discrimination and the priority of the country-of-origin principle over the country-of-destination principle should be guiding principles.

(iv)   The mediation of disputes by the WTO should be extended to include the environmental domain.

(v)   In the case of global environmental goods a consensus should be developed specifying the circumstances in which the polluter-pays principle and compensations should be applied.

V.   Approaches to Strengthen the World Order

The world trading order is permanently in a battle between forces that will weaken it by striving for a larger role of strategic behaviour of nation states and forces that attempt to contain and to push back the non-cooperative behaviour of national governments. As an international agreement among sovereign nation states, the world trading order requires mechanisms that stabilize the rule system. We distinguish:

---

[48]   H. Siebert, *Trade Policy and Environmental Protection. The World Economy, Global Trade Policy 1996* (Cambridge, MA, 1996), pp. 183–194.

(i)   negative incentives, ie sanctions, that enforce rule behaviour;
(ii)   adjusting existing rules and creating new rules to fill the void; and
(iii) positive incentives that improve the acceptance of rules and suggest joining the rule system.

V.1   Sanctions

An important mechanism in international contracts is sanctions which can be taken if rules are violated. The WTO dispute settlement procedure is such a mechanism. Relative to GATT, the dispute settlement procedure has been strengthened. Whereas the ruling of a panel set up to decide the dispute can be appealed before the Appellate Body, the decision of the Appellate Body is binding unless all parties are against its adoption. When the Dispute Settlement Body (DSB) has adopted the panel or the appellate report, the losing party must either propose a suitable implementation of the report's recommendations or negotiate compensation payments with the complaining party. If there is no agreement on compensation or if the losing party does not implement the proposed changes, the DSB can authorize the other party to impose retaliatory measures such as counter-tariffs. The retaliation can occur in the same sector, in other sectors or even in other agreements.

The litmus test of the settlement procedure is whether global players will accept the verdicts of the dispute panels and of the Appellate Body. The preliminary experience so far is a tentative yes. For instance, the EU has accepted the WTO dispute settlement panel decision from September 1997 concerning the EU import system for bananas and will change the import rules in accordance with the WTO trade agreement.[49] The USA has lost four cases in the WTO panels and has each time accepted the outcome.[50] The two major trading blocs have used the WTO settlement procedure frequently. The EU has brought cases to the WTO panels 21 times and the USA 35 times; this can be taken as an indicator of acceptance.

Still an open question is to what extent major players like the USA will use their own national sanctions such as the USA 'Super 301' from the Omnibus Trade Act of 1988 outside the WTO rule system or whether aggressive bilateralism can be controlled under the WTO roof. With an effective dispute settlement procedure firmly in place, there is no longer a need for clauses like the USA 'Super 301'. Bilateral negotiations outside the

---

[49]   In another case, the USA–EU dispute over growth hormones in cattle, on 13 February 1998, the DSB has accepted the Appellate Body report stating that the EU ban on imports of meat and meat products from cattle treated with hormones for growth promotion is inconsistent with WTO agreements unless qualified scientific studies are forwarded pointing to the health risks of such meat products.

[50]   Three minor cases concern silk shirts, underwear and imported gasoline, and a major case involved Fuji and Eastman Kodak in 1997. (Japan – Measures affecting consumer photographic film and paper WT/S44.) Kodak tried to prove that Japanese bureaucrats had given Fuji an advantage over Kodak in the Japanese market, impeding Kodak's access to Japanese retail outlets. But the WTO panel rejected the complaint, arguing that the Japanese government had not prevented Kodak from competing fairly in Japan.

WTO framework and under threat of national sanctions defy the foundations of the multilateral trading regimes. Therefore, developments like the application of the 'Super 301' or the Helms–Burton Act should be closely monitored and clearly denounced.

V.2   Positive mechanisms

Besides sanctions, the world trading order has to contain mechanisms that attempt to strengthen the institutional arrangement and to expand it. One such mechanism is the MFN clause which extends reductions of trade barriers to third parties and thus multilaterizes liberalizations. Another mechanism is reciprocity of concessions requiring that the tariff reduction of one country must be answered by other countries (even though the concept of reciprocity has its roots in a mercantilistic philosophy). Yet another mechanism is to bind tariffs so that the results of liberalization rounds are chiselled in stone and countries cannot easily walk away from agreements reached.[51] We have to look for other such principles which can strengthen the world trade order.[52]

V.3   Filling in the void

The rules must follow the problems and the rule-evading behaviour of participants. When new areas develop in the international division of labour an institutional vacuum exists where no rules apply. This void has to be filled, for instance, in the area of the trade in services. Participants may also find ways around the rules, ie they may substitute one means of protection for another. An example is quantitative restraints (including voluntary export restraints) as a way around bound tariffs. In the future, national legislation may play a more important role, as in product standards, licensing of activities, administered protection, competition policy, social standards and environmental norms. Care must be taken that the protectionistic content of domestic legislation is contained.

V.4   The prospect of an increase in future benefits

An essential condition for the creation and the stability of an international economic order is that the institutional framework must be acceptable to all countries. Therefore, the transition from non-cooperative to cooperative behaviour must have an advantage for each country. For this, an important prerequisite is that benefits are expected in the future.

---

[51]   A country that wants to raise the bound tariff has to negotiate with the countries most concerned; it may have to compensate for the trading partners' loss of trade.

[52]   J. Tumlir, 'Weltwirtschaftsordnung: Regeln, Kooperation und Souveränität' (Kieler Vorträge 87, Institut für Weltwirtschaft, Kiel, 1979) has proposed giving individuals the right to go to the domestic courts if rules of the world trading order are violated. Domestic courts would thus enforce the rules of the international system. I am, in principle, sympathetic to this proposal. However, it requires a clear-cut rule system for the international division of labour which does not exist. Practical experience with courts and labour laws in some European countries suggests that courts have limited efficiency. Moreover, in a time when the rule system for trade has somehow to incorporate environmental issues, the rule system is extremely unclear. The same holds for class action suits in domestic courts.

From an intertemporal perspective, the global rule system is a relational contract[53] in which countries interact along a time axis and in which a strategic gain from non-cooperative behaviour today must be confronted with the opportunity costs of retaliation in future periods. Honouring a rule system or violating it must be interpreted as a repeated game in which an agent accumulates or destroys reputation and in which the preparedness of the other agents to cooperate tomorrow is affected by the agent's behaviour today. These intertemporal linkages help to prevent reneging on the contract and give stability to the system.

For the stability of institutional arrangements it is therefore crucial that the individual country's cost–benefit calculations should not shift asymmetrically over time into the negative; quite to the contrary, the net advantage for each country should increase over time. If this condition is not fulfilled, there will be an incentive not to honour the treaty, but instead to withdraw from it. It must pay to stick to the rules because there will be a reward in the future. As a practical consequence, when the rule system is expanded by a new member, there must be net advantages to the old members of the club.

V.5 Packaging advantages and the single undertaking nature of the WTO

An institutional order consists of several suborders. Inevitably, the suborders are interdependent, in Eucken's sense.[54] A specific suborder may benefit one country more than another, while another suborder may be more advantageous for another country. A greater advantage from one suborder can compensate for the lesser advantage of another suborder. This aspect is significant for the acceptance of new suborders. Packaging advantages into one bundle is a promising approach in order to find acceptance for an international institutional framework in cases in which an agreement on suborders cannot be reached.

The single undertaking nature of the WTO reflects the concept of packaging the benefits arising in different areas of the international division of labour. In the past, plurilateral agreements, introduced in the Tokyo Round, allowed a subset of GATT members to sign contracts for specific areas.[55] Such a procedure, though easing a contract among at least some GATT members, represents an à la carte approach and entails the risk of fragmentation of the multilateral trading system.[56] In principle, it can be expected

---

53   I.R. MacNeil, 'Contracts. Adjustment of Long-Term Economic Relations under Classical, Neoclassical, and Relational Contract Law' (1978) 72 *Northwestern University Law Review* 854–905.

54   W. Eucken, *Die Grundlagen der Nationalökonomie* (Berlin, 1940), translated as *The Foundations of Economics: History and Theory in the Analysis of Economic Reality* (Berlin, 1992).

55   The Agreement on Civil Aircraft, the Agreement on Government Procurement, the International Dairy Agreement and the International Bovine Agreement (the two last terminated at the end of 1997).

56   R.J. Langhammer, 'Nach dem Ende der Uruguay-Runde: Das GATT am Ende?' (Kieler Diskussionsbeiträge, 228, Institut für Weltwirtschaft, Kiel, 1994), p. 11 shows that the à la carte approach led to a large variance in country coverage of individual agreements under the Tokyo Round umbrella.

that the single undertaking nature of WTO will strengthen the rule system because it forces countries to swallow less favourable rules in one area if they are compensated by rules allowing higher benefits in other areas. The approach of packaging is also helpful in focusing bargaining when a liberalization round is being concluded.

V.6   Preventing institutional domino effects

Packaging benefits stabilizes interdependent suborders. However, this all-or-nothing approach may have its drawbacks and some exceptions may indeed be helpful if they are associated with a process that leads to more liberalization over time.[57] The 'offsetting' between the advantages of suborders should not be carried too far. If in the course of time the advantages of countries shift asymmetrically in the individual suborders, a fragile structure of acceptance could collapse like a house of cards. To avoid domino effects, it makes sense that the suborders should basically legitimate themselves on their own and not be conditionally accepted.

The interdependence of suborders raises other issues. One is that the suborders may contradict each other. Apparently, they must be mutually consistent. One suborder must not lead to behaviour on the part of economic agents which contradicts and undermines some other suborder. As a consequence, suborders must have the same or similar objectives or philosophies. An important example of this consistency issue is the relation between the world trade order and the world environmental order (see above). In any case, the interdependence of suborders must be taken into consideration when an overall rule system is developed.

Another issue is to what extent the withdrawal of benefits from one suborder can be used as a threat or sanction to abide by the rules of the other suborder. In a game-theoretic approach threatening the withdrawal of benefits from one rule system may be an effective inducement to join (and to respect) another rule system. However, this approach makes one suborder contingent on another order. If one institutional system falls, the other falls too. This raises the risk that the overall rule system is endangered. Therefore, the advantage of threatening with the withdrawal of benefits of one suborder must be weighed against the risk of destroying the overall rule system.

Thus, the question to what extent the withdrawal of benefits of one suborder can be used to establish or stabilize another is open. A possible approach to this question is to distinguish explicitly between two different stages, namely the creation of an institutional arrangement and the implementation of the rule system associated with it. In establishing a new institutional framework, withholding benefits to non-members from another subsystem is a strong sanction that is positive for establishing the new order. Once an institutional arrangement is established, however, the validity of one suborder should – as a principle – not be contingent on the functioning of some other suborder in order to prevent institutional domino effects. This means that the instrumental levels should be

---

[57]   An analogous question relates to regional integration processes. For instance in European integration, integration at different speeds has been proposed to propel the integration process.

clearly separated.[58] As a rule, economic policy instruments available to an international institution should be limited to specific suborders. Trade policy instruments should not be employed for environmental policy purposes; the instrumental level should thus be modularly subdivided and demarcated.

V.7 Determining for which areas no rules should be developed

We have discussed several areas into which the WTO has to be expanded: services, investment, property rights and the use of the environment. Other areas are debated such as competition policy, labour and social standards. Quite clearly, the rule system has to respond to new issues. But somewhere there must be a line beyond which the WTO is not and should not be in charge. A more theoretical answer is that the WTO should be concerned with rules for the international division of labour, including trade in goods and services and international factor mobility and global public good environment. A basic principle is that differences in endowment are accepted as the starting point for the international division of labour arbitraged by trade and factor flows. This would exclude protectionism, harmonization and worldwide redistribution. A more practical answer is to look at which areas nation states are ready to accept being partly ruled by the WTO and which new areas of rules the WTO can absorb into its rule system without losing efficacy. This practical aspect may require some caution.

V.8 Banning distributional aspects from the world trading order

A rule system should allow countries to gain from the international division of labour, but it cannot possibly solve the issue of distribution of benefits between nation states. From trade, all countries can gain. Introducing distributional constraints will make the world order ineffective. Such issues including the alleviation of poverty have to be solved in other ways.[59]

V.9 Multilateralizing regional integrations

An exemption from the single undertaking nature of WTO is the waiver for regional integrations. Much has been written on the relationship between regionalism and multilateralism, especially on the question whether regionalism is the correct road that eventually leads to a strong multilateral order.[60] In the last 50 years, regionalism by and large has not been a hindrance to a multilateral trade order. But this is no guarantee for

---

[58] This raises the question of credibility. If the sanction of withdrawing the benefits from one subsystem is not the best policy response in the implementation phase, the threat of such a sanction in the phase of establishing the order may lose credibility.

[59] This also points out the difficulty which arises when an attempt is made to combine the world trading order and an international environmental order for global media. The allocation of property rights for using global environmental media is a distributional issue *par excellence*.

[60] J. Bhagwati, 'Regionalism and Multilateralism' (1992) *World Economy* 535–555.

the future. Regionalism can always become inward looking; as a 'hub and spoke' agreement[61] it can be part of an aggressive bilateralism.

Extending regional integrations with preference zones opens up regional integrations, but it may also strengthen a hub and spoke system where the hubs are the centres of a bilateral world. Thus, preference zones are not a sufficient guarantee of multilateralization. An important precondition for multilateralizing regional integrations is to keep regional integrations open for new members. A strong mechanism for this is for members of integrated regions to grant concessions to third countries, in the sense of conditional most-favoured-nation treatment where conditional means that the third countries have to grant similar concessions in order to benefit from the trade barrier reductions achieved within the integrated region.[62] This could be done on a voluntary basis, but the WTO could also agree on a timetable for multilateralization.[63] All this is not sufficient. A mechanism must be found by which the barriers erected by regional subsystems of the world are reduced in the course of time; there is no automatic mechanism serving that objective. In the past, the liberalization rounds have fulfilled that task. Possibly, specific criteria should be established for the waiver to be accepted such as applying the Kemp-Wan criteria[64] or allowing only customs unions with the lowest tariff level of members as the common tariff.[65] Another approach is to link regional integrations by agreements going further than the WTO system (see below).

V.10 Extending to new members

Enlarging the membership of the WTO club will generate additional benefits to the old members. The new members will have benefits as well. Enlargement of the membership is therefore an important mechanism to make the system more attractive.

In the long run, the optimal size of WTO is the world as a whole because then all potential benefits of the international division of labour are exploited. In the short run, however, there is one important condition for the extension of membership. The rule system should not be weakened but strengthened when a new member enters. The pending accessions of China and the Russian Federation illustrate that a new member can have a strong impact on the WTO rule system. New members must accept the rule system as a single undertaking; they must have a track record showing that they have followed the basic WTO philosophy for some time. Moreover, economic conditions in the

---

[61]   Richard Blackhurst, 'The WTO and the Global Economy' (1997) 20 *World Economy* 527–544 at 531.

[62]   H. Klodt et al., 'Standort Deutschland: Strukturelle Herausforderungen im neuen Europa' (Kieler Studien, 265, Tübingen, 1994), p. 118.

[63]   T.N. Srinivasan, 'Regionalism and the WTO: Is Nondiscrimination Passé?' in A.O. Krueger (ed.), *The WTO as an International Organization* (Chicago, 1998).

[64]   A.O. Krueger (ed.), *The WTO as an International Organization* (Chicago, 1998), p. 23. This requires trade volume with third countries to be higher after than before the customs union.

[65]   J. Bhagwati, *The World Trading System at Risk* (New York, 1991), p. 71.

potential new member countries must be such that the countries are fit to survive in the world market.

V.11 Extending the frontier by a WTO-Plus

Another positive mechanism is to allow new problems to be solved by a subset of WTO members. These countries could commit themselves to realizing attempted results of the WTO rounds 'more quickly than planned, liberalize more than agreed and employ the permitted exceptions less often'.[66] Such a WTO-Plus, a world integration *à deux vitesses*, could advance the integration process in the world economy. This also holds for dovetailing various regional blocs by establishing a free trade zone between the blocs, for instance in a transatlantic economic area.[67]

VI. Bibliography

Axelrod, R., 'An Evolutionary Approach to Norms' (1986) 80 *American Political Science Review* 1095–1111

Baldwin, R., 'Trade and Wages' (Symposium on 'Challenges for Highly Developed Countries in the Global Economy' of the Kiel Institute of World Economics, 20 March 1998)

Bhagwati, J., 'Splintering and Disembodiment of Services and Developing Nations' (1984) 7 *World Economy* 133–143

—— *The World Trading System at Risk* (New York, 1991)

—— 'Regionalism and Multilateralism' (1992) *World Economy* 535–555

Blackhurst, Richard, 'The WTO and the Global Economy' (1997) 20 *World Economy* 527–544

Dornbusch, R., 'Policy Options for Freer Trade: The Case of Bilateralism' in R.Z. Lawrence and C.L. Schultze (eds), *An American Trade Strategy: Options for the 1990s* (Washington, DC, 1990)

Ehlermann, C.D., 'The Role of Competition Policy in a Global Economy' in OECD, *New Dimensions of Market Access in a Globalizing World Economy* (Paris, 1995)

Eucken, W., *Die Grundlagen der Nationalökonomie* (Berlin, 1940), translated as *The Foundations of Economics: History and Theory in the Analysis of Economic Reality* (Berlin, 1992)

Finger, J.M., M.D. Ingco and U. Reincke, *The Uruguay Round – Statistics on Tariff Concessions Given and Received* (World Bank, Washington, DC, 1996)

---

[66] Sachverständigenrat zur Begutachtung der gesamtwirtschaftlichen Entwicklung, *Den Aufschwung sichern – Arbeitsplätze schaffen. Jahresgutachten 1994/95* (Stuttgart, 1994), p. 242.

[67] H. Siebert, R.J. Langhammer and D. Piazolo, 'The Transatlantic Free Trade Area – Fuelling Trade Discrimination or Global Liberalization?' (1996) 30 *Journal of World Trade* 45–61.

Fikentscher, W. and U. Immenga (eds), 'Draft International Antitrust Code' in *Kommentierter Entwurf eines internationalen Wettbewerbsrechts mit ergänzenden Beiträgen* (Baden-Baden, 1995)

Freeman, R.B., 'Are Your Wages Set in Beijing?' (1995) 9 *Journal of Economic Perspectives* 15–32

Graham, E.M., 'Competition Policy and the New Trade Agenda' in OECD, *New Dimensions of Market Access in a Globalizing World Economy* (Paris, 1995)

Grossman, G.M. and E. Helpman, 'Trade Wars and Trade Talks' (1995) 103 *Journal of Political Economy* 675–708

Gundlach, E., H. Klodt, R.J. Langhammer and R. Soltwedel, 'Fairneß im Standortwettbewerb? Auf dem Weg zur internationalen Ordnungspolitik' in *Fairneß im Standortwettbewerb* (Gütersloh, 1996)

Haggard, S. and B. Simmons, 'Theories of International Regimes' (1987) 41 *International Organization* 491–517

Hillman, A.L., 'The Political Economy of Migration Policy' in H. Siebert (ed.), *Migration: A Challenge to Europe* (Tübingen, 1994), pp. 263–282

Hoekman, B.M. and P.C. Mavroidis, 'Competition, Competition Policy and GATT' (1994) 17 *World Economy* 121–150

Immenga, U., 'Konzepte einer grenzüberschreitenden und international koordinierten Wettbewerbspolitik' (Kiel Working Paper 692, Institut für Weltwirtschaft, Kiel, 1995)

Klodt, H. et al., 'Standort Deutschland: Strukturelle Herausforderungen im neuen Europa' (Kieler Studien, 265, Tübingen, 1994)

Kowalczyk, C. and T. Sjöström, 'Bringing GATT into the Core' (1994) 61 *Economica* 301–317

Krueger, A.O. (ed.), *The WTO as an International Organization* (Chicago, 1998)

Langhammer, R.J., 'Nach dem Ende der Uruguay-Runde: Das GATT am Ende?' (Kieler Diskussionsbeiträge, 228, Institut für Weltwirtschaft, Kiel, 1994)

—— 'Die Weiterentwicklung der WTO: Wegbereiter einer weltumfassenden Harmonisierung von Regelwerken?' (1998) 27 WiST 121–126

Low, P., 'Market Access through Market Presence' in OECD, *New Dimensions of Market Access in a Globalizing World Economy* (Paris, 1995)

MacNeil, I.R., 'Contracts. Adjustment of Long-Term Economic Relations under Classical, Neoclassical, and Relational Contract Law' (1978) 72 *Northwestern University Law Review* 854–905

Mattoo, A. and P. Mavroidis, 'Trade, Environment and the WTO: How Real is the Conflict?' in *Welthandel und Umweltschutz – Wie handeln wir ökologisch?* (Münster, 1996), pp. 61–83

Mohr, E. and J. Thomas, 'Are Legality Constraints on International Sanctions a Codification of Economic Optimality?' (mimeo, 1998)

Moser, P., 'Toward an Open World Order: A Constitutional Economics Approach' (1988) 9 *Cato Journal* 133–147

Nicolaides, P., 'Towards Multilateral Rules on Competition. The Problems in Mutual Recognition of National Rules' (1994) 17 *World Competition*, issue 3, 5–48

North, D., *Institutions, Institutional Change and Economic Performance* (Cambridge, 1990)

Ostry, S., 'New Dimensions of Market Access: Challenges for the Trading System' in OECD, *New Dimensions of Market Access in a Globalizing World Economy* (Paris, 1995)

—— 'A New Regime of Foreign Direct Investment' (Group of Thirty, Washington Occasional Paper 53, 1997)

Ruggiero, R., 'From Vision to Reality: The Multilateral Trading System at Fifty' (Brookings Institution Forum on 'The Global Trading System: A Gatt 50th Anniversary Forum', 4 March 1998)

Sachverständigenrat zur Begutachtung der gesamtwirtschaftlichen Entwicklung, *Den Aufschwung sichern – Arbeitsplätze schaffen. Jahresgutachten 1994/95* (Stuttgart, 1994)

Sauvé, P. and A.B. Zampetti, 'New Dimensions of Market Access: An Overview' in OECD, *New Dimensions of Market Access in a Globalizing World Economy* (Paris, 1995)

Scherer, F.M., *Competition Policies for an Integrated World Economy* (Washington, DC, 1994)

Senti, R., *WTO. The New World Trade Order. Materialien* (Institut für Wirtschaftsforschung, ETH Zürich, 1997)

Siebert, H., *Außenwirtschaft* (6th revised edn, Stuttgart, 1994)

—— 'Ein Regelwerk für eine zusammenwachsende Welt' (Kieler Diskussionsbeiträge 251, Institut für Weltwirtschaft, Kiel, 1995)

—— 'On the Concept of Locational Competition' (Kiel Working Paper 731, Institut für Weltwirtschaft, Kiel, 1996)

—— *Trade Policy and Environmental Protection. The World Economy, Global Trade Policy 1996* (Cambridge, MA, 1996), pp. 183–194

—— *Weltwirtschaft* (Stuttgart, 1997)

—— 'An Institutional Order for a Globalizing World Economy' in Klaus Jaeger and Karl-Josef Koch (eds), *Trade, Growth, and Economic Policy in Open Economies – Essays in Honour of Hans-Jürgen Vosgerau* (Heidelberg, 1998), pp. 331–349

—— *Disziplinierung der nationalen Wirtschaftspolitik durch die internationale Kapitalmobilität. Zeitschrift für Wirtschafts- und Sozialwissenschaften des Vereins für Socialpolitik* (1998)

—— *Economics of the Environment. Theory and Policy* (5th revised edn, Heidelberg, 1998)

Siebert, H., R.J. Langhammer and D. Piazolo, 'The Transatlantic Free Trade Area – Fuelling Trade Discrimination or Global Liberalization?' (1996) 30 *Journal of World Trade* 45–61

Snape, R.H., 'Reading Effective Agreements Covering Services' in A.O. Krueger (ed.), *The WTO as an International Organization* (Chicago, 1998), pp. 279–295

Spinanger, D., 'The WTO after the Singapore Ministerial: Much to Do about What?' (Kieler Diskussionsbeiträge 304, Institut für Weltwirtschaft, Kiel, 1997)

Srinivasan, T.N., 'Regionalism and the WTO: Is Nondiscrimination Passé?' in A.O. Krueger (ed.), *The WTO as an International Organization* (Chicago, 1998)

Stähler, F., 'Reflections on Multilateral Environmental Agreements' in *Economic Policy for the Environment and Natural Resources* (Cheltenham, 1996), pp. 174–196

Tobin, J., 'A Proposal for International Monetary Reform' (1978) *Eastern Journal* 153–159

Tumlir, J., 'Weltwirtschaftsordnung: Regeln, Kooperation und Souveränität' (Kieler Vorträge 87, Institut für Weltwirtschaft, Kiel, 1979)

—— 'International Economic Order and Democratic Constitutionalism' (1983) 34 ORDO 71–83

Worth, D.C., 'Market Access in the Global Economy' in OECD, *New Dimensions of Market Access in a Globalizing World Economy* (Paris, 1995)

World Trade Organization, *Regionalism and the World Trading System* (Geneva, 1995)

—— *Annual Report 1997* (Geneva, 1997), vol. I, *Specific Topic: Trade and Competition Policy*

Chapter 13
Managing Liberalization, Regionalism and Globalization in the Next 50 Years

Augustine H.H. Tan

As we look back over the last 50 years, we cannot but agree that we have much to be thankful for: trade liberalization through the efforts of the General Agreement on Tariffs and Trade (GATT) and its successor, the World Trade Organization (WTO), has borne astonishing fruits in the fourteen-fold increase in merchandise trade and the nearly six-fold rise in world production. This accomplishment is all the more amazing when one recalls that the predecessor organization, GATT, had no real enforcement powers and unprecedented changes had to be accommodated in the global economy. More importantly, despite regional wars and conflicts, there has been no world war and no world depression. The long queue of 31 aspiring new members of WTO is further testimony to the importance and effectiveness of the organization. Nevertheless, we cannot be complacent. After the break-up of the Soviet empire, many new players have entered the global market place: the so-called transition economies, Latin America, parts of Africa, and India. China, of course, embarked on the global scene in 1979. In addition, according to the Director General of WTO, Mr Renato Ruggiero:

> 'The celebrations of the 50th anniversary are also taking place in a time of rapid expansion of regional trading systems. More than 90 preferential regional agreements are currently in place, and over three quarters of them entered into force in the last four years. More than a third of these agreements involve the European Community.'[1]

The new forces of liberalization, regionalism and globalization have unleashed new sources of tension and uncovered national, regional and global institutional weaknesses. Unless we manage these new forces wisely, trade and other conflicts may lead to economic breakdown, if not collapse and world war. The WTO fully deserves the support of member states and will need greatly increased funds to accomplish the arduous tasks ahead.

---

[1]   Renato Ruggiero, 'From Vision to Reality: The Multilateral Trading System at Fifty' (Address at the Brookings Institution Forum on 'The Global Trading System: A GATT 50th Anniversary Forum'), p. 7.

I. National Issues

At the national level political pressure arises from the demands of global integration. Countries that have significant trade or current account surpluses face international pressure to liberalize imports further and to pursue expansionary fiscal and monetary policies. Japan is a case in point: domestic politics constrain import liberalization and favour increased fiscal expenditure rather than a tax cut. There is a similar constraint on reform of the banking sector. Unfortunately, Japan's fiscal decisions will impact not only on its own economy but also on the global one. The financially troubled Asian economies are hoping for a stronger Japanese economy and a stronger yen to help them out of the crisis. A stronger Japanese economy would help them export more while a stronger yen will help prevent another round of currency devaluations.

The recent Asian currency crisis has uncovered institutional and other weaknesses. Before the crisis, orthodox economic thinking was that a current account deficit could be acceptable and sustainable provided that it was investment- and not consumption-driven; this was held to be even more so when the deficit was brought about by private sector decisions (ie, market-driven) and not by budget deficits. As it turned out, this thinking was grossly wrong. The foreign borrowing was indeed largely private but on a short-term basis. This exposed the Asian countries to a double jeopardy. On the one hand, there was a mismatch of maturities: liabilities were short-term while the assets generated were medium to long-term ones. On the other hand, there was a mismatch of currencies: borrowing was in foreign currency while receipts generated were in domestic currency. These mismatches virtually guaranteed a liquidity crisis which in turn led to widespread insolvency. The afflicted Asian countries suffered a triple deflation of stock market, property market and currency values. They were forced to turn to the IMF for assistance. Unfortunately, the International Monetary Fund (IMF) did not and perhaps could not take care of the most important problem of staunching capital flight by helping the countries come to terms with the short-term creditors. South Korea was helped directly by the USA, and Thailand to some extent by Japan. Indonesia was left twisting in the wind: large-scale unemployment and damaging inflation followed. Of course politics was at play. President Suharto was in the process of re-election by the Indonesian Parliament and needed the votes. The IMF-mandated reforms would have prevented financial help for his supporters. The USA and the IMF, on the other side, needed Congressional approval for the additional US$18 billion, and could not appear to soften the terms of the IMF loan.

The next political problem may arise when the afflicted Asian countries start running substantial trade surpluses to repay their loans: will protectionist pressures arise in the USA and elsewhere?

There are other institutional problems that came to light during the Asian currency crisis. One has to do with the exchange rate regime. Some countries' currencies were directly pegged to the USA dollar; others were pegged to a basket of currencies and managed in varying degrees. The direct and indirect pegging of Asian currencies contributed to the double jeopardy mentioned earlier, particularly the mismatch of currencies, by encouraging over-borrowing from abroad, especially on a short-term basis. Moreover, in 1994, China devalued the yuan 35 per cent, putting serious competitive pressure on the Asian economies. This was followed in 1995 by the substantial weakening of the yen. In 1996–1997 the electronics industry suffered a recession globally. In addition, the Japanese economy has stagnated since 1990. All these factors contributed to the worsening of the current account deficits of South Korea, Thailand, Malaysia, Indonesia and the Philippines, and triggered the crisis, beginning with Thailand.

From the experience of the Asian countries, developing countries need to learn how to manage the floating of their currencies.

Let us begin with the institution of the central bank. In what way can it be insulated from politics? It should be noted that the venerable Bank of England was granted independence only recently by the UK Government. In Asia, only now, under the IMF reform programme, is the Indonesian Government granting autonomy to the central bank but not before it increased the money supply by 160 per cent since last year: a sure recipe, indeed, for hyperinflation.

A further question relating to central banks has to do with the quality and professionalism of staff. By August 1997, the Thai central bank had reportedly lost US$15 billion (practically all its reserves) in foreign exchange interventions particularly in the forward market. In addition, there was poor supervision of financial institutions, resulting in liquidity problems and financial failures. There appears to be a number of reasons for this. In the first place, in 1990, Thailand began liberalizing the domestic financial system and removing controls on foreign exchange: among the key elements of the Thai liberalization programme were:

> '(1) three rounds of foreign exchange decontrol, (2) removal of all interest rate restrictions in June 1992, (3) encouragement of non-banking capital markets such as the bond, equity and derivative markets, and (4) the move to the capital adequacy standard as the principal means of bank supervision.'[2]

This led to a proliferation of financial institutions and a tremendous increase in the volume and variety of financial activities and instruments. In the process, the central bank lost a number of key professionals to the much better paid private financial institutions. Is it any wonder that the afflicted Asian countries found themselves with weak and poorly supervised financial institutions that crumpled readily in the face of the currency crisis? A study by Kaminsky and Reinhart uncovered 46 balance-of-payments crises from 1980–1995, 22 of which were associated with banking crises followed in turn by currency devaluations. The banking crises were preceded by a private lending boom triggered by financial liberalization.[3]

A further important question must be raised concerning financial liberalization: was the domain of the domestic currency compromised in the process of liberalization?

---

[2]   Manuel F. Montes, *The Currency Crisis in Southeast Asia* (Institute of Southeast Asian Studies, Singapore, 1998), p. 9.

[3]   G. Kaminsky and C.M. Reinhart, 'The Twin Crises: The Causes of Banking and Balance-of-Payments Problems' (Working Paper No. 17, University of Maryland at College Park, Center for International Economics, 1996).

Moreover, the freer mobility of capital meant that domestic financial institutions were no longer so constrained by central credit restrictions. Substantial capital inflows resulted in over-valued currencies, which not only made exports of goods and services uncompetitive but also led to asset inflation and massive resources being shifted to the non-traded goods sector. This produced the unsustainable euphoria that precedes a financial crash.[4] The private sector lending boom compounded the problem of monetary control. Subsequently, massive capital outflows resulted in severe asset deflation and the free-fall of currency values, and compromised the integrity of the financial system. International credit rating agencies such as Moody's and Standard & Poor then downgraded the afflicted Asian countries' financial institutions: the result was that their letters of credit were not accepted abroad, bringing trade to a standstill (particularly in the case of Indonesia). More recently, even Japan, the world's largest creditor nation, had her banks rerated from stable to negative. The yen consequently fell by nearly 3 per cent. At the global level, the question needs to be asked: why should private credit rating agencies have so much power?

II. Regional Issues

The proliferation of preferential trading agreements (PTAs) was mentioned earlier. The acceleration of this phenomenon in the last few years seems puzzling on the surface, coming as it did on the heels of a successful Uruguay Round and the achievements of the WTO in liberalizing telecommunications and financial services. Jagdish Bhagwati has suggested that there are only two valid reasons for PTAs:

> '1. that the members of a customs union wish to integrate very deeply, to the extent of free capital and labour mobility and even attempts at common parliaments and foreign policy ... and 2. that the MTN [multilateral trade negotiations] approach is not working to reduce worldwide trade barriers so that we must take the alternative PTAs path to worldwide free trade, as when the USA turned to a Canadian–USA FTA [free trade area] when the Europeans did not agree to a new Round of MTN in November 1982.'[5]

In my view there may be two other interrelated motivations for pursuing PTAs. One of these has to do with the effects of liberalization, globalization, the international diffusion of technology, and the international mobility of capital and labour, both skilled and unskilled. Bhagwati has described this phenomenon as:

> 'kaleidoscopic comparative advantage, a concept that gives meaning to the notion that globalization of the world economy has led to fierce competition:

---

[4]   Kindleberger, 1978.

[5]   Jagdish Bhagwati, *The Feuds Over Free Trade* (Institute of Southeast Asian Studies, Singapore, 1997), pp. 20–21.

slight shifts in costs can now lead to shifting comparative advantage, which is therefore increasingly volatile.'[6]

One might pose the question of whether regionalism is partly a response to this phenomenon of kaleidoscopic comparative advantage: a PTA may offer a partial shelter, a half-way house towards global competition.

The other motivation towards PTAs may stem from insecurity and the search for stability in a rapidly changing, and perhaps, polarized world. The rapidly expanding European Union (EU) plus the soon-to-be-implemented euro were rooted in the historical desire for political, economic and currency stability. The European roots go back to the nineteenth century – the Latin Monetary Union, the German currency union and the gold standard.[7] By 1962, four years after the Treaty of Rome, the European Commission had already mooted a single currency. Despite the problems of the Snake arrangement and the Exchange Rate Mechanism (ERM), the euro appears to be on schedule. Meanwhile, the world saw the birth of the Canadian–USA PTA followed by NAFTA.

The impetus for the formation of the Asia–Pacific Economic Cooperation Council (APEC) came from the establishment of the Canadian–USA PTA. The Asian-Pacific countries felt left out in a world dominated by two giant groupings. APEC was to be a balancing factor, a bridge, an insurance against exclusion. Moreover, APEC was conceived as a grouping that was based on open regionalism and committed to multilateralism, fully supportive of the WTO.

In contrast, the recent Asian currency crisis has set in motion new ideas which may lead to a new Asian grouping that may not be so conducive to multilateralism or open regionalism. It may be recalled that, at the onset of the crisis last year, Japan mooted an Asian Fund to help the afflicted Asian countries. Apparently, the idea was shelved after vigorous objection by the USA. However, despite the IMF rescue packages, the crisis has been unduly prolonged and unduly severe. Asian leaders have voiced several frustrations. One complaint was that there was undue delay; another was that not enough was done, especially by the EU; a third was that no help was given to help resolve the short-term corporate foreign debt of Thailand and Indonesia although it was given to South Korea. There is also the perception, rightly or wrongly, that speculators and/or conspiracies brought about the crisis and that Western economic and political interests were behind the tough IMF reform programmes. Some of the mandated reforms, indeed, appear to them to have no direct or immediate relevance to economic recovery or financial stability, at least in the short term. Witness the resentment expressed by some Asian leaders. The recently appointed Minister for Trade and Industry of Indonesia, in response to a question about the IMF-mandated ending of the ban on exports of palm oil, was reported as saying that his country 'is not the IMF Republic; this is the Republic of Indonesia.' The perception and fear is that foreigners will end up dominating and controlling the Asian

---

[6]   Ibid., p. 46.

[7]   Economist, 'A Survey of EMU', *Economist*, 11 April 1998, p. 4.

economies. Asian financial markets were already small by world standards before the crisis and the triple deflation means that many Asian assets are available at bargain-basement prices. Bill Gates's wealth is probably enough to buy up several Asian stock markets!

Asian leaders have also noted with dismay that the EU was largely silent and offered no help outside the IMF. The recent Asia–Europe Meetings summit in London produced some platitudes and a paltry effort to help Asian countries develop expertise in monitoring and controlling the financial sector.

Asian leaders are also frustrated that, since the floating of exchange rates last year, there has been great volatility. They have also discovered the dominant role played by the US dollar in world trade and finance: some are seriously seeking alternatives. There is talk of a yen bloc or a yuan bloc or else some kind of Asian ERM. Meanwhile, there is the euro shortly to be established. If the Asian crisis is unduly prolonged, an Asian bloc may well arise, with some kind of ERM and, perhaps, not so open regionalism. The world may then face a tri-polar configuration which may produce a fortress mentality. Multilateralism would surely ebb to everybody's detriment.

III.   Global Issues

III.1   New global players

At the global level several challenges lie ahead. The much publicized success and performance of the Asian newly industrializing economies plus the demise of the Soviet empire have resulted in several new players (some of them huge) on the global market. The competition is for foreign investment and markets for low-tech goods. The question and fear is whether the new players can be accommodated without triggering protectionism. The attempt to include the items of trade and social issues and trade and environmental issues on the WTO agenda at the last Singapore ministerial meeting is a case in point.

Several concerns need to be addressed. The first is whether kaleidoscopic comparative advantage, whereby competitive margins are so thin that comparative advantage is lost easily, may not lead to protectionism via competitive devaluations, a phenomenon which accentuated the miseries of the last Great Depression. The Asian countries afflicted by the current currency crisis are hoping that the Hong Kong peg will hold, that the Chinese yuan will not be devalued and that the yen will not weaken (the dollar strengthen) at least for a year or two. Otherwise, the fear and expectation is that there will be another chaotic round of competitive devaluations, possibly with disastrous consequences. Already Hong Kong is hurting with high interest rates and seriously deflated property and stock markets. There are also reports that China is hurting in her exports and inflow of foreign investments, especially at a time when she is reforming her state-owned enterprises and financial sector.

Meanwhile, the trigger for competitive devaluation may come from elsewhere. Brazil, the largest Latin American country, is having difficulties. Russia or some East European countries are also likely candidates. We can only hope there will be none.

An equally serious concern is whether all the low-tech exports will find enough markets without arousing protectionism in the importing countries. Add to this the need for the afflicted Asian countries to develop export surpluses in the next two to three years to pay off their loans and IMF obligations. Can America and Europe provide the market leeway? Japan is needed but has been struggling with stagnation for the last eight years. Recently, every stimulus package has met with a bad reception by the market. If Japan can revive, she can help absorb some of the Asian export surpluses. On the other hand, if Japan sinks into a serious recession, the question is whether the global economy will be pulled down either via demand deflation or via a financial crisis.

III.2   Trade as engine of growth?

The Director General of WTO has pointed out that, over the past 50 years, trade has been a powerful engine of growth.[8] The ratio of trade to GDP has grown from 7 per cent in 1950 to 23 per cent today. Obviously much credit belongs to the eight successive rounds of GATT which brought industrial tariff levels from an average of 40 per cent down to under 4 per cent. Two issues spring from this statistic. The first is that for most countries trade constitutes a high proportion of GDP. Changes in external demand, foreign competition, terms of trade etc have significant impact. If Professor Bhagwati is right about kaleidoscopic comparative advantage, fairly rapid and frequent changes in competitiveness impose social and political costs.

The removal or substantial reduction of most tariff barriers to trade has also exposed domestic policies, regulations etc as possible impediments to free trade and, hence, natural candidates for multilateral examination and subjection to international rules via the WTO. It may be recalled that the 1996 Singapore ministerial meeting of WTO agreed to establish working groups on issues relating to trade and investment and trade and competition. There was also agreement (i) to establish a working group to study the issue of transparency in government procurement practices, and (ii) to undertake exploratory work on trade facilitation, ie simplification of trade procedures like customs formalities and licensing procedures. Free traders and WTO have a lot of work in convincing sceptics that the loss of national sovereignty in some areas would be more than compensated for by enlarged economies and higher standards of living.

In the developed countries, the increasing importance of trade to GDP, the rapid adjustments necessitated by globalization, structural unemployment and visible inequalities in wages between skilled and unskilled workers result in protectionism and persistent attempts to include the Social Clause in the WTO agenda. The Samuelson-Stolper theorem, rather than Bhagwati's, is conveniently invoked: cheap imports produced by cheap and exploited labour must be depressing wages rather than labour-saving technical change. It is not easy to dispel the notion when cheap imports displace

---

8   Renato Ruggiero, 'From Vision to Reality: The Multilateral Trading System at Fifty' (Address at the Brookings Institution Forum on 'The Global Trading System: A GATT 50th Anniversary Forum'), p. 4.

local goods, and wages in developing countries are so much lower. Moreover, downsizing causes retrenchments and investments abroad have often taken the form of relocation of factories.

Blackhurst has pointed out that:

> 'To a large extent, governments have only themselves to blame for the backlash. Part of the problem is their frequent lack of candour regarding the fact that even though globalization clearly benefits the country as a whole, some groups in the economy will lose … More important is their reluctance to publicly acknowledge that while globalization creates tremendous opportunities, it also raises the cost of bad policies – such as labour market rigidities, over-regulation, substandard schools and educational policies, tax policies that discourage job creation, and chronic budget deficits that reduce investment by reducing national savings.'[9]

The political problem has always been that those who lose are better able to express their views and persuade law-makers than those who gain.

In fact, the competitiveness criteria and reports which are made periodically by the World Economic Forum and the International Institute for Management Development seem to some people to imply that trade is a zero-sum game.[10]

Internationally, inter-industry trade has been more vulnerable to protectionism than intra-industry trade. The former involves distinct industry groups while for the latter, gainers and losers are in similar groups. Even so, trade has not always been viewed as a positive-sum game in intra-industry trade: recall the strategic trade theory of first-past-the-post wins all.

The opening up of trade in services exposes another protectionist virus: countries want not only to trade merchandise but to engage in trading (services) as well. Here protectionism is more subtle and costly. Some trade in services requires hefty investments in infrastructure, eg ports, airports and railways. In south-east Asia we have witnessed several countries trying to be aviation hubs, sea port hubs and information technology hubs, resulting in costly replications. People tend to look at the merchandise trade balance separately from the balance in services and make policy to remedy deficits, regardless of comparative advantage. There is clearly a need for international education of policy makers.

III.3   Trade in financial assets

The domestic institutional problems arising from liberalization of financial services were referred to above. At the global level there are other issues. One is the short-term great

---

    [9]   Richard Blackhurst, 'The WTO and the Global Economy' (1997) 20 *World Economy* 531.

    [10]   Paul Krugman, 'Competitiveness: A Dangerous Obsession' (1994) *Foreign Affairs*, March/April.

impact of trade in financial assets on exchange rates, and, hence, comparative advantage in trade of goods and services. Developing countries are particularly vulnerable because of the smallness of their financial markets. There is indeed an urgent need for a new international financial architecture to deal with volatile short-term capital flows. Associated with this is the power of fund managers and speculators, who control billions of dollars, over exchange rates. If nothing is done, competitive devaluations might well be the order of the day, as in the inter-war period. Another problem related to this is the power of international credit rating agencies that I mentioned earlier. There should be a substitute global institution, perhaps the IMF, to issue the credit ratings, backed up, perhaps, by guarantees.

Index